NOTHING IS HIDDEN

To Ruth

NOTHING IS HIDDEN

Wittgenstein's Criticism of his Early Thought

————— Norman Malcolm —————

Basil Blackwell

© Norman Malcolm 1986

First published 1986

Basil Blackwell Ltd
108 Cowley Road, Oxford OX4 1JF, UK

Basil Blackwell Inc.
432 Park Avenue South, Suite 1503,
New York, NY 10016, USA

British Library Cataloguing in Publication Data

Malcolm, Norman
   Nothing is hidden : Wittgenstein's criticism
   of his early thought.
   1. Wittgenstein, Ludwig. Tractatus logico-
   philosophicus   2. Logic, Symbolic and
   mathematical   3. Languages—Philosophy
   I. Title
   160   BC135.W52

   ISBN 0-631-13744-0

Library of Congress Cataloging in Publication Data

Malcolm, Norman, 1911—
   Nothing is hidden.

   Bibliography: p.
   Includes index.
   1. Wittgenstein, Ludwig, 1889—1951.   I. Title.
   B3376.W564M23   1986   192   85—30661
   ISBN 0-631-13744-0

Typeset by Pioneer Associates, Perthshire
Printed in Great Britain by
TJ Press Ltd, Padstow

Contents

Beim Philosophieren muss man ins alte Chaos hinabsteigen, und sich dort wohlfühlen.

Wittgenstein, 1948

Preface

In his preface to the *Philosophical Investigations* Wittgenstein says:

> Four years ago I had occasion to read again my first book (the *Tractatus Logico-Philosophicus*) and to explain its thoughts. It suddenly seemed to me that I should publish those old thoughts and the new ones together: that the latter could be seen in the right light only by contrast with and against the background of my old way of thinking.

It is undoubtedly true that it greatly aids one's understanding of the *Investigations* if one comes to it directly from a close study of the *Tractatus*. The latter is a mighty work that tends to capture a serious reader: it is *convincing*. For various reasons the *Investigations* is more difficult to understand. Often one does not *see the point* of Wittgenstein's remarks. But when one who has been deeply impressed by the *Tractatus* begins to perceive the extent to which the *Investigations* is an assault upon the fundamental conceptions of Wittgenstein's first book, the feeling of 'not seeing the point' disappears, and one becomes aware of a dramatic conflict between two radically different philosophical outlooks.

Some writers have doubted both the accuracy and the validity of Wittgenstein's criticism of his earlier thinking. It has been said that when he wrote the *Investigations* he no longer understood the *Tractatus*; that he had lost interest in it; that what he criticizes are crude caricatures of its positions; that, in particular, he did not definitely reject what is perhaps the most basic thesis of the *Tractatus* — the picture theory of propositions; that apparently he had only a vague recollection of this theory; that, in short, his idea that his later thoughts could best be understood by contrasting them with the views of the *Tractatus* is greatly exaggerated.

I do not agree with any of this. I believe that when Wittgenstein wrote the *Investigations* he had an exact knowledge of the *Tractatus*. In the *Investigations*, and the other writings of his second period, there is a massive attack on the principal ideas of the *Tractatus*. According to my account the following positions are taken in the *Tractatus* and rejected in Wittgenstein's later thinking:

1   That there is a fixed form of the world, an unchanging order of logical possibilities, which is independent of whatever is the case.
2   That the fixed form of the world is constituted of things that are simple in an absolute sense.
3   That the simple objects are the substratum of thought and language.
4   That thoughts, composed of 'psychical constituents', underlie the sentences of language.
5   That a thought is intrinsically a picture of a particular state of affairs.
6   That a proposition, or a thought, cannot have a vague sense.
7   That whether a proposition has sense cannot depend on whether another proposition is true.
8   That to understand the sense of a proposition it is sufficient to know the meaning of its constituent parts.
9   That the sense of a proposition cannot be explained.
10   That there is a general form of all propositions.
11   That each proposition is a picture of one and only one state of affairs.
12   That when a sentence is combined with a method of projection the resulting proposition is necessarily unambiguous.
13   That what one *means* by a sentence is specified by an inner process of logical analysis.
14   That the pictorial nature of most of our everyday propositions is hidden.
15   That every sentence with sense expresses a thought which can be compared with reality.

Many, if not all, of these positions of the *Tractatus* are interlocking.

In the first eight chapters I expound the foregoing positions in the context of the *Tractatus*, and also Wittgenstein's sharp disagreement with them in his later thought. In the last three chapters I take up aspects of his new thinking that are not specifically confrontations with the *Tractatus*. Chapter 9 deals with his treatment of the concept of 'following a rule', and with some recent misunderstanding of his thinking on that topic. Chapter 10 brings some of Wittgenstein's views to bear on two prominent positions in the philosophy of mind—psycho-physical parallelism and mind-brain identity-theory. Chapter 11 extracts from Wittgenstein's last notebooks his thoughts on the concepts of certainty and knowledge, and compares the views of Descartes and Wittgenstein on the vexing philosophical problem of *certainty*.

I have great admiration for the *Tractatus*: it is truly a classic. I have even greater admiration for the way in which Wittgenstein purged himself of the thinking of the *Tractatus* and created a revolutionary new philosophy. The dominant currents in today's academic philosophy have been scarcely touched by the latter. The *Investigations* has been read but its message not digested. As has been aptly said, it has been assimilated without being understood. I have written the present book in the hope, perhaps vain, that somewhere some students of philosophy may be helped by it to a better understanding of that great work, and may have their own struggles in philosophy freshened and inspired by Wittgenstein's unmatched insights into the nature of philosophical confusion, and by the example of his extraordinary life as a philosopher.

There are many topics in the *Tractatus* I have not discussed. Among them are issues in formal logic, such as Wittgenstein's treatment of logical truth, general propositions, and formal series; also ethics and value, mathematics and science, the metaphysical I and the mystical. I hesitated over whether to include a chapter on solipsism. Many different writers have construed the remarks on solipsism of the *Tractatus* in many different ways. A plausible case can be made for interpreting the *Tractatus* as endorsing a highly original form of solipsism. But a plausible case can also be made for interpreting the *Tractatus*, not as endorsing solipsism, but instead as presenting it as a conspicuous illustration of metaphysical nonsense. Wittgenstein retained a strong interest in solipsism in his later thought. He was acutely aware of the temptation to think such a thing as 'Only my own experience is real.' In *The Blue Book* there is a long and brilliant study of the temptations of solipsism. This is, by implication, a criticism of the

Tractatus if the latter endorses solipsism — but if not then not. Being unable to resolve this question, I decided not to address the topic of solipsism, since I want the main focus of this book to be on Wittgenstein's later criticism of positions that were definitely held in the *Tractatus*.

Since coming to King's College in 1978 I have profited greatly from many discussions with Peter Winch on many philosophical problems. His skill in discussion and his keen insights have been a tonic for me. From chapter 2 it will be seen that we have disagreed in some interpretations of the *Tractatus*. I am indebted to him for his criticism of early drafts of chapter 1. This helped me to strengthen, I hope, the case for my reading of the *Tractatus*.

Dan Rashid has been a participant for several years in my seminars at King's. He has been a strong presence in those discussions. He has often come to my aid when I have floundered; and also by his criticism he has forced me to tighten my thinking. I have relied on his fine understanding of Wittgenstein's thoughts in the *Investigations* and elsewhere. In addition, he read through all of the chapters of the present book, correcting errors and infelicities, and giving me good advice — for all of which I am grateful to him.

Norman Malcolm
King's College London
September 1985

References to Wittgenstein's Writings and Discussions

Tractatus Logico-Philosophicus, English tr. D. F. Pears and B. F. McGuinness. Routledge & Kegan Paul: London, 1961. (Cited in the text by decimal numbers of propositions.)

Notebooks 1914—1916, 2nd edn, eds G. H. von Wright and G. E. M. Anscombe, English tr. G. E. M. Anscombe. Basil Blackwell: Oxford, 1979. (Cited in the text as *NB* followed by page number.)

Ludwig Wittgenstein: Letters to C. K. Ogden, ed. G. H. von Wright. Basil Blackwell: Oxford, 1973.

Ludwig Wittgenstein and the Vienna Circle, conversations recorded by Friedrich Waismann, ed. Brian McGuinness, tr. Joachim Schulte and Brian McGuinness. Basil Blackwell: Oxford, 1979. (Cited in the text as *WWK* followed by page number.)

Philosophical Remarks, ed. Rush Rhees, English tr. Raymond Hargreaves and Roger White. Basil Blackwell: Oxford, 1975. (Cited in the text as *PR* followed by page number.)

Philosophical Grammar, ed. Rush Rhees, English tr. Anthony Kenny. Basil Blackwell: Oxford, 1974. (Cited in the text as *PG* followed by page number.)

The Blue and The Brown Books, dictated by Wittgenstein to students. Basil Blackwell: Oxford, 1958. (Cited in the text as *BB* followed by page number.)

'Wittgenstein's Notes for Lectures on "Private Experience" and "Sense Data"', ed. Rush Rhees, *The Philosophical Review*, vol. 77, no. 3, July 1968. (Cited in the text as *NFL* followed by page number.)

'Wittgenstein, "Cause and Effect: Intuitive Awareness"', manuscript notes by Wittgenstein, ed. Rush Rhees, English tr. Peter

Winch, *Philosophia*, vol. 6, nos. 3—4, Sept.—Dec. 1976. (Cited in the text as *C&E* followed by page number.)

Remarks on the Foundations of Mathematics, revised and enlarged edn, eds G. E. M. Anscombe, Rush Rhees, and G. H. von Wright. Suhrkamp Verlag: Frankfurt am Main, 1974. (Cited in the text as *RFM* followed by page number.)

Philosophical Investigations, English tr. G. E. M. Anscombe. Basil Blackwell: Oxford, 1967. (Cited in the text as *PI* followed by paragraph number or page number.)

Zettel, eds G. E. M. Anscombe and G. H. von Wright, English tr. G. E. M. Anscombe. Basil Blackwell: Oxford, 1967. (Cited in the text as *Z* followed by paragraph number.)

Last Writings on the Philosophy of Psychology, eds G. H. von Wright and Heikki Nyman, English tr. C. G. Luckhardt and Maximilian A. E. Aue, vol. I. Basil Blackwell: Oxford, 1982.

On Certainty, eds G. E. M. Anscombe and G. H. von Wright, English tr. Denis Paul and G. E. M. Anscombe. Basil Blackwell: Oxford, 1969. (Cited in the text as *OC* followed by paragraph number.)

For the most part I follow the above translations: but sometimes I provide different translations.

———— CHAPTER 1 ————

The Form of the World

A fundamental conception of the *Tractatus* is: *the form of the world*. What is this conception? We are told that the form of the world is fixed, unalterable; and that it consists of the 'simple objects'. 'This fixed form just consists of the objects.' (2.023) To understand this we need to take a preliminary look at the concept of a (simple) object. An object, just like the form of the world, is fixed, unchanging, permanent (2.027). But an object enters into combinations with other objects. These combinations or configurations of objects are not, like the objects themselves, fixed and unchanging. They come and go. A configuration of objects is a state of affairs (2.0272). A possible configuration is a possible state of affairs; an actual configuration is an existing state of affairs. The actual world (at a certain time) is just the totality of existing states of affairs (at that time) (2.04).

It is essential to any thing (whether simple or complex) that it *can* be a constituent of a state of affairs (2.011). To take a crude example, a chair *can* be between a stool and a table; but it cannot be between a wall and the paint on the wall. If I know what a chair is I must realize that a chair can be between a stool and a table, that it can be a constituent of such a state of affairs. Here the *Tractatus* brings in the notion of 'the form' of an object: 'The possibility of its occurring in states of affairs is the form of an object.' (2.0141) I cannot know an object without knowing its form.

> In logic nothing is accidental: if a thing *can* occur in a state of affairs, the possibility of the state of affairs must already be presupposed in the thing. (2.012)

> If I know an object I also know all its possible occurrences in states

of affairs. (Every one of these possibilities must lie in the nature of the object.) A new possibility cannot be discovered later. (2.0123)

The *Tractatus* uses the metaphor of *a space* surrounding an object as an image of the object's possible combinations with other objects:

> Each thing is, as it were, in a space of possible states of affairs. I can conceive this space to be empty, but I cannot conceive of the thing without the space. (2.013)

We are now prepared to understand the notion of 'the form of the world'. Each object carries with it a space of possibilities. These possibilities are intrinsic to the object; they are its 'internal properties' (2.0231). Now if we conceive of *all* objects, taken together, we are conceiving of the *totality* of possible combinations of objects — which is the totality of possible states of affairs, situations. 'If all objects are given, then also with that all *possible* states of affairs are given.' (2.0124) 'Objects contain the possibility of all situations.' (2.014) This totality of possible states of affairs just is the form of the world. It consists of every possible state of affairs. It is identical with 'logical space'. 'The facts in logical space are the world.' (1.13) The possibilities that *exist* are the facts; the possibilities that do not exist are still there as possibilities. The totality of simple objects constitutes 'the substance' of the world (2.021). The objects are unchanging in themselves. Their actual combinations change, but not their possible combinations. This is the sense in which the fixed form of the world consists of the objects (2.023).

The form of the world cannot change over time, any more than can the possible combinations of an object. The form of the world could be said to be timeless, and in that sense eternal. The form of the world is the form of any conceivable world. 'It is obvious that a conceivable world, however different it may be from the real one, must have *something* — a form — in common with it.' (2.022) The form of the world is completely *a priori*. Logically speaking, it is *prior* to all discoveries or inventions — to all experience and all change. There is nothing empirical or contingent about it.

Here I will make a remark that some students of the *Tractatus* will find objectionable. The remark is that the form of the world, as conceived of in the *Tractatus*, is not dependent on *language* or on *thinking*. I mean that the form of the world is not a creation of language or thinking, but indeed is *presupposed* by language and thinking. I will spell out this interpretation by first taking a look at the theory of language of the *Tractatus*.

According to the *Tractatus*, language just *is* the totality of propositions (4.001). What is a 'proposition'? Any sentence that has sense is a proposition. But also a map, or a drawing, or a diagram, is a proposition. A sentence that has sense presents (depicts, describes) a possible state of affairs. The *sense* of a sentence just is the possible situation that it presents (2.221).

The basic propositions are the 'elementary' propositions. Every genuine proposition (every sentence with sense) is held to be a truth-function of elementary propositions, the latter being truth-functions of themselves (5).

An elementary proposition is composed solely of simple signs called 'names'. The simplicity of a name consists in its *meaning* a 'simple object'. Wittgenstein makes the striking remark that 'A name means an object. The object is its meaning.' (3.203) He makes another, equally striking remark about the relation between a name and an object: 'Der Name vertritt im Satz den Gegenstand.' (3.22) The verb *vertreten* means 'to deputize for', 'to substitute for', 'to act for'. If the president of a corporation could not attend a meeting of the board, he might send another official to deputize for him, to speak and vote for him. It does not adequately capture the sense of 3.22 to say that a name 'designates' or 'represents' or 'refers to' or 'stands for' an object. I prefer to translate 3.22 as follows: 'In a proposition a name deputizes for an object.' One could also say that a name 'substitutes for' or 'takes the place of' an object.

In another remark Wittgenstein says: 'Die Moglichkeit des Satzes beruht auf dem Prinzip der Vertretung von Gegenstanden durch Zeichen.' (4.0312) *Vertretung* is the noun that goes with the verb *vertreten*. It can mean 'substitution' or 'replacement'. A good translation of 4.0312 would be: 'The possibility of propositions is based on the principle of the substitution of signs for objects' or 'the replacement of objects by signs.'

The idea here is quite remarkable. In an elementary proposition a name *takes the place* of an object. Since an *object* is not a word or any other kind of sign, an object itself cannot occur in a sentence. The next best thing, therefore, is to have a sign in the sentence, that 'takes the place of', 'deputizes for', 'acts for' an object. The sign, a 'name', will have *all the powers* that the object has for which it deputizes. But the powers of a name will be exercised in the medium of language, not in the medium of reality. The possibilities that an object has of combining with other objects are *duplicated* by the possibilities that its name has of combining with other names in elementary sentences.

In an elementary sentence that has sense, the names that are the elements of the sentence are combined in a particular way. This combination pictures (presents, depicts) the corresponding simple elements of reality (the objects) as combined in the *same* way (2.15). Wittgenstein likens this combination to a *living picture*:

> One name stands for one thing, another for another thing, and they are combined with one another. In this way the whole — like a living picture — presents a state of affairs. (4.0311)

For example, the Last Supper might be depicted on a stage: one actor would deputize for Jesus, other actors for each of the disciples, and the way the actors were arranged would depict the arrangement at the Last Supper.

The arrangement of names in an elementary sentence depicts the corresponding objects as combined in that way. If the objects are combined that way in reality, the proposition is true; if not, false. Whether true or false, it has sense.

An elementary proposition is a picture. It presents a possible situation in logical space (2.202). This possibility is the *sense* of the picture (2.221). Since every proposition is a truth-function of elementary propositions, every proposition has one and only one complete analysis into elementary propositions (3.25). So, what *every* proposition does, whether elementary or non-elementary, is the same: it pictures a possible situation in logical space — a possible arrangement of simple objects.

Thus, to say anything meaningful, whether true or false, is to picture (depict, describe) some possibility or other in that totality of possibilities that constitutes the form of the world. This form, this aggregate of possible states of affairs, is unchanging. Therefore, *what can be said*, is unchanging. The possible configurations of the objects provide the boundary of what can be said.

The *Tractatus* says that 'A proposition *shows* its sense.' (4.002) That is, it shows (displays) a state of affairs, which may not exist but *could* exist (as a tableau vivant, shows an arrangement of those who were at the Last Supper — an arrangement that may not have existed, but could have existed). The same idea is conveyed by the remark that 'A proposition determines a place in logical space.' (3.4) I think this means that a proposition picks out (describes) one possibility in the totality of possibilities. Wittgenstein says:

> A proposition can determine only one place in logical space: nevertheless the whole of logical space must already be given by it. . . . A proposition reaches through the whole of logical space. (3.42)

This is hard to construe. I take it to mean that any *one* possible configuration of objects *presupposes* every possible configuration — perhaps in a sense similar to that in which the space enclosed by a single room presupposes the whole of space.

For my present purpose the important point is that the remark that a proposition 'determines' a place in logical space does *not* mean that the proposition *creates* that place. No. A place in logical space is simply one possibility in the timeless order of possibilities. One could say that a proposition focuses on a possibility by describing it.

Nor do *thoughts* create the possibilities of which they are thoughts. A thought is a picture (3). Like any picture it presents a possible situation in logical space (2.202). Whatever is thinkable is possible, for a thought just is a picture of a possibility (3.02). There cannot be illogical thoughts (3.03), since an 'illogical thought' would not be a picture of a possibility. To say that a state of affairs is thinkable (conceivable) means that we can make a picture of it (3.001).

Thus the boundary of language and of thinking is drawn against the background of the form of the world. The conception of the form of the world is not a *product* of the theory of language of the *Tractatus*, although it is articulated by that theory. I think that the conception that there is a fixed form of all possible worlds is one of the visions that inspired the *Tractatus*. It is presupposed by Wittgenstein's theories of language and thought.

The *Tractatus* could be said to conceive of three domains of possibility: what is possible in reality, what is possible in thought, what is possible in language. These domains are reflections of one another: given any possibility in one of these domains, there is a counterpart in each of the others.

In the *Philosophical Investigations* Wittgenstein characterizes the view of the *Tractatus* in the following way: 'These concepts: proposition, language, thought, world, stand in line one behind

the other, each equivalent to each.' (*PI* 96) He goes on to say of
his former view:

> The *a priori* order of the world, i.e. the order of *possibilities*, which
> must be common to the world and thought . . . is *prior* to all
> experience, must run through all experience; no empirical
> cloudiness can be allowed to affect it — it must instead be of the
> purest crystal. But this crystal does not appear as an abstraction;
> but as something concrete, indeed, as the most concrete, as it were
> the *hardest* thing there is. (*Tractatus Logico-Philosophicus* no.
> 5.5563) (*PI* 97)

It is significant, for two reasons, that here Wittgenstein explicitly
cites the *Tractatus*: first, it makes clear beyond doubt that he is
describing his former view; second, that he was able to cite the
actual *Tractatus* number indicates that he had a copy of the book
in front of him. I mention this because some commentators have
thought that when Wittgenstein wrote the *Investigations* he had
only a hazy recollection of the *Tractatus*.

To what in 5.5563 was he referring? No doubt to these remarks:
'That utterly simple thing, which we have to formulate here, is
not an allegory of the truth, but the complete truth itself. (Our
problems are not abstract, but perhaps the most concrete that
there are.)' What is this which is not abstract but absolutely
concrete? Two propositions earlier there occur these remarks:
'Empirical reality is bounded by the totality of objects. The
boundary shows itself again in the totality of elementary
propositions.' (5.5561)

Here the *Tractatus* is drawing the boundary of possible
experience, and also the boundary of language. The boundaries
of both are fixed by *the totality of simple objects*. The objects are
the substance of the world. They are the substratum of both the
possible and the actual. This is the sense in which they are 'form
and content' (2.025). Their possibilities of combination are the
substratum of all *possible* states of affairs. Their actual
combinations are the substratum of all *facts*. They are the
substratum of *thought* — for all thoughts are pictures of their
possible combinations. They are the substratum of *language* —
for every meaningful sentence has an analysis into an arrangement
of names, each name *meaning* an object. Without the objects
language would have no meaning, and so would not be language.

When Wittgenstein said in *Tractatus* 5.5563 that his 'problems'
were not 'abstract, but perhaps the most concrete that there are',

I think he was referring to the problems of what underlies and connects with one another, the concepts of possibility, fact, thought, experience, proposition, language, world. The solution of the *Tractatus* is that these underpinnings and interconnections are all provided by the enduring and indissoluble simple objects. They are 'the *hardest* thing there is'. They make up the *a priori* order of possibilities, that order which has the transparence of 'purest crystal'.

Let us think critically now about the conception of the form of the world — the totality of possible states of affairs. In the *Investigations* Wittgenstein says that the concepts of 'thought', 'language', 'world', and so on of the *Tractatus* were not concepts of ordinary language but were '*super*-concepts' (*PI* 97). That this was so is evident just from the fact that in writing the *Tractatus* he was unable to specify any *examples* of 'simple objects', or of 'names', or of 'elementary propositions', even though these concepts were basic to his theory of the nature of the world and of language. There is some pathos in his remark in the *Notebooks* that 'Our difficulty was that we always spoke of simple objects and did not know a single example of one.' (*NB*, p. 68) He wrote this in June 1915 — and the difficulty was never removed. If no certain example of a simple object could be produced, then also there could be no example of a 'name', or of an 'elementary proposition', or of 'complete analysis'. If a philosopher is unable to decide what are examples of his basic concepts, this shows that in a sense he does not know what he is talking about. In the *Investigations* Wittgenstein remarks that 'if the words "language", "experience", "world", have a use, it must be as humble a one as that of the words "table", "lamp", "door".' (*PI* 97)

This must be true also of the word 'possible' that looms so large in the *Tractatus*. Some of the statements in which this word occurs are the following. 'The possibility of its occurring in states of affairs is the form of an object.' (2.0141) 'Objects contain the possibility of all situations.' (2.014) 'A picture presents a possible situation in logical space.' (2.202) 'A thought contains the possibility of the situation of which it is the thought.' (3.02)

Let us consider again the statement that 'A proposition can determine only one place in logical space: nevertheless the whole of logical space must already be given by it. . . . A proposition reaches through the whole of logical space.' (3.42) As I said before, this seems to mean that although a proposition is a picture of only one possible state of affairs, it *presupposes* the totality of possible states of affairs. To put it another way: a proposition (or thought, or picture) has a *sense*. Its sense just is the possible situation it depicts. What 3.42 seem to mean is that the sense of any one proposition presupposes the sense of *every* proposition. Or put it like this: the possibility of one thought presupposes the possibility of *any* thought.

This would be an astonishing view. According to the *Tractatus, language* just *is* the totality of elementary propositions and of the non-elementary propositions that can be constructed out of them. What can be said in language coincides with what can be thought. Was Wittgenstein holding that if a human being, no matter how primitive, were to express by sounds or signs any thought whatever, this thought of his 'would reach through the whole of logical space'? Was he implying the *possibility*, for that person, of any thought whatever? Was Wittgenstein assuming that if a person could make a picture of one possible situation then he *could* make a picture of any possible situation? Does having one thought imply the possibility of having any thought?

It could be maintained that this is not a correct interpretation of the *Tractatus*. It might be held that Wittgenstein was not talking about what any individual person *could do*. Perhaps he was only meaning that a thought of the most primitive person would have a determinate place in the whole of language.

I think, however, that the view I have called 'astonishing' really is in the *Tractatus*. A relevant point is that the *Tractatus* speaks of 'knowing' an object. 'If I know an object I also know all of its possible occurrences in states of affairs.' (2.0123) This surely implies that one *can* 'know' an object. But how are we to understand this notion of 'knowing' an object? The German word, which is translated here as 'know', is *kennen* — which is commonly translated as 'to be acquainted with'.

In 1922 there was a correspondence between C. K. Ogden and Wittgenstein about the translation of the *Tractatus*. Ogden raised a query about the translation of *kennen* in 2.0123. He asked whether 'am acquainted with' would be better than 'know'. Wittgenstein replied that 'to be acquainted with' does not have, he thought, 'exactly the meaning I want, because it seems to me to imply somehow that one knows a lot about an object, while to know here just means: I know *it* but I needn't know anything *about* it.'[1] So to 'know' an object, in 2.0123, means: to know *it* without necessarily knowing anything *about* it. This implies that one can *know* a simple object without knowing anything about it — that is, without knowing what are any of its *actual* occurrences in states of affairs. The remainder of 2.0123 says that one *cannot* know an object *without* knowing its *possible* occurrences in states of affairs.

Wittgenstein was right about the ordinary use of 'acquainted with' in English. You would not say that you were *acquainted* with a person if you did not know *anything* about him. It is interesting that Russell had previously introduced the expression 'knowledge by acquaintance' into philosophy with the following meaning:

> Knowledge of things, when it is of the kind we call knowledge by *acquaintance*, is essentially simpler than any knowledge of truths, and logically independent of knowledge of truths.[2]

To say that 'knowledge by acquaintance' is logically independent of 'knowledge of truths' means that one *can* know something 'by acquaintance' without knowing any actual truths *about* it. Thus, the idea that Wittgenstein wanted to express in 2.0123, by the phrase 'to know an object', agrees with Russell's earlier technical definition of the phrase 'knowledge by acquaintance'.

Russell says: 'I say that I am *acquainted* with an object when I have a direct cognitive relation to that object, i.e. when I am directly aware of the object itself.'[3] He also says: 'To say that S has acquaintance with O is essentially the same thing as to say that O is presented to S.'[4] Thus 'acquaintance' with an object, in Russell's technical sense, involves the notion that the object is 'presented' to one, and also the notion that one is 'directly aware' of the object.

Russell had drawn a contrast between 'knowledge by 'acquaintance' and 'knowledge by description'. The latter always involves 'some knowledge of truths as its source and ground'[5] whereas 'knowledge by acquaintance' does not. Russell held that 'sense-data' are among the things with which one has 'acquaintance':

> Thus in the presence of my table I am acquainted with the sense-data that make up the appearance of my table — its colour, shape, hardness, smoothness, etc.; all these are things of which I am immediately conscious when I am seeing and touching my table.[6]

Russell says that when he sees his table, 'the particular shade of colour that I am seeing' is something with which he is 'acquainted':

> So far as concerns knowledge of the colour itself, as opposed to knowledge of truths about it, I know the colour perfectly and completely when I see it, and no further knowledge of it itself is even theoretically possible.[7]

Were the simple objects of the *Tractatus* conceived of by Wittgenstein as 'objects of acquaintance' in Russell's sense? There certainly is considerable agreement. From Wittgenstein's reply to Ogden it is clear that in 2.0123 to 'know an object' means to 'know *it*' without necessarily knowing anything *about* it. This agrees with Russell's *definition* of 'acquaintance'. Also, Russell's 'objects of acquaintance' are 'presented' to one. Wittgenstein speaks of the simple objects of the *Tractatus* as being 'given' — which looks like the same idea. Still another similarity is the following. Russell says that 'knowledge concerning what is known by description is ultimately reducible to knowledge concerning what is known by acquaintance.'[8] He says that 'the fundamental principle' in the analysis of propositions containing descriptions is this: 'Every proposition which we can understand must be composed wholly of constituents with which we are acquainted.'[9] There is a striking resemblance between Russell's 'fundamental principle' and the thesis of the *Tractatus* that every non-elementary proposition must have a complete analysis into elementary propositions consisting solely of names that deputize for simple objects. So there are good grounds for concluding that what Wittgenstein meant in the *Tractatus* by 'knowing an object' was close to what Russell meant by 'being acquainted with an object'.

Yet the similarity should not be pressed too far. The simple objects of the *Tractatus* could not include 'sense-data'. Sense-data are supposed to be 'fleeting': they quickly alter, come and go. The simple objects are not like that: they are enduring and unchanging (2.0271). It may be that Wittgenstein would not have agreed that any of Russell's various candidates for 'objects of acquaintance' could be accepted as 'simple objects'. Both agreed that there are things that are 'known' independently of any knowledge of facts about them; that these things are 'presented' or 'given'; that knowing these things is fundamental for sense and understanding. But there was no agreement as to what these things are.

Could one know a simple object only *partly*? Apparently not. A
simple object does not have a colour or a shape. It does not have
any 'material properties'. Material properties are constituted by
configuration of simple objects (2.0231). There does not seem to
be anything involved in knowing a simple object other than
knowing the *logical form* of the object — that is, knowing its
possibilities of combination with other objects. Wittgenstein calls
this 'knowing its internal properties', in contrast with 'knowing its
external properties'. The latter would be knowing its actual
configurations with other objects. To know an object requires a
complete knowledge of its internal properties. 'In order to know
an object, though I need not know its external properties, I must
know all of its internal properties.' (2.01231) 'If I know an object I
also know all of its possible occurrences in states of affairs.'
(2.0123) Thus, it appears that one cannot 'know' a simple object
only *partially*.

As previously noted, the *Tractatus* employs the metaphor of 'a
space' to refer to an object's possibilities of occurrence in states
of affairs. 'Each thing is, as it were, in a space of possible states of
affairs. I can conceive this space to be empty, but I cannot
conceive of the thing without the space.' (2.013) This surely
means that I cannot conceive of the thing without conceiving of
the whole of its space of possibilities. To know an object requires
that one knows *all* of its possibilities of combination with other
objects. Now this seems to imply that knowing an object requires
knowing *all* the objects with which it can combine — and also,
knowing *all* the objects with which it cannot combine. Knowing
one object seems to require knowing *all* objects.

As previously said, the *Tractatus* speaks of objects as being
'given'. 'If all objects are given, then with that all possible states of
affairs are also given.' (2.0124) To *whom* are objects given? Surely
they are given as objects to anyone who thinks. Remark 2.0124
does not say that *all* objects are given. But this *is* said elsewhere:
'If objects are given, then with that we are given *all* objects. If
elementary propositions are given, then with that are given *all*
elementary propositions.' (5.524) Surely this means that if *any*
objects are given to us, then 'we' (human beings) are given *all* of
the objects. Knowing any of them involves knowing all of them.
Remark 5.524 also appears to declare that if it is given to a person
to understand *any* elementary proposition then it is given to him
to understand *every* elementary proposition.

All of this argues for the 'astonishing' interpretation of the *Tractatus*. A person cannot know some objects without knowing all objects. If he can understand one possible state of affairs he can understand every possible state of affairs. He cannot have a grasp of just a part of logical space: he must have a grasp of the whole of it. Even the most primitive thought 'reaches through the whole of logical space'. One cannot think at all without catching on to the form of the world — the totality of *a priori* possibilities.

The form of the world is independent of human thinking and human language. It is a possibility that human beings might never have existed: but it is not a possibility that the world might not have had a fixed form. 'Logic is *prior* to every experience — that something *is so*.' (5.552) I take this to imply that the totality of possibilities is presupposed by any experience whatever. An experience would be the perception that one or another of the *a priori* possibilities is realized.

The knowledge of the possible configurations of objects cannot be acquired through education. It is prior to all experience and therefore to all learning. Hence it is prior to the learning of any natural language. This would appear to assume that a child will have a grasp of the *a priori* possibilities before it learns to speak.

In the *Investigations* Wittgenstein says that Augustine describes the learning of human language in such a way as to imply that a child can *think* before it can speak (*PI* 32). Some present-day philosophers hold that one must have 'a language of thought' *before* one can learn any natural language. The same view appears to be assumed in the *Tractatus*. A child can *think* every possible arrangement of the substance of the world before it knows a single word.

Since the words 'possible' and 'possibility' play so large a role in the *Tractatus* it may be helpful to consider how they are used in ordinary speech. They belong with other words, such as 'can', 'could', 'might', 'is able to'. When we use these words in ordinary life they often mean different things. In his later writings Wittgenstein calls attention to some of the *different* meanings that these words have *in different circumstances*. In *The Brown Book* he notes that the question 'Can he speak?' (when asked of a doctor about a patient who suffered a throat injury) might mean 'Is his throat all right?'; whereas the same words (when addressed to the parent of a small child) might mean 'Has he learned to speak?' (*BB*, p. 114)

Consider the following example. I ask a friend, 'Can you go to the football game this afternoon?' Looked at from the viewpoint of the static *a priori* possibilities of the *Tractatus*, this would seem a strange question. Of course any person *can* go to a game! In the *Tractatus* the only impossibility is *logical* impossibility (6.375). So also, the only possibility is *logical* possibility. Any sentence that has sense presents a possibility.

But in ordinary life I would not have been asking about a logical possibility. If my friend had recently been ill, my question might mean 'Are you well enough to go?'; if he has a job, it might mean 'Do you have to work this afternoon?'; if he had previously told me that he would try to get a ticket for the game, the question might mean 'Do you have a ticket?' If he were to reply 'I can go', this would in the first case come to the same as 'I am well enough'; in the second case to 'I don't have to work'; in the third to 'I have a ticket.'

It might be objected that the two sentences 'I can go to the game' and 'I have a ticket for the game' certainly do not have the same meaning (same sense). Wittgenstein's reply would be that *in general* they do not have the same sense, but in the circumstances described they would have the same sense (*PI* 183; *BB*, pp. 113–15). The friend and I wish to go to the game together. The only obstacle we are aware of is that he does not have a ticket, and he agreed to try to get one. In the light of those circumstances, either of the sentences 'Can you go?' and 'Do you have a ticket?' would serve exactly the same purpose — namely, to inquire whether that particular obstacle had been removed.

It might be felt that this cannot be right: for the first sentence asks whether something is *possible*; the second sentence asks whether something is *actual* (does he have a ticket?). Surely the possible and the actual are different concepts.

The issue here reflects a striking difference between the *Tractatus* and Wittgenstein's second philosophy, in respect to what determines the *sense* of a sentence. The *Tractatus* says that anyone understands a sentence who understands its constituent parts (4.024). Nothing else is required. Two sentences with different constituent parts will differ in sense. The sense of a sentence is *fixed* — fixed by its constituent parts. If the sentence is composed of constituents you understand, then you understand the sentence. (I examine 4.024 more closely in chapter 5.)

In his new thinking Wittgenstein rejects this conception. To understand a sentence it is not enough that its constituent parts be understood. What must be added is a knowledge of *the circumstances*, previous and present, in which the sentence is employed.

If we merely *look* at the sentences 'He *can* go to the game', 'He is *able* to go', 'It is *possible* for him to go', not reflecting on the differing circumstances of their actual use, we may feel that they refer to something that is *on a plane above* such details as whether the person has a ticket, or has received permission, or is feeling well, and so on. The nature of this something, this 'possibility', may seem intangible, mysterious. If, however, we consider some of the actual occasions of life in which the sentence 'He can go to the game' is uttered, the sense of what is said will not appear to be elusive or intangible. We will realize that this sentence does not have a fixed meaning, but in various circumstances refers to different, specific, down-to-earth, obstacles, hindrances, prohibitions — none of which is mysterious.

It could be objected that here I am not dealing with the conception of 'possibility' that is central to the *Tractatus*. This is true. I was not referring to the *a priori* possibilities that comprise 'the form of the world'. The sentence 'He cannot go to the game without a ticket' expresses only an *empirical* impossibility. It means that as a matter of contingent fact the gatekeepers will not allow him to enter the stadium without a ticket. In contrast, the *a priori* possibilities are not a matter of what is empirical or contingent. According to the *Tractatus*, the enduring substance of the world consists of the simple objects. The objects can enter into combinations with one another. The totality of these possible combinations is the form of the world. This totality is fixed, unchangeable. It is prior to the existence of human beings, of experience, of thought, of language.

According to the *Tractatus*, if a name is assigned to an object, the use of that name in sentences must duplicate the form of that object. The possibilities of combination of that name with other names, in sentences that have sense, are determined by and exactly match the possibilities of combination of that object with other objects in states of affairs. What makes sense in language and thought is dependent on and derived from the nature of the objects. Language does not *create* what is thinkable: it can only *say* what is thinkable. What makes sense in language is based on the possible combinations of the simple elements of reality.

There is a profound difference here between the *Tractatus* and the *Investigations*. In the latter work a distinction *is* drawn between what is 'conceptual' or 'grammatical' on the one hand, and what is empirical or contingent on the other. Wittgenstein speaks of 'grammatical propositions', of 'grammatical differences', of the 'grammar' of a word. But in this second philosophy he rejects the idea that the grammar of language is determined by some underlying reality.

Undoubtedly there is a strong philosophical temptation to think for example, that the grammar of the word 'thinking' is determined by the nature of thinking, the grammar of the word 'pain' by the nature of pain, the grammar of the names of colours by the nature of the colours, and so on. Wittgenstein opposes this conception. Early in the *Investigations* he remarks that 'the word "meaning" is used incorrectly if one uses it to designate the thing that "corresponds" to the word. This confuses the meaning (*Bedeutung*) of a name with the bearer (*Träger*) of the name.' (*PI* 40) Of course this is a criticism of the assertion of the *Tractatus* that 'A name means an object. The object is its meaning.' (3.203) But the remark of *PI* 40 has a *generality* that is not always appreciated. It implies not only that the meaning of a proper name of a person is not *that person*, but also that the meaning of the name 'red' is not the colour *red*, the meaning of the name 'north' is not the direction *north*, the meaning of the word 'thinking' is not *thinking*, the meaning of the word 'pain' is not *pain*. With these words, as with any others, their meaning is not any thing, occurrence, or process, that 'corresponds' to the word, but instead is the *use* of the word.

In the *Investigations* there is this striking remark: '"Once you know *what* the word stands for, you understand it, you know its whole use."' (*PI* 264) Wittgenstein puts this remark in inverted commas to mark it as something one is inclined to say or think. The remark occurs in his treatment of the notion of the 'privacy' of sensation, in particular connection with the idea that if I 'inwardly' fix my attention on a sensation and name it 'pain', then I shall henceforth know how to use the word 'pain'. But the remark also applies to the conception of the *Tractatus* that when a name is given to a simple object the syntax of the name (its use in sentences) is thereby fixed. The remark also applies to the notion that if I focus my attention 'outwardly' on a sample of red colour, and am told that this is called 'red', then I shall know how to use that word.

The general assumption underlying these particular examples is that the grammar of language is determined by the things in the world to which the expressions of language refer. In opposition to this assumption Wittgenstein holds in his second philosophy, not merely that language is formed by human conventions and practices, but also that the grammar of language is, in a sense, *arbitrary*. What does he mean by that? Here is a luminous quotation from *Zettel*:

> Why don't I call the rules of cooking arbitrary, and why am I tempted to call the rules of grammar arbitrary? Because 'cooking' is defined by its goal, whereas 'speaking' is not. That is why the use of language is in a certain sense autonomous as cooking and washing are not. You cook badly if you are guided in your cooking by rules other than the right ones; but if you follow other rules than those of chess you are *playing another game*; and if you follow grammatical rules other than such-and-such ones, you are not saying something wrong, but are speaking of something else. (*Z* 320)

Why is Wittgenstein here only 'tempted' to say that the rules of grammar are arbitrary? Why doesn't he straightforwardly assert it? The answer is indicated by something he says about the rule of propositional logic that a double negation is an affirmation. He says: 'It looks as if it followed from the nature of negation that a double negative is an affirmative.' (*PI*, p. 147, fn.) It is clear that he thinks this is wrong. But he adds that '*Our nature*' is connected with this rule (ibid.). Perhaps he has in mind our tendency to imagine a proposition as an arrow pointing to a state of affairs. Given this image, a double negation of the proposition would be a rotation of the arrow through 360 degrees, thus returning it to its original position.

Consider another example. Could not the rules of chess be augmented by the rule that a move had to be made in ten seconds? Certainly. But this rule would spoil chess *for us*. If chess were played so swiftly people of normal mental powers would not be able to think out a series of moves and counter-moves, would not be able to plan a strategy. That rule would deprive the game of interest. The rejection of that rule would not be arbitrary but would have a justification. Someone might say that this rule would be 'incompatible with the nature of chess': but what this would amount to is that the rule would be incompatible with *our* nature. It is something about *us* that makes the rule of double negation acceptable, and the ten-second rule of chess unacceptable.

Let us go to an example that has more depth. We all have an inclination to think that the correct use of the word 'pain' is dictated by *the nature of pain*. This is why Wittgenstin's remark 'You learned the *concept* "pain" when you learned language' (*PI* 384) is felt to be so shocking! But let us go to the example. In *Zettel* 380 Wittgenstein imagines a tribe with a word that is used, at first sight, like our word 'pain'. When a person with visible injuries displays natural pain-behaviour, the other people respond with concern and help. Their word is connected with all of this, and so we translate their word with our word 'pain'. But later we discover that the response of concern and help occurs only if the complaining person has *perceptible* bodily damage; otherwise he is regarded with indifference, or even with contempt and ridicule. If there is no perceptible bruise, laceration or swelling, those people regard the pain-behaviour as pretence, or as illusion. (Their difference in attitude may appear *less* outrageous if we remember that *we too* tend to react with *more* pity, anxiety and help where there is perceptible bodily damage — after a child has had a fall, say — than where there is none. So this difference affects our reactions too: only we don't draw as sharp a line as they do.) We will probably say of these people that their *concept* of 'pain' is different from ours. Their word has a different grammar. They regard it as nonsense to apply it in the absence of perceptible injury.

Let us suppose that we reason with these people in order to bring them round to our viewpoint. We say, 'Don't you see that the *sensation* can be the *same* even if there is no perceptible injury?' They reply: 'Of course it cannot be the same!' So, they have a different grammar for 'same sensation'. We tell them that there are internal organs, veins, intestines, which can cause pain when infected, injured, blocked, or swollen. Those people concede that such internal parts can be impaired: but they believe that this causes, not pain, but only complaining behaviour! So they also have a different grammar for the word 'cause'. The difference in their concept of pain reverberates through many of their concepts. We say to them: 'Why should pain be produced solely by external damage?' They reply: 'Why should pain be produced by internal physiological conditions, and not mere pain-like behaviour?'

We can imagine that this arguing back and forth might get nowhere. We could say that we have *information* they don't have. But the difference in the two attitudes is so great that we cannot *teach* them our information. We are *certain* of something and they are *certain* of the opposite. This difference in certainties goes deeper than information or reasoning. It goes down to a difference in *natural reaction*.

Most of us tend to respond with concern when someone displays the behaviour of pain, largely in disregard of whether there is perceptible bodily injury. Those people respond with concern only when they perceive bodily injury. This is the difference that results in two different grammars of 'pain'.

The following might be a specific grammatical difference between their concept and ours: if one of us were to declare to one of them, in all sincerity, 'I really was in pain yesterday, even though I had no visible injury', he might be told, 'You only *thought* you were in pain!' Our concept of pain does not permit such a remark to be taken seriously. Their language of 'pain' allows for a logical possibility of illusion or error that our language does not allow. (A similar case is this. A person declares in fright, 'I saw a ghost in my room last night!' Another person calmly says: 'You couldn't have seen a ghost. There is no such thing.' These two employ a different grammar for the word 'ghost'.)

Wittgenstein's example of an invented natural history helps to make it clear that what is *a priori* possible or impossible, what is empirical or contingent, what is sense and what is not, is *relative* to the grammar of a language, and that this grammar will be shaped by attitudes, tendencies, reactions, which are natural for the speakers of the language. To imagine differences in natural reactions enables one to imagine *different boundaries* of sense and nonsense, of possibility and impossibility. As Wittgenstein puts it:

> If anyone believes that certain concepts are absolutely the correct ones, and that having different ones would mean not realizing something that we realize — then let him imagine certain very general facts of nature to be different from what we are used to, and the formation of concepts different from the usual ones will become intelligible to him. (*PI*, p. 230)

But what becomes then of Wittgenstein's vision, in the *Tractatus*, of the form of the world, of the one logical space, of the fixed order of possibilities — which is *prior* to human societies and languages, and is changeless? Nothing has become of it. It was a vision of something that never was. It was a metaphysical illusion.

It tends to be assumed without question by logicians and philosophers that *logical possibilities* belong to a realm that is entirely sealed off from the way things are in the actual world. The order of logical possibilities must be *prior* to whatever is contingent and empirical. This assumption is embedded in the *Tractatus*. In his second philosophical career Wittgenstein turned this assumption upside down. He saw that the formation of concepts, of the boundaries of what is thinkable, will be influenced by what is *contingent* — by facts of nature, including human nature.

─────── CHAPTER 2 ───────

Language and the Objects

The *Tractatus* is an enigmatic work. It is possible for different readers to have quite different impressions of what the relationships are between the basic conceptions of the book. In chapter 1 I put forward the view that the theory of language of the *Tractatus* is based on the conception that there is a fixed form of the world which consists of the simple objects. On my interpretation, the form of the world and the objects are independent of language and thought. Some students of the *Tractatus* take a different view. According to their interpretation, at least as I understand it, the *Tractatus* contains first and foremost a theory of language, a theory in which language is conceived of as being entirely *autonomous*: that is to say, language does not presuppose a reality that is independent of language. In this theory of language (or theory of logical syntax, or 'semantic theory') there have to be elementary propositions composed of primitive (undefined) signs, called 'names'. The 'meaning' of such a sign is said to be an 'object'. But, according to the interpretation of the *Tractatus* under consideration, there is no assumption that the so-called 'objects' have any existence independent of language. In the present chapter I will respond to this interpretation. In chapter 3 I will undertake a closer study of the concept of an object, and of Wittgenstein's reasons for thinking that there have to be objects.

My friend and colleague, Peter Winch, read an early draft of chapter 1 and made serious objections to it, which he set forth in an unpublished paper. Winch holds that my interpretation of the *Tractatus* is in conflict with something that Wittgenstein says in his preface to the *Tractatus*. Winch holds, and I agree, that this preface should be read as a part of the *Tractatus*. The passage to which he refers is the following:

The whole sense of the book might be summed up in the following words: what can be said at all can be said clearly; and whereof one cannot speak, thereof one must be silent.

Thus the aim of the book is to draw a boundary of thinking, or rather — not of thinking, but of the expression of thoughts: for in order to draw a boundary of thinking, we should have to be able to think both sides of the boundary (we should have to be able to think what cannot be thought).

It will therefore only be in language that the boundary can be drawn, and what lies on the other side of the boundary will be plain nonsense.

Winch says, rightly, that Wittgenstein was in these remarks spelling out the general purport of the book. Winch thinks I am holding that in the *Tractatus* the logical syntax of language is what it is because of 'the nature of the world'. Now this remark is ambiguous. It can be taken in a sense which would be entirely wrong. But before explaining this, let us see more of Winch's view. According to him, when Wittgenstein says that the boundary of the expression of thoughts can be drawn 'only in language', he means that the boundary itself must be thought of as a linguistic boundary. That is to say, we cannot decide that one form of words makes sense and another does not, by comparing these linguistic expressions with something non-linguistic. We can make the distinction only by referring to features of the linguistic expressions themselves. I believe that I can agree with Winch here, but in a sense that is compatible with my interpretation. Winch calls attention to *Tractatus* 4.114—4.115, where Wittgenstein is describing the role of philosophy:

> It must set the boundary of what is thinkable and, by that, the boundary of what is unthinkable.
> It must set the boundary of what cannot be thought from within through what can be thought. (4.114)

> It will indicate what cannot be said, by presenting clearly what can be said. (4.115)

Let us consider the remark that philosophy 'will indicate what cannot be said, by presenting clearly what can be said'. Presenting clearly what can be said consists in expounding the nature of genuine propositions. Genuine propositions, as distinguished from pseudo-propositions, describe or present possible states of affairs. If such a state of affairs exists, it *might not* have existed. If it does not exist, it *might have* existed. Every genuine proposition is *contingent*. The same is true of every genuine thought. By setting forth the nature of genuine propositions one is 'drawing the boundary' between what can be said and what cannot be said; between what can and what cannot be thought.

This boundary, however, is drawn against, or on, the background of certain assumptions: for example, that all possible worlds possess one and the same form; that there are simple elements of reality (objects); that these combine to form states of affairs; that if there is to be language it must be possible to form elementary propositions composed of signs that deputize for objects.

One role of philosophy is to draw attention to these assumptions or presuppositions — which, since they are *a priori* (non-contingent), cannot be expressed in genuine propositions. Philosophical remarks are pseudo-propositions. Nevertheless, they can clarify the nature of language and thought. 'The result of philosophy is not "philosophical propositions", but the clarification of propositions.' (4.112)

A philosopher-logician may pose certain questions which he would like to have answered *a priori*. He may want to know what are all of the possible forms of elementary propositions; or how many names there are with different meanings (5.55). He may want to know, for example, whether it is possible that there should be a state of affairs that could be described only by employing a relation containing 27 terms (5.5541). Wittgenstein's response is that such questions *cannot* be answered *a priori*.

> Our fundamental principle is that whenever a question can be decided by logic at all, it must be possible to decide it without more ado.
>
> (And if we get into a position where we have to look at the world for an answer to such a problem, that shows that we are on a completely wrong track.) (5.551)

Winch seems to think that this passage is a refutation of my view that, according to the *Tractatus*, language presupposes a fixed form of the world, which consists of the objects (2.023), and which is independent of language. But the above passage does not sustain such a reading. Wittgenstein was saying there that 'problems of logic' cannot be answered by 'looking at the world'. By 'looking at the world' he means observing whether this or that state of affairs *exists*. This would be an observation of what is contingent, of what happens to be the case. But the problems of logic are *a priori*. They concern what *must* be or *cannot* be.

Wittgenstein's thought is spelled out in the remarks that immediately follow 5.551:

> The 'experience' that we need in order to understand logic is not that there is such-and-such a situation, but that something *is*: that, however, is *not* an experience.
> Logic is *prior* to every experience — that something *is so*.
> It is prior to the *How*, not prior to the *What*. (5.552)

Wittgenstein was clearly holding here that logic is prior to every perception that such-and-such *is the case*. It is prior to any observation of *how* things are related to one another.

But when he says that logic is *not* prior to the *What*, and that the 'experience' we need in order to understand logic is that something *is* — these remarks are difficult to construe. By the *What* and the *is*, does he mean *a* world — not this or that *kind* of world, but just *a* world? Or by the *What* and the *is* does he mean *substance*, the *objects* — that which is independent of what is the case, and which constitutes the form of any possible world?

On the first interpretation the existence of *a* world would be an *a priori* necessity. On the second interpretation the existence of any world at all would be contingent. It would be logically possible that nothing whatever should *be the case* — that there should be no existing states of affairs. The simple objects would be there, but they would not have entered into any combinations with one another.

This second interpretation seems baffling. How could the objects exist without being in any relation with one another? Nevertheless, this second interpretation may be the right one. Dan Rashid has pointed out to me that 2.013 seems to imply the second interpretation:

> Each thing is, as it were, in a space of possible states of affairs. I can conceive of this space as empty, but not of the thing without the space. (2.013)

The remark 'I can conceive of this space as empty' certainly appears to mean that *none* of the states of affairs into which a thing (and therefore an object) *could* enter, might exist. If this is possible for one object, it would be possible for every object.

Therefore the whole of logical space could have been empty: there might have been no existing states of affairs — that is, no world at all.

I think the second interpretation is the right one. The existence of any particular state of affairs is contingent. The existence of that particular grouping of states of affairs, which is the actual world, is also contingent. Going back to 5.552, the *What* that is presupposed by logic is not *the* world, or *a* world, but *substance*. Substance is composed of the simple objects (2.021). The objects (substance) constitute the fixed form of any possible world (2.021, 2.022). So one can say that the *What* which is presupposed by logic is just the fixed form of the world, i.e. the totality of logical possibilities, i.e. the whole of logical space.

On this interpretation, the feeling that the objects must be 'related' to one another in *some* way, is satisfied by the idea that they might be related only in the sense that together they constitute logical space. They might not have been related to one another in the special way of constituting existing states of affairs.

Since logical space (the totality of possibilities) is given, it can be determined *a priori* (i.e. by logic) that a state of affairs is a linking of objects, that a fact is an existing state of affairs, that the objects are simple, that human beings can make pictures of facts, that a picture is a structure composed of elements, that a picture and what it depicts must have the same form, that thoughts and propositions are pictures, and so on. That something *is* (the fixed form of the world) gives rise to all of these *a priori* determinations of logic.

On my interpretation of the *Tractatus*, its theory of language *presupposes* such conceptions as that there is a fixed form of the world, that there are simple objects, and so on. As I have said, the *a priori* remarks that express these conceptions do not 'state facts'.

Winch refers to the remark that 'A name means an object. The object is its meaning.' (3.203) He thinks that on my view this remark 'states a relation between something linguistic, a name, and something non-linguistic, an object'. That is correct. Winch goes on to say that 'Wittgenstein did not think of those sentences as "stating facts" at all.' That is also correct. The two remarks in 3.203 are both *a priori*. Wittgenstein was saying that the meaning of a simple sign is something entirely different from the meaning of a sign that refers to a complex. He was saying that the meaning of a simple sign (a name) *has to be* the object for which it deputizes in an elementary sentence. Remark 3.203 is a general one about the meaning of *any* name. The meaning of a name *is* the object that it means. The object that it means is a simple element of reality. The object is not a linguistic entity. Winch says that in so far as one can speak of a 'relation' holding between a name and an object it would be an '*internal* relation', not an '*external* relation'. I think there is an ambiguity here. When A and B stand in an 'internal' relationship it is inconceivable that they might not stand in that relationship. But when a simple sign of language designates a particular object it is conceivable that that sign might have designated a different object. What *is* 'internal' is that the *meaning* of a name is *an* object. One could regard this as the *definition* of the phrase 'the meaning of a name'. That names *mean* objects, and that objects are their *meaning*, is an internal property of names, and an internal relationship between names and objects. Internal relations are *a priori* and so cannot be stated in genuine propositions:

> The existence of such internal relations cannot be stated in propositions, but shows itself in the propositions that present the relevant states of affairs and are concerned with the relevant objects. (4.122)

Wittgenstein gives an example that illustrates his meaning:

> A property is internal if it is unthinkable that its object should not possess it.
> (This shade of blue and that one stand, *eo ipso*, in the internal relation of lighter to darker. It is unthinkable that *these* two objects should not stand in this relation.) (4.123)

It is unthinkable, inconceivable, that *this* shade and *that* shade should not be related as lighter to darker. Therefore, the sentence 'This shade is lighter than that one' does not express a genuine proposition: for the negation of any genuine proposition is conceivable.

Winch says, rightly, that the words 'name' and 'object' express *formal* concepts. He refers to the following remark:

> When something falls under a formal concept as one of its objects, this cannot be expressed by a proposition. But it shows itself in the very sign for this object. (A name shows that it designates an

object, a sign for a number that it designates a number, etc.)
(4.126)

But note: 'A name shows that it designates an object.' If, for example, the word 'red' were a name, the sentence 'The word "red" is a name' would not express a genuine proposition. The role of the word 'red' in the language (its logical syntax) would *show* that it is a name — that is, would show that it designates an object.

Winch thinks it wrong to suppose that, according to the *Tractatus*, 'the meaning of any particular name consists in its standing in relation to something extra-linguistic, an object.' But an object is certainly not a linguistic entity: it is not a word, or phrase, or sign. Objects are unchanging, enduring things (2.027). They persist through all change (2.0271). Their configurations constitute states of affairs in the world (2.0272). The objects would remain the same in every possible world, including a world in which there was no language.

On Winch's interpretation of the *Tractatus*, as I understand it, language does not depend on anything outside of language, on anything 'extra-linguistic'. He refers to the following remark in support of his view:

> In logical syntax the meaning of a sign should never play a role. It must be possible to establish logical syntax without mentioning the *meaning* of a sign: only the description of expressions may be presupposed. (3.33)

I think the position is the following: the task of describing the logical syntax of expressions can be undertaken, and understood, only by people who *know* the meaning of those expressions. The explanation of the *meaning* of a particular expression would belong to the *teaching* of language, not to describing logical syntax. A description of logical syntax would not refer to any individual expression, and therefore not to the meaning of any individual expression. It would refer to a *class* of expressions. It would be formal, abstract. It could be stated in purely logical notation. An example of a description of logical syntax would be Russell's formal analysis of what he called 'definite descriptions'. This analysis does not mention any particular definite description (except as an illustration). It purports to set out the form of *all* definite descriptions. Other propositions of logical syntax might state conditions that any sentence must satisfy in order to have sense. For example, the statement that 'In a proposition there must be exactly as many distinguishable parts as in the situation it presents' (4.04) may have been regarded by Wittgenstein as belonging to logical syntax. Perhaps he would even have regarded 3.203 as belonging to logical syntax.

Since descriptions of logical syntax are general and abstract, it is clear that those descriptions will not, as 3.33 says, mention the meaning of any particular sign. But this does not deny or diminish the view of the *Tractatus*, that 'objects' are non-linguistic entities, that they are the simple elements of which everything is composed, that they would 'exist' even if there were no human beings or any language, and that *the meaning* of a primitive sign of language *is* the object for which it deputizes in an elementary sentence.

Winch's view is that 'A name has meaning if it behaves in language just as though it had one; in fact, its having a particular meaning just consists in its having a "significant use" (*sinnvollen Gebrauch*).' He refers to the following remark:

> The rules of logical syntax must go without saying, once we know how each individual sign signifies. (3.334)

Winch's comment is: 'It is important that Wittgenstein writes "*how*" rather than "*what*" here. The "what" will already be settled once the "how" is established.' Winch adds that what *corresponds* to the meaning of an expression 'is not some peculiar sort of extra-linguistic entity, but a certain syntax. Having such a syntax is what "meaning an object" comes to.'

What Winch says here is true of some linguistic expressions, but seems to be clearly wrong in respect of those expressions that are the primitive signs of language, and are called 'names'. An object *does* 'correspond' to a name; an object is *not* a linguistic entity; an object *is* the meaning of a name. According to the *Tractatus*, the syntax of a name will indeed *match* the form of the object that the name means. But the name has that particular syntax *because* of the nature of the object for which it deputizes. The syntax of the name is *derived* from the object. Having that syntax is *not* what 'meaning that object' comes to: although a name would not *mean* a certain object if the syntax of the name did not correspond to the form *of* the object. One could say that the syntax of a name *models* the form of the object for which the name deputizes.

Winch seems to have the impression that on my view the correlations between names and objects are established *before* the names are used in propositions. Such a view would imply that a simple sign can name an object *outside of* any proposition. This does not accord with the *Tractatus*, and is not my view. The *Tractatus* says that 'only in the context of a proposition does a name have meaning.' (3.3) 'It is impossible for words to appear in two different roles: by themselves, and in propositions.' (2.0122) 'A name occurs in a proposition only in the context of an elementary proposition.' (4.23)

I take it that if you were to utter a name just by itself, without any propositional context being implied, that utterance would be meaningless. You would not be referring to anything. This would be so with any word. If you uttered the word 'queen', but had no propositional context in mind, you did not *mean anything*. Thus, there cannot be a preliminary preparation for language, consisting of correlating signs with objects, outside of propositions. A sign means a certain object only when its use in a sentence reflects something of the form of the object. Nevertheless, when a sign is so used, what it means (designates, deputizes for) is something that is independent of language. Language can have sense only if it mirrors the fixed form of the world, which consists of the objects.

Winch's interpretation of the *Tractatus* is similar to one put forward several years previously by Hidé Ishiguro, in her essay 'Use and Reference of Names'. She says that 'The "objects" of the *Tractatus* are not particular entities in any normal sense, but entities invoked to fit into a semantic theory.'[1] Now it is true that the 'objects' of the *Tractatus* are quite peculiar entities. They are not the sticks and stones that we encounter in daily life. They have the extraordinary properties of being unchangeable, indestructible, of enduring through all change. But that doesn't mean that they were not assumed to be real entities, or that they were parasitical on Wittgenstein's theory of logical syntax.

Ishiguro says, quite correctly, that 'a word or a symbol cannot have the role of referring to a fixed object without having a fixed use.'[2] She thinks the key to the relation between names and objects is to be found in the remark of the *Tractatus* that 'only in the context of a sentence does a name have meaning.' (3.3) She infers from this that 'One cannot look for the references of Names independently of their use in propositions.'[3]

This last remark of hers is somewhat puzzling. I don't think one 'looks for' the reference of a name. Names occur only in elementary propositions (4.23); that is, only in propositions that are 'completely analysed' (3.2, 2.201). You don't start out with a completely analysed proposition and then look for objects to correspond to the names of which it is composed. The idea of the *Tractatus* seems to be that you may wish to provide an analysis of some state of affairs that is described by an unanalysed sentence of ordinary language. You want to analyse that state of affairs in terms of the simple objects that compose it. As you proceed in the analysis you will provide a name for each of the objects: you will substitute a name for each object. You will also try to arrange the names in a combination that will match the configuration of the objects in that state of affairs. If you succeed in all of this, you will have produced an elementary proposition that correctly pictures that state of affairs, and which is logically equivalent to the original unanalysed proposition of ordinary language.

Ishiguro has the idea that when the logical syntax of a name is settled, then the object that corresponds to the name will be whatever it is that satisfies that logical syntax. This idea is not wrong in itself: but she seems to think that what has *priority* is the syntax. She says 'The *Tractatus* view entails that it is the use of the Name which gives you the identity of the object rather than vice versa.'[4] 'In the *Tractatus* catching on to the use of a Name *is* grasping the identity of the reference of the name.'[5] She says that 'Names in the *Tractatus* are like dummy Names', and also that 'the identity of an object can be determined only by settling the sense of the propositions in which the Names occur.'[6]

Ishiguro seems to have an incorrect view of the relation between names and objects. She is right in saying that a name cannot refer to 'a fixed object without having a fixed use'. But she is wrong about *the direction of determination*. In the *Tractatus* view the objects are real things: they are the substance of the world; they are that which stands fast, endures, no matter what is the case (2.024). An object has a *form* that consists of its possibilities of combining with other objects in states of affairs. In order for a name to 'deputize for', or to be a 'proxy' for an object, the name must have a syntax that reflects the form of the object. The name must have the same possibilities of combining with other names in elementary propositions as the object has of combining with other objects in states of affairs. The name itself has to have a 'form' (a syntax) that is patterned after and conforms to the form of the object. It is by virtue of this that the form of picturing of propositions is the same as logical form, i.e. the form of reality (2.18). Although a name and its object have the same 'form', the 'form' of the name (its logical syntax) is dictated by the form of the object — not the other way round. The logical syntax of names is determined by the nature of their objects.

Ishiguro says:

> The simple objects whose existence was posited were not so much a kind of metaphysical entity conjured up to support a logical theory as something whose existence adds no extra content to the logical theory.[7]

She seems to be saying that the simple objects, if considered as actual entities, really have no role to play in the *Tractatus*. Perhaps this is what she means by saying that the names are like 'dummy' names. In contrast, I think that the objects are the *foundation* for the theory of logical syntax of the *Tractatus*. Wittgenstein had various reasons for believing that there *had to be* simple elements of reality. (I examine these reasons in chapter 3.) These elements, or objects, are 'metaphysical entities' in the sense that their existence is deduced as a necessary presupposition of the form of the world, and of thought and language. The objects are indeed not 'conjured up to support a logical theory': instead, the conception that complex things and states of affairs are *composed* of objects was thought to *require* the theory of language and of logical analysis of the *Tractatus*. Substance (the objects) does not 'add extra content to the logical theory': rather, it provides both the form and the content of the world (2.025). An adequate theory of language must explain how language is capable of portraying the configurations of the objects.

Brian McGuinness, in an essay entitled 'The So-called Realism of the *Tractatus*', takes a position similar to the one stated earlier by Ishiguro. He endorses her view that (as he puts it) 'reference cannot be determined independently of how we settle or understand sense. To understand the reference of a name is to know something about the truth-conditions of some propositions.'[8]

It is true, as I have said, that when a name designates a particular object the use of that name in propositions is thereby settled. McGuinness goes on to say: 'Use determines reference in the *Tractatus*.'[9] Like Ishiguro he has reversed the direction of determination. He seems to want to say that 'reference is defined solely in terms of semantic role.'[10] I presume that by the 'semantic role' of a name he means its 'logical syntax'. His view seems to be that which object a particular name designates is to be found out solely by seeing how that name is employed in sentences.

There may be a first-person/third-person ambiguity here. If I heard a person utter a word and thought he was using it as a name, but did not know to which object the name referred, then I might observe how he uses that name in various sentences, and infer that such-and-such an object is meant by that name. But it could not work like that in my own case. I would not find out what object is designated by a name *I* am employing, by observing how *I* combine that name with other names in various elementary sentences. No! When I construct an elementary proposition in order to analyse some state of affairs, I correlate names with objects. For any given object I know its possible combinations with other objects. When I correlate a name with an object it is thereby settled for me in what linguistic contexts that name can occur. The name carries a definite grammar: but it has that specific grammar only because it is correlated with a specific object. On the view of the *Tractatus* it would be senseless to suppose that I *might not know* which object I meant by a name, and had to infer this from an observation of how *I* employ that name in sentences.

McGuinness says that 'Objects are . . . beyond being, and it is therefore misleading to regard Wittgenstein as a realist in respect of them.'[11] It is true that, according to the *Tractatus*, it cannot be 'said' that the simple objects 'exist'. Only complex things and states of affairs can be said to exist or not exist. Nevertheless, the *Tractatus* comes close to saying that the objects exist: 'Only if there are objects can the world have a fixed form.' (2.026) The world has a fixed form; therefore there are objects.

It seems that Wittgenstein was drawn in two different directions. On the one hand he wanted to say that objects *have to exist*; on the other hand he wanted to say that it is nonsense to speak of the objects as either 'existing' or 'not existing'. (I discuss this tension in chapter 3.)

The fact that in the *Tractatus* there is a peculiar difficulty about stating that the objects do or do not exist, is no warrant for McGuinness's remark that since the objects are 'beyond being' it is therefore 'misleading to regard Wittgenstein as a realist in respect of them'. If a philosopher conceives of the world as composed of unchangeable, simple elements, then he is going to be in difficulties concerning what can be *said* about those elements. But this does not mean that doubt must be allowed as to their reality.

On my interpretation of the *Tractatus*, its theory of language rests on a metaphysical underpinning. It is often remarked, and with some justice, that the *Tractatus* is an 'anti-metaphysical' work. This may give rise to the feeling that it must be wrong to think that the theory of language in the *Tractatus* is given a metaphysical foundation. A clear statement of the anti-metaphysical position of the book is the following:

> The correct method in philosophy would really be: To say nothing except what can be said . . . and then, whenever another person wanted to say something metaphysical, to demonstrate to him that he had failed to give a meaning to certain signs in his propositions. (6.53)

Did Wittgenstein recognize that some of the conceptions and assertions of the *Tractatus* were metaphysical? Perhaps not. He does say that anyone who understands him will in the end recognize 'my propositions' as 'nonsensical': 'He must overcome these propositions, and then he will see the world aright.' (6.54) In saying that his own propositions were nonsensical, did he mean that they were metaphysical? Not necessarily. Perhaps he only meant that they were *a priori*, and therefore not 'genuine' propositions. It is possible that even though his posture was anti-metaphysical, none the less he introduced metaphysical conceptions into his work without recognizing them as metaphysical.

The *Tractatus* does in fact contain a number of metaphysical conceptions: for example, that the world has a fixed form (2.023, 2.026), and that there is an essential nature of all propositions (4.5, 5.471). Probably the most striking and far-reaching metaphysical conception is that of a simple object. In his brilliant criticism of this conception, in the *Investigations* (*PI* 46—8), Wittgenstein demonstrates the metaphysical character of the idea that something might be simple in an 'absolute' sense. Given that the conception of a simple object is metaphysical, it follows that several other conceptions are metaphysical — a 'name', an 'elementary proposition', an 'elementary state of affairs', and also the claim that every genuine proposition has a 'complete analysis' into elementary propositions. Was Wittgenstein aware of the metaphysical character of these conceptions? It doesn't seem likely. I think that if he had been aware of this the *Tractatus* would never have been written. What was later perceived as metaphysics in the *Investigations* was embraced as solid reality in the *Tractatus*.

The interpretation of the *Tractatus* which I am contesting holds that it is a misunderstanding of the *Tractatus* to suppose that the meaning of a 'name' is something other than and prior to the name's logico-syntatical role. I should mention, however, that Winch does not agree with Ishiguro's remark that *Tractatus* names are 'like dummy names' — for the reason that her remark suggests that *Tractatus* names don't really *refer* to anything, whereas Winch's view is that they certainly do refer, but their referring is nothing other than their role in the symbolism. If we leave aside Ishiguro's remark about 'dummy names', I think the central idea of the Ishiguro-McGuinness-Winch interpretation of the *Tractatus* could be put like this (as Winch did put it to me): 'The discussion of what it is for a name to function in a certain way in a symbolism *is* a discussion of what it is for it to have a reference.'

I would be willing to agree that Wittgenstein *ought* to have understood by 'the meaning of a name' nothing other than the role of a name in the symbolism. If he had understood the matter in this way the view of the *Tractatus* would have been much closer to that of the *Investigations*. I also agree that in the *Tractatus* the syntactical role of a name *is* the meaning of the name, *if* one understands by this *just* that the logical syntax of a name must exactly *match* the form of the object that it names.

I think that Wittgenstein was confused about 'objects' and 'names'. This is evident in the *Notebooks*, where he racked his brain trying to decide what an example of an 'object' would be — but without success. One might *suppose* that this confusion was present only in those preliminary studies, and that in perfecting his thinking in the *Tractatus* he had got rid of this unclarity — had come to realize that it was senseless to look about in the world for examples of 'objects', since the meaning of a name was nothing other than the name's syntactical role.

There is plenty of evidence against this supposition. First, there is Wittgenstein's own testimony. I quote from my *Memoir*:

> I asked Wittgenstein whether, when he wrote the *Tractatus*, he had ever decided upon anything as an *example* of a 'simple object'. His reply was that at that time his thought had been that he was a *logician*; and that it was not his business, as a logician, to try to decide whether this thing or that was a simple thing or a complex thing, that being a purely *empirical* matter! It was clear that he regarded his former opinion as absurd.[12]

According to this account it was Wittgenstein's conception when he wrote the *Tractatus* that it required an *empirical* investigation to determine whether any given thing was simple or complex. One would have to study the phenomena of physical nature, or of sensation or of sense-experience. This would mean that it could not be determined solely from the way a word functioned in a symbolism, whether what it designated was a simple object.

There is also Wittgenstein's testimony in the *Investigations*. He quotes the description in the *Theaetetus*, by Socrates, of a conception he has heard of — namely, that there are primary elements of reality, out of which we and everything else are composed; that there can be no description or account of the primary elements; that they can only be *named*. And Wittgenstein remarks that the 'objects' of the *Tractatus* were conceived of as such primary elements (*PI* 46). It seems pretty obvious that in this conception described by Socrates the primary elements of reality are independent of language. The philosophical idea that there are 'primary elements of reality' is linked with but not identical with the idea that an adequate symbolism must contain indefinable signs.

The *Tractatus* itself contains evidence that tells in favour of the view that 'objects' are ontologically independent of 'names'. As I mentioned in the first chapter, Wittgenstein states the relationship between 'names' and 'objects' by employing the verb *vertreten* and the noun *Vertretung*. The idea is that a name 'deputizes for', or 'is a proxy for', or 'replaces', or 'takes the place of' an object. 'In a proposition a name deputizes for an object.' (3.22) 'Objects can only be *named*. Signs deputize for them.' (3.221) 'The possibility of propositions is based on the principle of the replacement of objects by signs.' (4.0312) There is also the striking image of 'a living picture':

> One name stands for one thing, another for another thing, and they are combined with one another. In this way the whole — like a living picture — presents a state of affairs. (4.0311)

Wittgenstein's insistence on saying that a name 'deputizes for', 'is a proxy for', 'takes the place of' an object, makes it quite clear that he thought of an 'object' as something apart from the syntax of a name. The secretary of a corporation can deputize for the president of the corporation at a meeting of the executive committee. But the president and the secretary are two different persons. A name deputizes for an object; but the name and the object are two different things. It is true, in a sense, that whether a word deputizes for an object is a question of what kind of logico-syntactic role that word has in the symbolism. But whether a word does deputize for an object is also a matter of whether there *is* an object for which it *can* deputize — just as the secretary cannot deputize for the president unless there *is* a president. And when we consider the comparison of a proposition with a tableau vivant, it can hardly be doubted that the 'objects' have an existence prior to and independent of the 'names' which are their proxies.

Finally, it is said in the *Tractatus* that a simple object can be *known*. It was pointed out in chapter 1 that what Wittgenstein meant by 'knowing an object' agreed with Russell's *definition* of 'knowledge by acquaintance'. A simple object can be 'known' in the sense that one can 'know *it* without knowing anything *about* it'. Obviously, this could not be said of the syntax of a word, of the role of that word in a symbolism. One could know the syntax of a word: but to know this would require knowing a lot *about* the way that word actually functions in the symbolism. Thus, 'knowing a simple object' must be something other than knowing the logical syntax of the name of the object.

CHAPTER 3

The Elements of Reality

Although Wittgenstein did not offer a single example of a 'simple object' in the *Tractatus*, this does not mean that he did not struggle hard to try to decide on an example, and also to understand the thinking that drew him to a belief in simple objects. The *Notebooks* present ample evidence of such a struggle. There he said:

> What is my fundamental thought when I talk about simple objects? Do not 'complex objects' in the end satisfy the demands which I apparently make on the simple ones? If I give this book a name 'N' and now talk about N, is not the relation of N to that 'complex object', to those forms and contents, *essentially* the same as I imagined only between name and simple object? For note: even if the name 'N' vanishes on further analysis, it still indicates a single common thing. (*NB*, pp. 59–60)

But in an entry of the same day (14 June 1915) he goes on to say:

> It seems that the idea of the *simple* is already contained in that of the complex and in the idea of analysis, and in such a way that we come to this idea quite apart from any examples of simple objects, or of propositions which mention them, and we realize the existence of the simple object — *a priori* — as a logical necessity.
> So it looks as if the existence of the simple objects is related to that of the complex ones as the sense of not-*p* is to the sense of *p*: the *simple* object is *presupposed* in the complex. (*NB*, p. 60)

It is surely correct that the idea of something's being 'complex' presupposes the idea of something's being 'non-complex' (i.e. 'simple'), just as the sense of 'not-*p*' is presupposed by the sense of '*p*', or as the idea of 'high' presupposes the idea of 'low'. But it does not follow that anything is 'high' or 'low', or 'complex' or 'non-complex', in an *absolute* sense.

Wittgenstein continued to try to give an example of a simple object. He wondered whether 'this watch' did not satisfy the conditions for being a simple object (*NB*, p. 60). He even wonders whether *all* names might not be *genuine names* — that is, whether all objects 'were in a certain sense simple objects' (*NB*, p. 61).

In this connection he makes a curious remark:

> When I say this watch is shiny, and what I mean by this watch alters its composition in the smallest particular, then this means not merely that the sense of the sentence alters in its content, but *also* that *the statement about this watch* straight-way alters its sense. The whole form of the proposition alters. (*NB*, p. 61)

This seems to be a paradoxical view. Consider the statement 'This watch belonged to my father.' This statement would have a different sense for every change in the watch, e.g. if the watch became less shiny. Would it even be *true* that *this* watch was my father's watch?

Fortunately, Wittgenstein rejects this idea a few pages later.

> If, e.g., I say that this watch is not in the drawer, there is absolutely no need for it to *follow logically* that a wheel which is in the watch is not in the drawer, for perhaps *I had not the least knowledge* that the wheel was in the watch, and hence could not have meant by 'this watch' the complex in which the wheel occurs. (*NB*, pp. 64—5)

It appears that in his thinking about the sense of a sentence, his focus was shifting from the physical sentence to what one *means* by it when one uses it. He said: 'All I want is only for *my meaning* to be completely analysed!' (*NB*, p. 63) He begins to emphasize that what one *means* by a sentence must be clear and definite.

> When I say, 'The book is lying on the table', does this really have a completely clear sense? (An *extremely* important question.) But the sense must be clear, for after all we mean *something* by the sentence, and as much as we *certainly* mean must surely be clear. If the proposition 'The book is lying on the table' has a clear sense, then I must, whatever *is the case*, be able to say whether the proposition is true or false. But there could very well occur *cases* in which I should not be able to say straight off whether the book is still to be called 'lying on the table'. Then — ? (*NB*, p. 67)

It is easy to think of cases where one does not know whether to

say of a book that it is 'lying on the table': e.g. one end of it is on
the table but the other end is supported by some other books.
Wittgenstein deals with this difficulty in an interesting way. He
says that it can be that

> the sentence 'The book is lying on the table' presents my meaning
> completely, but that I am using the words, e.g. 'lying on', with a
> *special* meaning here, and that elsewhere they have another
> meaning. What I mean by the verb is perhaps a quite special
> relation which the book now actually has to the table. (*NB*, p. 68)

Wittgenstein is suggesting that although there can be many
situations where it is unclear whether or not a book can be said to
be 'lying on' a table, yet in a particular situation where he asserts
the proposition, he may mean by 'lying on' just that actual relation
that the book has to the table. The *general* meaning of 'lying on'
may be vague, but in a particular case I can give it a precise
meaning. Wittgenstein says that he wants to *justify* the vagueness
of ordinary sentences, and declares that it *can* be justified (*NB*,
p. 70). The justification seems to be this: taken generally a
sentence may be vague, but when a person uses the sentence to
make an assertion, what he *means* is not vague! 'It seems clear
that what we *mean* must always be "*sharp*".' (*NB*, p. 68) 'It is clear
that *I know* what I *mean* by the vague sentence.' (*NB*, p. 70)

> I tell someone 'The watch is lying on the table', and now he says:
> 'Yes, but if the watch were in such-and-such a position would you
> still say it was lying on the table?' And I should become uncertain.
> This shows that I did not know what I meant by 'lying' *in general*. If
> someone were to drive me into a corner in this way in order to
> show that I did not know what I meant, I should say: '*I know* what I
> mean; I mean just *this*', pointing to the appropriate complex with
> my finger. And in this complex I do actually have the two objects
> in a relation. (*NB*, p. 70)

It is a strange contention that people (in conversation, say) always
know what they mean, and that what they mean always has a
sharp, definite sense. This is far from being true. For example, if I
were speaking to you about an acquaintance of mine, I might say,
'He is a peculiar chap.' You might ask, 'Peculiar? In what way?' I
might ponder this, and finally answer, 'I can't really explain it. But
he certainly is peculiar.' Did I *know* what I meant? Did I mean
something *definite*? Or consider this actual incident. A radio
announcer was giving the weather forecast for the following day.

He said, 'The probability of rain is 100 per cent.' He paused to reflect, then said: 'What does that mean? It means that it *must* rain!' After another brief pause he said: 'No. It doesn't mean that. It just means that the probability of rain is 100 per cent!' The announcer did not know very well what his statement meant. Yet the statement was not entirely meaningless: for someone who planned an outing for the next day might reasonably cancel his plan on the basis of that information. Vague sense can still be sense.

In both the *Notebooks* and the *Tractatus* Wittgenstein was explicitly denying this — that vague sense can still be sense. In the *Tractatus* he said: 'A proposition must determine reality one way or the other: yes or no.' (4.023) There can be no *in between*. Wittgenstein is characterizing this notion in the *Investigations*, when he says:

> The sense of a sentence — one would like to say — may, of course, leave this or that open, but the sentence must nevertheless have *a* definite sense. An indefinite sense — that would really not be a sense *at all*. — This is like: an indefinite boundary is not really a boundary at all. (*PI* 99)

In both the *Notebooks* and the *Tractatus* the requirement that sense be definite provides a basis for postulating simple objects. 'The requirement of simple things *is* the requirement for definiteness of sense.' (*NB*, p. 63) 'The requirement that simple signs be possible is the requirement that sense be definite.' (3.23) The *Notebooks* contain an argument to the effect that there must be simple objects because reality, the world, is definite:

> *And it keeps on* forcing itself upon us that there is some simple indivisible, an element of being, in brief a thing. It does not go against our feeling, that *we* cannot analyse *propositions* so far as to mention the elements by name; no, we feel that the *world* must consist of elements. And it appears as if that were identical with the proposition that the world must be what it is, it must be definite. (*NB*, p. 62)

If reality is unambiguous, definite, then it would seem that our propositions, our thoughts, must be equally definite, for otherwise they would not be descriptions of reality. But is the world always definite — the weather, for example? Can't it be that it is neither definitely raining, nor definitely not raining? To say that the weather 'must be what it is' means nothing: even if the weather is ambiguous, 'it is what it is.'

The idea that *the world* must be definite is not stated in the *Tractatus*. But I think this was assumed. For it is stated that 'A proposition must determine reality one way or the other: yes or no. In order to do that it must describe reality completely.' (4.023) This seems to imply that *only* if a proposition *describes reality completely* can it be a 'yes or no' proposition. And that seems to imply that the reality (the state of affairs), which the proposition describes, must itself have a 'yes or no' property. Furthermore, it is a *requirement* that the sense of a proposition be definite (3.23). But the sense of a picture, and therefore of a proposition, just *is* the possible situation that it presents (2.202, 2.221). Thus, the demand that the sense of propositions be definite, is at the same time a demand that situations, states of affairs, be definite.

It appears that Wittgenstein was insisting that the Law of Excluded Middle must hold for every proposition, for every thought, for every state of affairs either possible or actual. This insistence on the Law of Excluded Middle was not based on any observation of reality, or of how people actually think and speak: it was purely an *a priori* requirement.

The assumption that reality is composed of simple elements appears to be the only way of satisfying the requirement of Excluded Middle. There is nothing fuzzy about a simple element: it has a determinate nature. Two elements can either combine with one another — or they cannot. Each element has a specific 'form', which consists of its possible combinations with other objects in states of affairs.

Simple signs of language ('names') can deputize for the simple elements of reality. Names can be combined in a sentence in such a way that the sentence depicts a possible configuration of the corresponding simple elements of reality (3.2, 3.201, 3.21). This is the *sense* of the sentence. A possible configuration of simple elements is something absolutely precise: either it exists or it does not exist. The sense of the sentence that describes it will be equally precise. This is how the demand of Excluded Middle for definiteness of sense in propositions is satisfied.

So also for *thoughts*. A thought, like a sentence, is a picture (3). A thought is composed of elements that deputize for simple elements of reality (2.131). A thought depicts a possible configuration of reality-elements. Such a configuration is something that is absolutely precise. A thought that depicts it must be equally precise.

Thus, the conception that reality is composed of simple elements satisfies, in a remarkably elegant way, the 'yes or no' demand of the Law of Excluded Middle. This conception enables one to understand how there can be perfect exactness, definiteness, in reality, language and thought.

The fact is, however, that the Law of Excluded Middle does not provide any support for this assumption of definiteness, but only *seems* to. Consider the question whether dogs have dreams. If my dog begins to bark in his sleep, and his body wriggles and jerks, I may say with a smile, 'He is dreaming of chasing a rabbit.' If someone said, 'Do you *really* think he is dreaming?', I should be taken aback: I had not meant my words to be taken so seriously. Suppose the person went on to say: 'It must be either the case that he is dreaming or the case that he is not dreaming!' I should probably feel paralysed by this injecting of Excluded Middle into the conversation. Why so? Because the remark conveys a picture which seems to guarantee a definite *sense* for the question 'Is the dog dreaming?' — but at the same time I do not grasp what that sense is. Concerning some different examples Wittgenstein, in the *Investigations*, says the following:

> The law of excluded middle says here: it must either look like *this*, or like *that*. So it really — and this is a truism — says nothing at all, but gives us a picture. And the problem ought now to be: whether reality agrees with the picture, or not? And this picture *seems* to determine what we have to do, what to look for, and how — but it does not do so, just because we do not know how it is to be applied. Here saying 'There is no third possibility', or 'But there can't be a third possibility!' — expresses our inability to turn our eyes away from this picture: a picture which looks as if it must already contain both the problem and its solution, while at the same time we *feel* that it is not so. (*PI* 352)

Excluded Middle *seems* to guarantee that the sentence 'The dog is dreaming' has a definite sense. But it does not actually do this, because it does not tell us 'what to do, what to look for' to determine whether the dog is or isn't dreaming. If we already knew this there would be no objection to the appeal to Excluded Middle. If we need to know whether a stick is a foot long, but are not sure whether it is, then the remark 'Well, either it is or it isn't' can prod us into employing an accepted procedure for determining the length of a stick. But when there is no accepted procedure, and the sense of a sentence is in doubt, the appeal to Excluded Middle is useless.

It appears that in the thinking of the *Tractatus* one route to the deduction of simple elements of reality is from the Law of Excluded Middle. But the ticklish problem is whether in this use of the Law, Wittgenstein was conceiving of it as a Law of Reality, or only as a Law of Propositions. I am suggesting the first interpretation. This is in accord with the *Notebooks*, where Wittgenstein says: 'We feel that the *world* must consist of elements. And it appears as if that were identical with the proposition that the world must be what it is, it must be definite.' He goes on to say: 'It looks as if to deny things were as much as to say that the world can, as it were, be indefinite.' (*NB*, p. 62) To say that the *world* must be definite seems to be equivalent to saying that any state of affairs must be definite: either it exists or it does not exist. If this is so then our propositions, all of which describe possible states of affairs, must be equally definite: they must be 'yes or no' propositions: they must be true or false. According to this interpretation, the application of the Law of Excluded Middle to propositions is *derived from* its application to reality. Furthermore, if the definiteness of reality demands the existence of simple elements of reality, then the propositions that depict reality must be analysable into combinations of simple signs that correspond to the simple elements of reality.

Whether or not this is a correct interpretation of the use of the Law of Excluded Middle in the *Tractatus*, it is still the case that paragraph 352 in the *Investigations* provides a fundamental criticism of the *Tractatus*. The Law of Excluded Middle cannot *prove* that the sentence 'My dog is dreaming' has a definite, sharp sense; nor can it prove this of any other sentence. This Law applies only to sentences that *have* a clear sense: for sentences that do not it is pointless to invoke Excluded Middle. If the grammar of a sentence is confused or unsettled, this Law can do nothing to clarify it. Invoking the Law may be at most a spur to *giving* a sentence a clear sense: but this is something that *we* do, not that the Law does.

There is a remark in *On Certainty* that is akin to the one in the *Investigations*:

The use of 'true or false' has something misleading about it, because it is like saying, 'It agrees with the facts or it doesn't', and the very thing in question is what 'agreement' is here. (*OC* 199)

If we say something that does not have a clear sense for us, then we don't understand when to say that it *agrees* with the facts or that it doesn't. We may *decide* to give the sentence a clear sense. But — to take again the example 'The dog is dreaming' — whatever decision we make, we will not be giving this sentence the same sense that 'He is dreaming' has when applied to a human being: for in this case the sense of the sentence is *connected* with the phenomenon of 'telling a dream', whereas in the case of the dog it is not.

Let us turn to another source of the idea that there must be simple elements of reality. This is the ancient problem of 'false judgement' or of 'thinking what is not'. In Plato's *Theaetetus,*[1] Socrates presents the problem as follows. If a man sees he must see something, and something that *is*. If he hears he must hear something, and something that *is*. Likewise, if a man thinks he must think *something*. He cannot think nothing; for to think nothing is the same as not to think at all. Therefore, to think falsely is to think *something*, and something that *is*.

This reasoning makes it appear impossible to think what is not, i.e. to make a false judgement or to have a false belief. This paradox continued to perplex philosophers through the Middle Ages and into the present century. Russell proposed several different theories to solve the paradox, none of which was satisfactory.

One of the merits of the *Tractatus* is that it provides a simple solution for the problem of thinking what is not. The solution is this. To think is to have a thought. A thought, whether it is expressed in a physical sentence or not, is a picture of a *possible* state of affairs. If the state of affairs exists, the thought is true; if the state of affairs does not exist, the thought is false. But a thought can be a picture only by virtue of being composed of thought-elements that correspond to simple elements of reality. A combination of thought-elements depicts the corresponding reality-elements as combined in the same way as are the thought-elements (2.15). If that particular relationship of reality-elements does exist the thought is true; if not, false. What the solution eliminates is the need for an *existing* something to correspond with the *whole* thought.

The solution of the *Tractatus* is a *compromise* with the paradox. On the one hand, it does away with the requirement that there must be an actual something ('something that *is*') corresponding to the whole thought. On the other hand, it does require that there be an actual something (namely, an element of reality) corresponding to each element of the thought.

One of the doctrines concerning the simple elements of reality is that they can only be *named*: they cannot be *described* (3.221). The only kind of thing that can be described is something *complex* — namely, a combination of simple elements, i.e. a state of affairs. The *Investigations* (*PI* 46) connects this doctrine with the *Theaetetus*, where Socrates reports a conception he has heard of.[2] The conception is that the primary elements, out of which everything is composed, can only be *named*: it is impossible to give any 'account' of a primary element — 'its name is all it has.' Whatever consists of primary elements is complex. A complex can be described by putting together the names of the elements that compose it. 'For the essence of speech is the composition of names.' Wittgenstein says that the 'objects' of the *Tractatus* were such 'primary elements' (*PI* 46). This is certainly true.

A few paragraphs later he gives expression to a related notion, a notion that contains an argument for the existence of the enduring primary elements:

> What the names in language stand for must be indestructible; for it must be possible to describe the situation in which everything destructible is destroyed. And this description will contain words; and what corresponds to these cannot then be destroyed, for otherwise the words would have no meaning. (*PI* 55)

In the *Tractatus* there is no mention of this reasoning. But it fits in with the view that any imagined world, no matter how different from the actual one, must have the same form as the actual one (2.022). Therefore, a world in which everything destructible was destroyed, must be describable.

I take it that a world in which everything destructible had been destroyed, would be a world in which there were no physical things — no mountains, seas, earth, planets, sun, stars — not even any molecules. There might still be arrangements of the primary elements (and so, states of affairs); but these arrangements would not constitute physical things. I will leave aside the question of whether it would make sense to speak of such a state of the world, and also the objection mentioned in *PI* 55 that 'the description would have to exclude itself from the destruction.'

The point of the reasoning quoted in *PI* 55 is to 'prove' that the simple elements of reality, for which the simple signs of language (the 'names') stand, must be indestructible. The *Tractatus* does accept the conclusion: the simple objects are enduring and unchangeable (2.027). The fact that Wittgenstein *quotes* the reasoning in *PI* 55 suggests that he may have thought of and accepted that reasoning when working on the *Tractatus*. Whether or not this suggestion is correct, the reasoning is interesting. For it appears to provide a *proof* that the objects of the *Tractatus* are simple (2.02). The proof is that if the objects were complex things, then they could be destroyed; then their names would have no meaning; therefore, a *possible* state of affairs would not be describable. But every possibility is describable; so the objects must be simple.

This reasoning may help us to grasp a cryptic line of thought for the simplicity of the objects, that actually is presented in the *Tractatus*. It is the following:

> Objects constitute the substance of the world. For that reason they cannot be complex. (2.021)

> If the world had no substance, then whether a proposition had sense would depend on whether another proposition was true. (2.0211)

I am inclined to think that these two numbers present *two* arguments. The argument of 2.021 I understand this way. Substance just is the objects. Everything that has a composition is composed of substance. Substance cannot have a composition, for if it did it would be composed of itself. Therefore, the objects cannot be complex.

The argument of 2.0211 is much more original. I understand it as follows. If there were no simple objects, then the words of language could stand for complexes. If the complexes did not exist then the words would have no meaning. Therefore, a proposition would have sense only if another proposition was true — namely, a proposition asserting that those complexes do exist. The latter proposition would be a contingent proposition.

From the standpoint of the *Tractatus* this is intolerable. Whether a proposition has sense cannot depend on what is the case. Furthermore, an infinite regress would be involved: for if a proposition had sense only if a second proposition were true, then also the sense of the second proposition would depend on the truth of a third proposition, and so on. Therefore, there must be simple and indestructible things that correspond to the simple signs of language. These simples constitute substance, which exists independently of *what is the case* (2.024).

Another way of understanding 2.0211, suggested to me by Peter Winch, is the following. Suppose it were possible for object A not to exist. Then I might *ask* whether it exists, and conduct an enquiry to find out. The result of the enquiry might be negative. In that case A would not exist, and the (assumed) name of A in my original (presumed) question would be meaningless. Then that *question* would have had no sense and the 'enquiry' conducted to answer it can have been no genuine enquiry.

What criticism is there in the *Investigations* of the reasoning of *Tractatus* 2.0211, and of the quoted argument in *PI* 55? First of all, there is the observation of *PI* 40 (already referred to in chapter 1) that the word 'meaning' is (in all cases) used incorrectly if it is used to designate the thing that 'corresponds' to a word.

But another criticism employs a brilliant distinction between two different senses in which something may 'correspond' to a word. This distinction is introduced in *PI* 48 in connection with a table or chart that is used in providing descriptions of complexes of coloured squares. The table consists of columns of squares of different colours, each square being correlated with a simple sign: 'R' is correlated with a red square, 'G' with a green one, 'B' with a black one, 'W' with a white one. In describing a complex of coloured squares let us suppose that a person consults the table and then writes down a series of these signs in a sentence. Such a sentence might consist of the sequence 'RBGGWR'. This would be a description, right or wrong, of a complex of six coloured squares. If the table of paradigms or samples, with the correlated names, were lost — or if it were defaced in such a way that there was only a column of signs, the column of samples being erased — then of course the table could no longer be used as a guide in describing a complex. The samples of the table are used as *objects of comparison*. For any given square in a complex that is to be described, a person decides which sign to write down solely, we have supposed, by comparing it with the samples of the table: when he finds a matching sample he writes down the correlated sign. If the sample that goes with the sign 'W' has been erased, then he won't be able to use 'W' in a description. The sign 'W' will have become useless: that is, it will have become meaningless in the procedure of describing the complexes of squares.

Let us turn to the question of whether it is meaningful to say of a primary element that it 'exists'. In his lectures entitled 'The Philosophy of Logical Atomism', Russell argued that the name 'Romulus' is not a *genuine name*.

> If it were really a name, the question of existence could not arise, because a name has got to name something or it is not a name, and if there is no such person as Romulus there cannot be a name for that person who is not there.[3]

This is like saying that if a name is a genuine name, then the thing that corresponds to it *has* to exist.

The acute observation made about this reasoning in the *Investigations* is:

> To say 'If it did not *exist*, it could have no name' is to say as much and as little as: if this thing did not exist, we could not use it in our language-game. — What looks as if it *had* to exist, is part of the language. It is a paradigm in our language-game; something with which comparison is made. And this may be an important observation; but it is none the less an observation concerning our language-game — our method of representation. (*PI* 50)

This same observation is brought to bear on the argument of *Tractatus* 2.0211, which implies that the things that correspond to the names of language must be simple and therefore indestructible: for if the things that give the names their meaning could be destroyed and were destroyed, then the names would have no meaning. A corollary of this is that then it would be impossible to describe the state of affairs in which everything destructible is destroyed.

Wittgenstein responds by pointing out *two different ways* in which a thing may correspond to a name:

> But this man is surely what, in a sense, corresponds to his name. He is, however, destructible; and his name does not lose its meaning when the bearer is destroyed. — An example of something corresponding to a name, and without which it would have no

meaning, is a paradigm that is used in connection with the name in the language-game. (*PI* 55)

This powerful thrust takes the wind out of the metaphysical argument for the claim that the real names of language must stand for things that are simple and indestructible. For in regard to most names it is not true that the name loses its meaning if what corresponds to it is destroyed. There might, however, be a special case in which the use of a name was strictly tied to a paradigm, without which the name would have no meaning — as in the language-game of *PI* 48.

But let us note, first, that it is not *necessary* that any word should be strictly tied to a paradigm, as in *PI* 48: rarely are we actually guided by tables or charts in speaking or writing. Second, in the special case where the use of a word was tied to a paradigm it would be *irrelevant* whether the paradigm was something 'simple' or something 'complex'! As Wittgenstein notes in *PI* 48, the most natural thing to say is that the coloured squares which serve as paradigms are 'the simples', and that an arrangement of them is 'complex'. Yet those paradigms could be destroyed; in which case their names would lose their meaning. This shows that when a name is so tied to a thing that if the thing ceased to exist the name would lose its meaning, it does not follow that the *thing* corresponding to the name must be indestructible. Thus we are released from the grip of the metaphysical thought that what is 'simple' must be *indestructible*.

It is to be noted that the argument of 2.0211 is an argument from *the possibility of language*. What it says is that language is possible only if there are simple objects. The corollary argument *quoted* in *PI* 55 is also an argument from language. It says that it must be possible to describe the situation in which everything destructible is destroyed; but the possibility of such a description requires that there be indestructible things corresponding to the words of the description.

The rebuttal of these two arguments, in the *Investigations*, is also based on considerations of language. So it meets these arguments on their own ground. Wittgenstein reminds us of the possibility of a method of description that relies on paradigms. This is one of those 'reminders' that is, at the same time, both a commonplace observation and a deep philosophical point (see *PI* 127). What is the philosophical light cast by this observation? First, it makes us realize that the only clear case where a name would lose its meaning is the case where the paradigm corresponding to the name is lost or destroyed. (A similar case, mentioned in *PI* 57, is when we can no longer *remember* the colour that corresponds to a name.) Second, it shows that *Tractatus* 2.0211 is actually *in error* in assuming that whether a proposition (i.e. a sentence) has sense cannot depend on an empirical fact: for whether a sentence in language-game *PI* 48 has sense does depend on the empirical fact that the table contains a paradigm for each of the names of that language. Third, it shows that when a name loses its meaning because the corresponding paradigm no longer exists, it does not follow that the paradigm was not a true simple. In relation to the method of description of *PI* 48, the paradigms of the table really are the simple or primary elements. Yet they are destructible. We could put the point like this: something that serves as a primary element in a certain method of description is not, by virtue of that, indestructible.

In the *Investigations* there is a further discussion of whether the primary elements of reality can be said to 'exist'. Paragraph *PI* 58 begins with the quoted remark: 'I want to restrict the term "*name*" to what cannot occur in the combination "X exists." — Thus one cannot say "Red exists", because if there were no red it could not be spoken of at all.'

I wish to make two comments on this remark. First, it does represent the position taken by Wittgenstein in the *Tractatus*, and also by Russell in 'The Philosophy of Logical Atomism'. *Tractatus* 3.221 says: 'Objects can only be *named*.' In the *Tractatus* only a complex, a state of affairs, can be said to exist or not to exist. I might say to you, 'Does the beautiful table you used to have in your study still exist?' You might answer: 'No, it was destroyed in a fire' or 'Yes, it still exists.' This would be a meaningful use of 'exists' because, according to the *Tractatus*, a table is a complex, a state of affairs, an arrangement of simple elements.

Second, in the quoted remark of *PI* 58, the colour *red* is being taken as an example of a simple element, and the word 'red' as an example of a *name*. In the *Tractatus*, however, Wittgenstein decided that colours were not simple objects. In 6.3751 he says: 'The statement that a point in the visual field has two different colours at the same time is a contradiction.' In 4.211 he asserts that an elementary proposition cannot be contradicted by another elementary proposition. Now if colours were simple objects, then the propositions 'This point is red' and 'This point is green' would be elementary propositions: in which case there would be no contradiction in the statement 'This point is now both red and green.' But it is a contradiction: so colours are not simple objects.

We want, however, to consider the question of whether it makes sense to say of a simple element that it 'exists'. If we leave aside the thesis that elementary propositions cannot contradict one another, then I believe that almost any person who thought about the matter naïvely would regard a colour (or at least a *pure* colour, e.g. a pure red) as a *plausible* candidate for the role of a simple element of reality. I believe this is why the discussion in *PI* 58 employs the example of *red*.

Let us return to the discussion in *PI* 58. Wittgenstein says: 'It looks to us as if we were saying something about the nature of red in saying that the words "Red exists" do not yield a sense. Namely that red does exist "in itself" (*an und für sich*).' In saying 'it looks to us', he is referring to a temptation almost anyone will have: but also he is giving an account of how he, and Russell, actually thought about the primary elements — as I will show in a moment. Wittgenstein goes on to say:

> But what we really *want* is simply to take 'Red exists' as the statement: the word 'red' has a meaning. Or perhaps better: 'red does not exist' as '"Red" has no meaning.' Only we do not want to say that that expression *says* this, but that *this* is what it would have to be saying *if* it meant anything. But that it contradicts itself in the attempt to say it — just because red exists 'in itself'. (*PI* 58)

We have to keep in mind that *red* is being treated here as a supposed example of a 'simple object' (what Russell called an 'individual'). And the word 'red' is being regarded as a *genuine name*. If it is a name then the object it stands for *is its meaning*, as stated in *Tractatus* 3.023. In that case, the statement 'Red does not exist' would seem to say that the name 'red' has no meaning. Thus, if the statement were true it would follow that the statement itself was senseless. In this peculiar way the statement would 'contradict itself'. Hence, it appears that we are compelled to affirm the proposition 'Red exists.' But this is not a genuine proposition, since it does not have a negation that makes sense.

The required conclusion seems to be that it does not make sense to say that the simple elements of reality either 'exist' or 'do not exist'. Both Wittgenstein and Russell accepted this conclusion. On the other hand, they felt compelled to say that the simple elements *are there* — they have *being*, they 'subsist'. This is like saying that they have a *super-existence* — existence on *a higher plane* than the existence of complex things and states of affairs. In the thinking of both Russell and Wittgenstein there was a marked *ambivalence* about whether the simple elements could be said to exist.

In his lectures on 'The Philosophy of Logical Atomism', Russell said the following: 'So the individuals that there are in the world do not exist, or rather it is nonsense to say that they exist and nonsense to say that they do not exist.'[4] This is a curious statement. For what does the phrase 'the individuals that *there are in the world*' mean if not just 'the individuals that exist' or 'the existing individuals'? The whole sentence seems to say: 'Of the existing individuals one cannot say either that they exist or that they do not exist.' This statement appears to contradict itself. It *says* both that 'individuals' exist *and* that it cannot be said that they exist.

In the *Tractatus* there is the same vacillation about whether the primary elements can be said to *exist*. Strictly speaking, only a possible arrangement of elements can be said to exist or not. But 2.024 says: 'Die Substanz ist das, was unabhängig von dem, was der Fall ist, besteht.' Pears and McGuinness translate this as: 'Substance is what subsists independently of what is the case.' The trouble with translating *besteht* as 'subsists' is that the latter is such a hazy word. One could translate *besteht* as 'exists', or 'remains', or 'endures'. The most natural translation of the sentence would be: 'Substance is what exists independently of what is the case.' Substance just is the totality of simple objects. So 2.024 is saying that simple objects *exist* — though one is not supposed to say that.

Saying what cannot be said also crops up in 2.027: 'Only if there are objects can the world have a fixed form.' Since the world does have a fixed form, acording to *Tractatus*, what 2.026 is saying is that 'the existence' of simple objects is required by that fixed form.

Thus, a believer in simple elements of reality is drawn in two directions at once: towards saying that they must exist 'in themselves' (i.e. independently of what is the case) in order for the world to have a fixed form, and in order for language to be possible; and towards saying that it is nonsense to speak of those elements as either 'existing' or 'not existing'.

I will summarize the various arguments of the *Tractatus* that appear to force on us the view that there are primary elements of reality, together with the criticisms of those arguments in the *Investigations*.

I   *Argument*   Anything complex is an arrangement of elements. The destruction of a complex is simply the separation of its elements. There must be elements that are not complex, but simple. These are the primary elements or 'objects'. They are the substance of the world. They are indestructible and unchangeable, for all change consists in new combinations of the objects (2.02, 2.021, 2.027, 2.0271).
   Criticism (*PI* 59)   We encounter complex things composed of parts, and sometimes we observe that a complex thing changes or is destroyed while its component parts remain unchanged. But experience does *not* present us with elements that are unchangeable and indestructible. The assumption that there are such elements is a metaphysical picture. The forming of this picture is a leap that has no empirical justification.

II *Argument*   If there were no objects (indestructible elements) then whether a proposition had sense would depend on whether another proposition was true (2.0211). For if the words of language designated only complexes and not simples, then what corresponds to a word might be destroyed. In this case the word would have no meaning, since nothing would correspond to it. Thus it would have to be *true* that the corresponding complexes do exist, in order for a sentence to have sense.
   Criticism (*PI* 40, 50, 55)   First, it is a mistake to suppose that the meaning of a word is the thing that corresponds to the word. Second, there could be a method of description that employed names connected with paradigms: if the paradigms were destroyed the names would lose their meaning. Consequently, that special method of description could no longer be used. But this provides no ground whatever for assuming that there must be indestructible things in order for language to have sense. Third, it *can* be the case that whether a sentence has sense depends on whether a proposition is true. This is in fact the case when a method of description relies on paradigms.

III   *Argument*   There must be simple, indestructible elements of reality in order for the world to have a fixed form. If all things were complex and destructible, then what is logically possible could change (2.0214, 2.023, 2.026).

      Criticism   The fundamental criticism (expounded in chapter 1) is that it is an illusion to suppose that there is a fixed, unchangeable order of logical possibilities, prior to all experience and all language.

IV   *Argument*   Propositions can have a *definite sense* only if there are primary elements of reality with which simple signs of language can be correlated (3.23).

      Criticism   It is a mistake to think that a sentence cannot have a *vague* sense, or that what we *mean* by it cannot be vague. We only *imagine* that underneath *apparent* vagueness, strict and clear rules are hidden (*PI* 99—102). It is doubtful whether *any* sentence of ordinary language satisfies the ideal of the *Tractatus* of 'perfect logical order'.

In addition to the foregoing specific criticisms of specific arguments in the *Tractatus*, the *Investigations* contains a sweeping argument that demolishes all of the reasoning of the *Tractatus* concerning the simples. In his first book Wittgenstein had assumed that the terms 'simple' and 'complex' had *an absolute sense*. A thing is simple or it is complex. If it is not the one, it is the other. In *PI* 47 Wittgenstein destroys this absolutism by showing in numerous examples that *one and the same thing* can be regarded as simple, or as complex, depending on the decisions that one makes for a particular purpose or for a particular comparison. For example, I draw a line with a smooth upward and then downward curve. Is this line simple or complex? You might want to say that it is complex in comparison with a straight line; on the other hand you might want to say that it is a simple line in comparison with a jagged line or convoluted figure. If you say it is complex, what are its constituent simple parts? You might say that it consists of two parts, the ascending curve and the descending curve. Or you might say that its parts are one-inch segments; or that its parts are points. When I walk across the room, what are the parts of this motion? Would a part be a full stride or a half-stride? Obviously this motion of walking could be analysed in different ways (e.g. by a time and motion study), thus giving different answers.

In *PI* 47 Wittgenstein asks, 'What are the simple constituent parts of a chair?' If a chair was built out of little pieces of wood glued together, we might be inclined to call those pieces the simple parts or elements of the chair. If it was not built that way, but had been cut up into little pieces of wood, you might call those the parts of which the chair had been composed. For some scientific purpose you might say that the molecules composing those pieces of wood were the elements of the chair. If you were employed in assembling chairs out of a seat, a back, and four legs, you would naturally speak of those as the parts of a chair. In contrast, if there were metal chairs that were not assembled in this way but were cast whole in a mould, you might say that those chairs did not have any constituent parts.

Wittgenstein imagines someone saying: 'But isn't a chessboard, for instance, obviously and absolutely composite?' His reply is:

> You are probably thinking of the composition out of thirty-two white and thirty-two black squares. But could we not also say, for instance, that it was composed of the colours black and white and the schema of squares? And if there are quite different ways of looking at it, do you still want to say that the chessboard is absolutely 'composite'? (*PI* 47)

In a factory where chessboards are produced by gluing together the 64 black and white squares, one would naturally refer to these individual squares as the simple elements of a chessboard. But suppose it turned out that in handling and storage the squares broke rather easily. Triangular half-squares are found to be less fragile. So the manufacturing process is changed to the production of triangular half-squares, which are then called the simple elements of a chessboard.

In a bakery loaves of bread are sliced before being wrapped and sold: a loaf is said to be composed of 12 slices. But in another connection and for a different purpose, a loaf is said to be composed of the flour, milk, sugar, and salt from which the dough is made. For still another purpose the heat energy that is required for baking a loaf is counted as a constituent part of a loaf.

As Wittgenstein remarks: 'We use the word "composite" (and therefore the word "simple") in an enormous number of different and differently related ways.' And he asks:

> Is this length of 2 cm simple, or does it consist of two parts, each

1 cm long? But why not of one bit 3 cm long, and one bit 1 cm long measured in the opposite direction? (*PI* 47)

Wittgenstein has given a brilliant and (I think) decisive refutation of the conception that the distinction of simple and complex is fixed and absolute. This is an overwhelming blow to the *Tractatus*, but also to much of traditional metaphysics: for example, to Descartes's assumption (first stated in *The Rules for the Direction of the Mind*, and retained throughout his life) that there are 'simple natures', absolute 'primitive notions'; and to Leibniz's assumption in *The Monadology* that 'there must be simple substances, since there are compounds', and that these simple substances (the Monads) are 'the elements of things'.

Not all of those philosophers who have made a close study of the *Tractatus* would agree that the criticism in *PI* 47 is an 'overwhelming blow' to the *Tractatus*. Alexander Maslow wrote an early book on the *Tractatus*. He thought that there was a metaphysical trend in the *Tractatus* which could be discounted when interpreting the book's theory of language. An example of this trend is Wittgenstein's use of the word 'object'. Maslow says that 'at times he means by "object" the ultimate ontological simple entities out of which the real world "in itself" is made.'[5] Maslow says:

> But, as this metaphysical strain of Wittgenstein is not in accord with the general tenor of my interpretation of him, I will not pursue it here and will consider it as merely an unfortunate holdover from traditional metaphysical terminology.[6]

Maslow's own view is that

> It is logically perfectly arbitrary what we shall choose to consider as simple elements . . . the criterion of simplicity is to be established by ourselves, not found in the world. The practical considerations of convenience, habit, or usefulness may, of course, guide us in our grammatical determinations, but are logically irrelevant . . . We can take any object whatsoever in our experience and consider it as an element. This simplicity of object is imposed by our language upon the brute 'given' of experience and is thus relative to our language . . . There is no sense in speaking of absolute simples.[7]

Erik Stenius wrote an elaborate, painstaking, study of the *Tractatus*. He says:

The idea of substance as what is persistent in the course of time brings out a fundamental obscurity in the *Tractatus*: in what sense are the 'things' common to all 'possible worlds'? We will examine two possible answers to this question.

(a) That all 'possible' worlds have their substance in common is to be understood in an *absolute* sense. There is a definite system of atomic 'things' forming the substance; and a world the substance of which is not this is unthinkable.

(b) That all 'possible' worlds have their substance in common is to be understood only in a *relative* sense. The formation of the system of atomic states of affairs is, to be sure, *prior* to a description of the world, and forms a framework for it, but this framework can be chosen in different ways, and every choice determines a separate system of possible worlds.[8]

Stenius acknowledges that many of the statements of the *Tractatus* 'seem to confirm' that Wittgenstein assumed alternative (a). Stenius refers specifically to 2.022, 2.023 and 2.024. He also notes that the *Investigations* 'seems to attack' the view of alternative (a).[9]

Stenius then poses several questions, which he takes to be objections to the conception that substance is 'uniquely determined', i.e. is to be understood in an absolute sense. One question is, 'By what *method* we are to decide what things the substance consists of?'[10] The answer surely is that Wittgenstein had *no* method for deciding this. Another question is, 'How are we to decide what atomic states of affairs there are in the logical space?'[11] The answer of the *Tractatus* is that this cannot be determined *a priori*. Still another question is, 'How are we to decide what *forms* of atomic states of affairs there are? This question corresponds on the linguistic plane to the question: *by what method are we to decide what forms of elementary sentences* a description of the world is to contain?'[12] The *Tractatus* gives an explicit answer, namely, that there cannot be an *a priori* determination of the possible forms of elementary propositions (5.55).

The view of the *Tractatus* is that what is *a priori* is the following:

1 That there is a fixed form of all possible worlds
2 That this fixed form consists of the simple objects, i.e. substance

3   That in language it must be possible for there to be *names*, which stand for the simple objects
4   That in language it must be possible for there to be elementary sentences, which consist solely of configurations of names.

According to the *Tractatus* it is impossible to determine *a priori* how many simple objects there are, or of how many objects any possible state of affairs must be composed, or how the objects must be arranged in any possible state of affairs. Thus it is impossible to determine *a priori* any limit for the number of names there may be in an elementary sentence, or to specify *a priori* how the names must be arranged. As Wittgenstein says, 'we cannot give the composition of elementary sentences.' (5.55) He means: we cannot do this *a priori*.

The *Tractatus* says: 'The *application* of logic decides what elementary propositions there are.' (5.557) This is a difficult remark. I understand it as follows. Let us suppose that I perceive a state of affairs which I report in the words 'A donkey is in the garden!' I know *a priori* that there are simple objects. Suppose that now I turn logician. I attempt a complete analysis of this state of affairs as I perceive it. I think this state of affairs is composed of *n* simple objects configured in a certain way. I name the objects and combine the names in a sentence in such a way that the sentence will (I think) depict that perceived state of affairs. Thus, an elementary sentence will have emerged from my attempt to apply logical analysis to the situation I perceive. This sentence will be, at the level of final analysis, a picture (correct or incorrect) of that situation. This is an example of how the application of logic decides what elementary propositions there are. 'What lies in its application logic cannot anticipate.' (5.557)

Stenius holds two positions, which must be distinguished. One position is *his own view* about the question of whether the distinction between being simple and being complex is to be understood in an absolute sense. His answer is that 'there is no absolute difference between complexes and elements.'[13] His view is that 'whether a thing appears as a complex or not is a question of how' a situation 'is analysed.'[14] I have no disagreement with Stenius about this view.

Stated in terms of 'concepts' and 'symbols' his view is the following:

Only in a logical system — as for instance that of geometry — is there a definite difference between 'defined' and 'primitive' concepts. And here too, *which* concepts are chosen as primitive and *which* are taken as defined is a matter of convention. In most systems of geometry the concept of a circle is considered defined, whereas the concept of a straight line is considered primitive, but there is nothing to prevent us from taking the concept of a circle as primitive and the concept of a straight line as defined. Hence there cannot be any absolute and intrinsic difference between defined and primitive symbols.[15]

I think this position is entirely correct. The second view of Stenius, with which I disagree, is *how the Tractatus* is to be understood. As said previously, Stenius believes there are statements in the *Tractatus* which 'seem to confirm' that the distinction between the simple and the complex is to be taken in an absolute sense. He puts this (rather obscurely) as the view that 'substance is uniquely determined.' He then declares that 'Wittgenstein in other contexts in the *Tractatus* expresses himself in a way which seems to contradict the idea of a uniquely determined substance.'[16] But Stenius does not cite any statements from the *Tractatus* which even *seem* to contradict the idea that the simples are simple in an absolute sense.

What Wittgenstein does say is that it is impossible to determine *a priori* 'the number of names with different meanings' (5.55). Which is to say that it is impossible to determine *a priori* the number of simple objects. This view by itself shows that, in the conception of the *Tractatus*, simple objects are not created by human convention, as are the primitive concepts of a system of geometry. Wittgenstein's thought was that it cannot be determined in advance how many names will be required in an elementary sentence in order for that sentence to depict some not yet encountered state of affairs. It cannot be known in advance whether such a sentence will contain five, ten, or 15 names. When experience presents you with a particular situation in the world you may undertake to describe that situation at the bottom level of complete analysis. When you have done this to your satisfaction you may find that the elementary sentence you have produced contains 27 names. In this *application* of logic you discovered that an elementary sentence containing that many names was needed for the description of that particular state of affairs. This application of logic was *a posteriori*, not *a priori*.

Stenius quotes from 5.557 the two sentences 'The *application* of logic decides what elementary sentences there are. What lies in its application logic cannot anticipate.' Stenius then makes the following statements, which he apparently thinks is what Wittgenstein was saying in 5.557:

> Substance, which forms the framework of the description of the world, is in so far *prior* to experience, as [*sic*] a question about experience can be *stated* only within a certain framework. Nevertheless the choice of a framework is not independent of experience. How the framework is to be chosen is a question about the application of logic.[17]

This comment on 5.557 is quite obscure. In contrast, 5.557 itself is comparatively luminous! Substance just is the totality of simple objects. Simple objects are designated by names in elementary sentences. To repeat, 5.557 is saying that the number of names that may be needed in an elementary sentence, and their arrangement, cannot be decided *a priori* but only *a posteriori*. That is what is meant by 'the *application* of logic decides what elementary propositions there are.'

Let us consider the comments of Stenius on 5.557, quoted above. He says that substance 'forms the framework of the description of the world'. This is vague. Perhaps it is to be understood as follows: when situations in the world are being described at the level of elementary sentences, each name in such a sentence will designate a simple object. In this sense the simple objects might be called 'the framework' of that kind of description. Next, Stenius says that substance is '*prior* to experience'. This is true: for substance 'exists' or 'subsists' (*besteht*) independently of what is the case (2.024); and experience is experience *of* what is the case. Next, Stenius seems to give a reason for saying that substance is prior to experience: the reason appears to be that 'a question about experience can be *stated* only within a certain framework.' Stenius has shifted from speaking of '*the* framework' to speaking of 'a certain framework'. Substance is *the* 'framework' of elementary description, in the sense I indicated: but it is not '*a certain* framework' or '*a* framework'. The latter expressions suggest that there might be more than one framework. And indeed this is what Stenius means: for he goes on to say that 'the choice of a framework is not independent of experience. How the framework is to be chosen is a question about the application of logic.'

But in the only sense which, I think, can be given to saying that the simple objects are 'the framework of the description of the world', this framework is not *chosen*. Stenius is influenced by the model of a system of geometry in which one chooses which concepts are primitive and which ones are non-primitive: which terms are taken as undefined and which terms are defined. But this model does not apply to the *Tractatus*. Since the simple objects are prior to all human experience, how could it be a matter for human choice whether something is, or is not, a simple element of reality?

I will try to state as clearly and briefly as possible why the interpretation that Maslow and Stenius give to the *Tractatus* is incorrect. Both of these writers hold that the distinction of simple/complex *should not* be understood in an absolute sense, and here I agree with them. It is of course this position that Wittgenstein later argued for, with such telling examples, in *PI* 47. In the preceding paragraph (*PI* 46), he quotes the famous remarks of Socrates about the primary elements of reality, and then *explicitly* says that the 'objects' of the *Tractatus* 'were such primary elements'. When Wittgenstein goes on in *PI* 47 to declare that it makes no sense to speak in an absolute sense of 'the simple parts of a chair', or of anything else, there can be no doubt that he is addressing the view of the *Tractatus*. When Stenius says that Wittgenstein in the *Investigations* 'seems to attack' the view that the objects are simple in an absolute sense, he makes a misleading understatement.[18]

Maslow says that 'at times' Wittgenstein in the *Tractatus* means by his 'objects' the 'ultimate ontological simple entities' out of which the actual world is composed. Maslow says that 'this metaphysical strain' is not in accord with Maslow's own interpretation of the *Tractatus*, and therefore he will disregard it.[19] Maslow says that whether anything is simple or complex is 'relative to our language' and that 'there is no sense in speaking of absolute simples.'[20] And Stenius, as we have seen, thinks that the best interpretation of the *Tractatus* is one in which the distinction of simple/complex is relative to a framework which we choose. He says that 'the picture theory of sentence meaning' (of the *Tractatus*?) is 'independent of the idea that there is an absolute difference between complexes and "atomic" things'.[21]

I find it difficult to understand how anyone can study the *Tractatus* and come away with the impression that the objects owe their nature *as simple* to human convention or choice. Let us recall some of the basic positions of the *Tractatus*. One of the most basic is that the world has a fixed, unchangeable form. Not just the actual world, but any world that we can imagine or conceive of, must have the same form (2.022). This fixed form consists of the objects (2.023). The fixed form of the world just is the totality of possible states of affairs. This totality of possibilities derives from the possible combinations of objects. If all objects are given, then with that all *possible* states of affairs are also given (2.0124). The totality of possibilities is as fixed and unalterable as are the objects. Actual states of affairs come and go; but possibilities are there for ever.

Let us be reminded of what a *picture* is in the *Tractatus*. A picture is a picture of a possible state of affairs. 'A picture presents a possible situation in logical space.' (2.202) A picture depicts one of those possibilities in the totality of possibilities. A picture certainly does not create the possibility that it depicts. The possibility is prior to the picture.

Let us remember that *thoughts*, whether expressed in language or not, are conceived of as pictures. A *proposition* in language is a thought expressed in a sentence (3.1). 'We use the perceptible sign of a proposition (spoken or written, etc.) as a projection of a possible situation. Thinking the sense of the proposition is the method of projection.' (3.11) *Every* thought is a picture. *Every* proposition is a picture. A picture presents a possible situation (2.202), and the possible situation that it presents is the *sense* of the picture (2.221). Thus, all thought, all thinking, consists in depicting some possibility or other that belongs to the totality of possibilities, which is the fixed, unalterable form of the world.

Now if you could *decide* which things were simple and which were complex, would that not have to mean that you were *choosing* the logical form of the world? This itself would mean that the form of the world (the totality of possible situations) was not unalterable, as the *Tractatus* says it is (2.023, 2.026). Furthermore, this choosing would have to be done in thought and language. The choosing would involve thinking. This means that there would have to be thinking *before* there could be thinking! The notion that what is simple and what is complex could be *relative* to human conventions and decisions would be, according to the basic ideas of the *Tractatus*, a self-contradictory notion. An accurate reading of the *Tractatus* must, I think, lead to the

The Elements of Reality

conclusion that the simple elements of reality are simple in an *absolute* sense: their simplicity is not derived from thought and language, but is presupposed by it. The decisive refutation of this conception by the *Investigations* does indeed demolish the foundations of the *Tractatus*.

CHAPTER 4
Thoughts

At the beginning of the *Tractatus* Wittgenstein speaks of facts, objects, the form of an object, the form of the world, states of affairs. His first remark about *pictures* is the following: 'We make pictures of facts.' ('Wir machens uns Bilder der Tatsachen.') (2.1) A picture is composed of *elements*. The fact that is pictured is also composed of elements (objects). The picture-elements deputize for the objects (2.131). The picture-elements are related to one another in a definite way, and this presents (depicts) the objects as related in the *same* way (2.14, 2.15).

Wittgenstein says that, according to his conception, the picturing relationship (*die abbildende Beziehung*) 'belongs to the picture' (2.1513). What *is* the picturing relationship? Wittgenstein says that it is 'the correlations of the picture-elements with things' (2.1514), and he adds a remarkable piece of imagery: 'These correlations are, as it were, the feelers of the picture-elements with which the picture touches reality.' (2.1515) A picture is connected with reality by these feelers which 'touch' the objects in the state of affairs being pictured. Even if the picture is incorrect it still has that much contact with what is pictured.

The *picturing relationship* must be distinguished from the *form* of picturing (*die Form der Abbildung*). Just as 'the form' of an object consists of its *possible* combinations with other objects, so 'the form' of a picture consists of the *possible* combinations of the picture-elements.

The next step is to say that there must be something *common* to a picture and to what it depicts (2.161). This common thing is the picture's form of picturing (2.17). This means that the possible combinations of picture-elements must be the *same* as the possible combinations of reality-elements. What is implied is at least this much — the *number* of picture-elements must be the same as the number of reality-elements. For example, a picture containing only five elements could not depict a state of affairs containing six elements: the number of possible combinations (the form) would not be the same in the two cases. Wittgenstein makes this numerical identity explicit when he says: 'In a proposition there must be exactly as many distinguishable parts as in the situation it presents.' (4.04) A consequence is that if one picture contains a different number of elements than does another picture, then the two do not have the same form of picturing, and cannot depict the same situation. This poses an important problem: how many elements are there in a picture? How many elements are there in a state of affairs? How is this to be determined? How do we *count* elements? The *Tractatus* appears to present no answer. If this is true, it is a crucial weakness in the picture theory.

Having the same number of elements is necessary for two pictures to have the same form of picturing. But is it sufficient? I think not. Not only must they have the same number of elements, but also their respective elements must be able to be arranged in the same number of combinations. Consider a picture whose elements consist of five blocks of wood, and a picture whose elements are five colours. Is the number of possible arrangements of wooden blocks the same as the number of possible arrangements of colours? Apparently we cannot answer this until we know both the 'form' of a wooden block and the 'form' of a colour: for the number of arrangements possible for a given number of elements must be a function of the logical form of the elements.

Let us turn now to *thoughts*. It is noteworthy that the picture theory is applied to 'thoughts' (*Gedanken*) *before* it is applied to 'propositions' (*Sätze*). Every picture is 'a logical picture' (2.182): and 'A logical picture of facts is a thought.' (3) '"A state of affairs is thinkable", means: we can make a picture of it.' (3.001) 'The totality of true thoughts is a picture of the world.' (3.01)

What is the *nature* of a thought? Is it just a sentence of language that has sense? Since a thought is a picture, it must have a composition out of elements. What is the nature of these elements? Are they words? Is a thought a structure of physical signs? Here the *Notebooks* are of help. In an entry of September 1916 there occurs the following:

Now it is becoming clear why I thought that thinking and language were the same. For thinking is a kind of language. For of course a thought *too* is a logical picture of a proposition, and therefore it just is a kind of proposition.[1]

These remarks are highly interesting, but also somewhat confusing. If a thought is a proposition then it cannot be a *picture* of a *proposition*. A proposition is a picture of a state of affairs. A proposition, according to the *Tractatus*, *shows* its sense (4.022). And what can be shown *cannot* be said (4.1212). A proposition cannot describe or state the sense of another proposition. If two different propositional structures have the same sense, then they are the *same* proposition (see 5.141). What Wittgenstein could have been wanting to say in the *Notebooks* is that a thought is a structure in a certain medium, and a word-proposition is a structure in a different medium; and that these two structures can have the same sense, i.e. they can be the same proposition.

Wittgenstein's conception, in the *Tractatus*, of the nature of *thoughts* is greatly illuminated by an exchange of letters between Russell and Wittgenstein in August 1919. Russell had asked: what are the constituents of a thought, and what is their relation to those of the pictured fact? Wittgenstein replied:

I don't know *what* the constituents of a thought are, but I know *that* it must have such constituents which correspond to the words of language. Again the kind of relation of the constituents of the thought and of the pictured fact is irrelevant. It would be a matter of psychology to find out. (*NB*, p. 130)

To Russell's question, 'Does a thought (*Gedanke*) consist of words?', Wittgenstein replied:

No! But of psychical constituents that have the same sort of relation to reality as words. What those constituents are I don't know. (*NB*, p. 131)

These remarks throw a great deal of light on to the relation between *thoughts* and sentences of language, i.e. word-propositions. Notice that Wittgenstein said, *without qualification*, that *thoughts* (*Gedanken*) are composed of 'psychical constituents'. He did not say that there are two kinds of thoughts, one kind composed of mental ('psychical') elements, and another kind composed of non-mental elements. The straightforward interpretation of his remarks is that *all* thoughts are composed of mental elements. *No* thoughts consist of words, i.e. physical signs.

But, according to the *Tractatus*, a thought can be *expressed* in physical signs. 'In a sentence a thought (*Gedanke*) is expressed in a way that is perceptible to the senses.' (3.1) 'We use the perceptible sign of a proposition (spoken or written, etc.) as a projection of a possible situation. Thinking the sense of the sentence is the method of projection.' (3.11) 'I call the sign with which we express a thought a propositional sign. — And a proposition is a propositional sign in its projective relation to the world.' (3.12) 'What constitutes a propositional sign is that in it its elements, the words, stand in a definite relation to one another.' (3.14)

When we take these statements together with the remarks to Russell, we see that in the *Tractatus* thoughts (*Gedanken*) are *more basic* than word-propositions (Sätze). A thought does not *have* to be expressed in a physical sentence. A thought is always a configuration of mental elements. This configuration depicts a possible state of affairs, which is the sense of the thought. If a thought is expressed in a physical sentence, what happens is that the sense of the thought is *thought into* the sentence. 'An applied, thought, propositional sign, is a thought.' (3.5) The physical sentence is given the same sense that the thought already has. Thus, there are two structures with the same sense. One structure is composed of mental elements, the other of physical signs (words). Since these two structures have the same sense, they are one and the same proposition.

Given this understanding of the *Tractatus* conception of the relation of thought to language, there are two statements in the *Tractatus* that can be confusing and misleading. One is this: 'An applied, thought, propositional sign, is a thought.' (3.5) It is clear from 3.12 that a 'propositional sign' is a physical sentence. If 3.5 is taken as an identity statement, then the implication would be that a thought *has* to be expressed in a physical sentence. I think the correct interpretation is that 3.5 is not an identity statement. It does not imply that thoughts can occur *only* in physical sentences. It says instead that when a physical sentence is invested with a sense, the sentence becomes a thought. There is nothing wrong with this way of speaking: in ordinary language we often say such a thing as, 'That thought is to be found on page 98 of this book.'

Another possibly misleading statement is: 'A thought is a sentence with a sense.' (4) This might be read as meaning that *only* a physical sentence with a sense is a thought. I think this would be a wrong reading. In the *Notebooks*, when Wittgenstein says that a thought 'just is a kind of proposition' (*NB*, p. 82), I believe that by 'a thought' he means a configuration of mental elements. I think the correct interpretation of this passage and of *Tractatus* 4 is that there are *two kinds* of *propositions*: thoughts (composed of mental elements), and physical sentences that have been given sense. Both can be called 'propositions', since both are pictures of possible situations.

When we put together the statements of the *Tractatus* itself, the remark from the *Notebooks*, and what Wittgenstein said in the letter to Russell, there emerges a conception of the relationship between thought and language which is much more complex than appears on the surface of the *Tractatus*. It turns out that the picture theory of propositions is a theory about thoughts as well as physical sentences, and that it gives a *priority* to thoughts. I will present this enlarged version of the picture theory in a sequence of statements:

I   Thoughts are composed of mental elements.
II   A thought is, *by virtue of its intrinsic nature*, a picture of a possible situation. The pictured situation is its sense.
III A physical sentence is not intrinsically a picture, but can be made into a picture. For this to happen the sense of a thought must be bestowed on the physical sentence.
IV   How does that occur? Presumably in this way: correlations already exist, or are newly established, between the elements of a thought, the elements of a propositional sign, and the elements composing the situation depicted.
V   In this way a thought becomes 'perceptible to the senses' (3.1).

Let us see how the foregoing statements fit with what Wittgenstein explicitly says. First of all, a picture is a fact (2.141) and, since thoughts are pictures (3), they are facts. Every fact is ultimately composed of simple objects (2.0272): so this is true of thoughts. The objects of which a thought is composed are mental elements ('psychical constituents'). This is statement I.

Statement II says that a thought is a picture of a possible situation, and that this pictured possibility is its sense. This agrees with 2.202, 2.221 and 3. But statement II says that a thought is a picture of a particular situation 'by virtue of its intrinsic nature'.

This is controversial and I will come back to it.

Statement III appears to agree with 3.11 and 3.12. A physical sentence (a 'propositional sign') becomes a projection of a possible situation (becomes a picture) by being invested with the thought of that situation.

Statement IV connects with 3.2 and 3.201. 'In a proposition a thought can be expressed in such a way that elements of the propositional sign correspond to the objects of the thought.' (3.2) From 3.201 it is clear that in 3.2 Wittgenstein is talking about a 'completely analysed' proposition, i.e. a sentence consisting solely of *names*.

The phrase 'the objects of the thought' in 3.2 is confusing. Does it mean the objects of which the thought is composed? Or does it mean the objects composing the situation which the thought is about? Anthony Kenny interprets the phrase in the first way. He says: '"The objects of the thought" will be the psychic elements whose relation to each other constitutes the thought. A proposition is fully analysed when the elements of the propositional sign correspond to the elements of the thought.'[2] This interpretation fits with Wittgenstein's remark to Russell that the constituents of a thought 'correspond to the words of language' (*NB*, p. 130). It is doubtful, however, that in 3.2 the phrase 'the objects of the thought' refers to the objects of which the thought is composed. It is more likely that it refers to the objects that compose the situation of which the thought is a picture. For in the statements immediately following 3.2 Wittgenstein speaks of 'the objects', and clearly means the objects composing the situation which the thought is about. For example, in 3.21 Wittgenstein says: 'The configuration of objects in a situation corresponds to the configuration of simple signs in the propositional sign.'

Nevertheless, it is clear from Wittgenstein's remark to Russell about a thought having 'constituents which correspond to the words of language' that a simple sign of language (a 'name') must have *two different directions of correspondence*. It corresponds *both* to a thought-element and to a reality-element. This way of stating the matter might be confusing: for thoughts are facts in the world, and in this sense elements of thoughts *are* elements of reality. But it is necessary to distinguish between 'thoughts' and 'reality'. For a thought is a picture of a situation in reality. A thought consists of elements, and the situation it depicts consists of elements. A configuration of thought-elements depicts a configuration of reality-elements. The relation of depicting goes in one direction only — from the thought-configuration to the reality-configuration, and not vice versa. In order for depiction to take place there must be *two* configurations, whatever might be the ultimate nature of their respective elements.

When we come to a fully analysed propositional sign, we have a *third* configuration composed of simple signs (names). What I am arguing for is that a name must correspond both to a thought-element (a psychical constituent) and to a reality-element (a simple object). Is the relation of 'correspondence' the same in the two cases? This is a difficult question. From 3.203 we know that a name 'means' a simple object: 'The object is its meaning.' Does a name also 'mean' the thought-element with which it corresponds? There is nothing in the *Tractatus* that supports an affirmative answer. All we have to go on is Wittgenstein's vague remark to Russell that the psychical components of thoughts 'correspond' to the words of language. I think the safest procedure is to leave this relation as vague as Wittgenstein did. I will merely say that a name 'corresponds to' or 'is correlated with' a thought-element.

Statement V is a consequence of the previous steps. If a thought is not expressed in physical signs it is not perceptible to the senses. It is a configuration of mental elements, picturing a possible situation in the world. If the thought-elements (the objects that compose the thought) are correlated with simple signs of language (names), and if these signs are put into the same configuration that the thought-elements already have, then the linguistic configuration becomes a picture of the situation depicted by the thought. The linguistic configuration will be a spoken or written sentence (or map, blueprint, diagram). In this way a thought becomes perceptible to the senses. It is given physical clothing.

It may be felt that it is wrong to give so much importance to the notion of a 'thought composed of psychical constituents', on the ground that this produces a distorted impression of the *Tractatus*, being radically different from anything one reads in the book itself. In the letter to Russell, Wittgenstein does say that a thought consists of 'psychical constituents'; but if this notion is as central to understanding the *Tractatus* as I am making it out to be, why does Wittgenstein seem to show so little interest in it?

My reply is, first, that the concept of a *thought* (*Gedanke*) certainly does figure in the *Tractatus*, and indeed is introduced *before* the concept of a *Satz* (sentence or proposition) appears. Second, Russell asked Wittgenstein a straightforward question, 'Does a thought consist of words?': and he received a straight-forward, unhesitating answer: 'No! But of psychical constituents that have the same sort of relation to reality as words. What those constituents are I don't know.' This answer surely means that a thought consists of purely mental elements — even though it *can* be expressed in words. Wittgenstein's prompt, emphatic, and unambiguous reply to Russell does not suggest that the conception of 'psychical constituents' had first occurred to him in 1919, one year after the completion of the *Tractatus* — but rather that this conception had been *assumed* in the writing of the *Tractatus*.

Wittgenstein does not dwell on the possible nature of the 'psychical constituents', or on their relation to that which the thought pictures. Why not? Because this would be, he thought, an inquiry belonging to *empirical psychology*, not to logic! He wrote to Russell:

> I don't know *what* the constituents of a thought are but I know *that* it must have such constituents which correspond to the words of language. Again the kind of relation of the constituents of the thought and of the pictured fact is irrelevant. It would be a matter of psychology to find out. (*NB*, p. 130)

Philosophy should be dealing with logical questions, not empirical ones. The *Tractatus* says:

> Psychology is no more closely related to philosophy than any other natural science.
> Theory of knowledge is the philosophy of psychology.
> Does not my study of sign-language correspond to the study of thought-processes, which philosophers held to be so essential for the philosophy of logic? Only they usually became entangled in unessential psychological investigations, and with my method too there is an analogous danger. (4.1121)

It is worth noting that the question 'Does not my study of sign-language correspond to the study of thought-processes?' is a rhetorical question implying an affirmative answer. He thinks that his study of language does correspond to those previous studies of thought-processes. But there is a warning against becoming entangled in unessential psychological investigations. I think he believed that an inquiry into the nature of the 'psychical constituents' of a thought, and into their relation to what the thought pictures, would be 'unessential psychological investigations'.

If I am giving a correct interpretation of the *Tractatus*, it reveals that the conceptions of the *Tractatus* belong to a traditional framework of philosophical ideas about the relation of thinking to language. John Locke, for example, declared that a man's thoughts 'are all within his own breast, invisible and hidden from others, nor can of themselves be made to appear'. In order for there to be a communication of thoughts 'it was necessary that man should find out some external sensible signs, whereof those invisible ideas, which his thoughts are made up, might be made known to others.'³ This is substantially the same as Wittgenstein's idea that thoughts, composed of 'psychical constituents', have an existence apart from physical signs, but can be given an expression in physical signs, by which the thoughts are made perceptible to the senses. The notion is that thoughts are independent of spoken or written language.

The same notion is present in Augustine's *Confessions* where he gives an account of how he had 'learnt to speak':

I noticed that people would name some object and then turn towards whatever it was that they had named. I watched them and understood that the sound they made when they wanted to indicate that particular thing was the name which they gave to it, and their actions clearly showed what they meant.⁴

According to this account Augustine *began* his learning of language, by questioning in his mind what the adults *meant* by this or that sound; and by dint of numerous *observations* of their behaviour, he *concluded* that the sounds they made were *names* for this or that thing. He did much questioning, observing, and inferring — that is, a lot of thinking — before he had learned a single word. As Wittgenstein remarks in the *Investigations*:

Augustine describes the learning of human language as if the child came into a strange country and did not understand the language of the country; that is, as if it already had a language, only not this one. Or also: as if the child could already *think*, only not yet speak. (*PI* 32)

We recall that in the *Notebooks*, when Wittgenstein was trying to describe the relations between *thinking* and *language*, he said that thinking itself 'is a kind of language' (*NB*, p. 82). Presumably he meant that thinking, *before* it is expressed in physical language, *is* 'a kind of language'.

Now it is immensely interesting to note that in the present-day philosophy of mind and language inspired by the work of Noam Chomsky, such a view is taken literally. For example, J. A. Fodor, who is influenced by Chomsky, explicitly asserts that before one can *learn* any language one must already be in possession of an innate language, which Fodor calls 'the language of thought'. Fodor also calls the innate language of thought an 'inner code' or an 'internal representational system'. He says that 'learning, including first language learning, essentially involves the use of an *un*learned internal representational system.'[5]

I have made this scattered reference to various writers in order to emphasize the fact that when we begin to spell out the *Tractatus* view of the relation between thinking and language, we see that this view belongs to an old philosophical conception that retains its power to the present day. There is, and probably always will be, a natural and almost irresistible inclination to assume that thinking comes *before* language and underlies it — that a spoken or written sentence cannot *say* or *mean* anything unless a thought is injected into it. In a well-known passage of *The Blue Book* Wittgenstein describes this conception in a striking way:

> It seems that there are *certain definite* mental processes bound up with the working of language, processes through which alone language can function. I mean the processes of understanding and meaning. The signs of our language seem dead without these mental processes; and it might seem that the only function of the signs is to induce such processes, and that these are the things we ought really to be interested in. Thus, if you are asked what is the relation between a name and the thing it names, you will be inclined to answer that the relation is a psychological one, and perhaps when you say this you think in particular of the mechanism of association. — We are tempted to think that the action of language consists of two parts; an inorganic part, the handling of signs, and an organic part, which we may call understanding these signs, meaning them, interpreting them, thinking. These latter activities seem to take place in a queer kind of medium, the mind; and the mechanisms of the mind, the nature of which, it seems, we don't quite understand, can bring about effects which no material mechanism could. (*BB*, p. 3)

Wittgenstein is characterizing in this passage an idea that presents itself to virtually everyone as natural and inevitable. But, according to me, he is also characterizing his own conception in the *Tractatus*. This conception is perhaps most clearly stated in *Tractatus* 3.11, the first sentence of which is: 'We use the perceptible sign of a proposition (spoken or written, etc.) as a projection of a possible situation.' How to read the second sentence of 3.11 is somewhat problematic. The German is: 'Die Projectionsmethode ist das Denken des Satz-Sinnes.' This can be read in two ways. In the first way it would be translated: 'The method of projection is thinking the sense of the proposition.' Taken in this way it would be an explanation of what 'thinking the sense of a proposition' is — namely, it would be applying an appropriate method of projection to a sentence. In the second way of reading, the German will be translated: 'Thinking the sense of the proposition is the method of projection.' Taken in this way the remark would be an explanation of what 'a method of projection' is — namely, thinking the sense of proposition.

I favour the second reading for the reason that 3.11 provides the first occurrence of the word 'projection' in the *Tractatus*. It says that we use a sentence as 'a projection' of a possible situation. What does that mean? An explanation of the term 'projection' is needed *for this context*. According to the second reading the explanation is this: *thinking* the sense of the proposition *is* the method of projection. I take it that 'thinking' is being identified with 'having a thought'. Earlier in the *Tractatus* it is said that a thought is a picture (3, 3.01), and that it contains the possibility of the situation of which it is the thought (3.02). A thought already has sense; it is already a picture of a possible situation. The question now is: how does a physical sentence become a picture? The answer of 3.11 is that a sentence becomes a picture (a projection) by virtue of a thought's transmitting its own sense to the physical sentence. A sentence, by itself, is 'dead': it is without sense, it says nothing. Sentences without thoughts are lifeless, 'inorganic'. But when a sentence is filled with a thought it takes on life: it becomes a visible or audible thought.

In his *Philosophical Grammar, The Blue and The Brown Books*, and throughout his later writings, Wittgenstein frequently resorts to the imagery of the *deadness* of the physical instruments and signs of language, considered in themselves. Here is a sequence of passages from the *Investigations*:

'Put a ruler against this body; it does not say that the body is of such-and-such a length. Rather it is in itself — I should like to say — dead, and achieves nothing of what thought achieves'. (*PI* 430)

'There is a gap between an order and its execution. It has to be closed by the understanding.'
'Only in the understanding is it meant that we have to do *this*. The *order* — that is of course only sounds, ink-marks'. (*PI* 431)

Every sign *by itself* seems dead. *What* gives it life? — In use it is *alive*. Does it there have the living breath in itself? — Or is the *use* its breath? (*PI* 432)

In such passages Wittgenstein is holding up, for examination and criticism, the idea (which I think was his own in the *Tractatus*) that words and sentences are lifeless, until meaning and sense is injected, or projected, into them by mental events, acts, processes.

Let us scrutinize the details of how, according to the *Tractatus*, sounds and ink-marks can acquire meaning and sense. (In the *Investigations* it is remarked that if you think that a mouse may have been spontaneously generated out of grey rags and dust, you should examine those materials closely! (*PI* 52)) There are three types of elements to be considered: first, thought-elements (the components of thoughts); second, names (the components of elementary sentences); third, reality-elements (the simple objects that compose states of affairs).

We know that a propositional sign (a sentence) is supposed to acquire sense by being invested with thought (3.11, 3.5). But how does a 'thought' acquire sense? Or does it? I said previously that a thought should be conceived of as being *intrinsically* a picture of a possible situation. This is David Favrholdt's interpretation of the *Tractatus*. Favrholdt says:

It is a characteristic of the concept of 'thought' that a thought always deals with something different from itself. A thought is a fact, because it consists of objects only. But thoughts are the only facts that point to something different from themselves. A thought is always a thought *of* something. This is an empirical fact. We cannot think without thinking of something. In order to make the thought represent something, we need not do more than think the thought. We need not decide that it has to represent something nor in which way it has to represent. A thought has, *qua* thought, a relation to 'what it is about'. It does not contain an indication of how it represents something, since it consists of psychical elements only. That these elements have a certain relation to one another

constitutes the necessary and sufficient condition of the representation of something different from the thought itself.[6]

There is some confusion in Favrholdt's remarks. He starts out by
saying that he is going to characterize the *concept* of thought. But
then he says it is an 'empirical fact' that a thought is *of* something.
If that is a feature of the *concept* of thought then it is not an
'empirical' fact about thoughts. Also, Favrholdt gives the
impression in these remarks that he himself subscribes to the view
that a thought is a structure which, unlike any other structure,
intrinsically points to something different from itself.

Leaving these points aside, I believe that Favrholdt gives a
correct account of the thoughts, composed of 'psychical
constituents', of the *Tractatus*. If a physical sentence becomes a
projection of a possible situation by virtue of the *thinking* of that
situation, then the thought of that situation did not *become* a
thought of that situation by virtue of the work of a previous
thought — for this would result in an infinite regress. The view
that physical sentences get their sense from thoughts seems to
require that the latter do not *get* their sense from anything! When
a thought occurs its sense is inherent to it. It cannot first occur
and then later acquire a sense. When it occurs it is already a
picture of a possible situation.

Let us probe more deeply into the mechanism of the picture
theory of propositions. At the elementary level (the level of
complete analysis) there are three things to be considered: a
thought composed of mental elements; an elementary word-
proposition composed of names; an elementary state of affairs
composed of simple objects. Let us *assume* that the elementary
proposition is *true*. Then there are three configurations with the
same structure: the thought; the word-proposition; and the fact
in the world. The first two structures are both pictures of the
third structure. The question to be considered is: how are the
elements of these three structures related to one another?

Wittgenstein says that the picturing relationship, which makes
a picture into a picture, belongs to the picture (2.1513). And also
that the picturing relationship 'consists of the correlations of the
picture's elements with things' (2.1514). Since there are three
structures composed of three different types of elements, there
will have to be correlations between the elements of these three
types.

Let M designate a mental element, S a simple sign (name), and

O a reality-element (object). I wish to argue that the 'correlation' between M and S is entirely different in nature from the 'correlation' between M and O. I have already claimed that a thought is *intrinsically* a picture of a certain possible situation. If this is correct, then I think that a mental element M must intrinsically *mean* an object O. It cannot *come* to mean O by any stipulation or convention. There is no *act* of making a correlation between M and O. M, by its inherent nature, *means* O. This is required in order for a configuration of Ms to be *intrinsically* a picture of a configuration of Os. In the language of 2.1511 and 2.1515, a thought 'reaches right out to' reality, and the mental elements 'touch' the reality-elements.

We are trying to view the matter from the standpoint of a completely analysed proposition. This will be an elementary proposition consisting of a concatenation of simple signs (names). In calling a sign 'simple' Wittgenstein does not mean that the sign has no physical complexity. The simplicity of a name consists in its deputizing for, 'going proxy for', a simple object. 'In a proposition a name deputizes for (*vertritt*) an object.' (3.22) On my interpretation a thought *underlies* a proposition composed of names. The thought is composed of thought-elements each of which, by its own nature, *means* a simple object. A thought-element M is correlated with a linguistic sign S by stipulation or convention. Since M already means O, S automatically means O by virtue of S's correlation with M.

The process by which a sign comes to mean a simple object may be spelled out in stages as follows:

1 M intrinsically means O.
2 S is correlated with M by stipulation or convention.
3 As a consequence of 1 and 2, S comes to mean O.

Wittgenstein did not articulate these complexities in the *Tractatus*, or in what has survived of the *Notebooks*; and it may be doubted whether he had clarified them in his thinking. But once it is assumed that thoughts, composed of psychical elements, underlie word-propositions, then it seems to me that the foregoing account becomes highly plausible. One could think of it as the 'hidden' philosophy of mind and of language of the *Tractatus*.

An especially perplexing feature of the above account is the notion that a thought-element has an *intrinsic* reference to a certain object (reality-element). Richard Miller argues persuasively in support of this interpretation. He says:

> If a thought is an arrangement of psychic representatives, thought-elements must stand for objects independently of all conventions and decisions. Otherwise, when a thought about X has occurred one must admit that in another context, involving different conventions and decisions, the same concatenation of thought-elements, and hence the *self-same thought*, would not have been about X but about something else. And that is nonsensical. A thought about something else must be another thought.[7]

It would of course be a matter of stipulation or convention which *words* were correlated with which objects. But, as Miller remarks,

> Since a thought, unlike a sequence of sounds or marks, would not be the same were its reference different, the elements of which a thought is composed are not correlated with objects simply by convention. . . . Words require conventions to connect them with parts of the world. Thought-elements refer, as it were, without outside help.[8]

In an earlier, unpublished version of Miller's essay, he gave a concrete and, I think, cogent reason for holding that a thought-element *cannot* be correlated with an object by decision or convention. The reasoning is simple. In order to assign a thought-element to an object, I should already have to *mean* that object. I could not correlate a thought-element with that object unless I was referring to *that* object 'in my mind'. In my thought of such a correlation there would have to be an element that meant that object. In order to *make* a correlation between a thought-element and an object, the correlation must *already* exist. The conclusion is that thought-elements do not have their reference assigned to them, or acquire their reference by association. No. A thought-element has an *inherent* reference to the simple object to which it refers.

Previously I referred to an essay by Kenny. He rightly distinguishes the elements of a propositional sign from the elements of a thought. He says, correctly, that 'Meaning is conferred on signs by *us*, by our conventions.'[9] But then he is vexed by the question of how the thought-elements get *their* meaning. He makes the suggestion that the elements of a thought have their meaning conferred on them by 'the metaphysical I' of

---

the *Tractatus* (5.641), the I or subject that 'does not belong to the world' (5.632). Kenny says:

> In the thought itself, perhaps, we can distinguish between the particular mental configuration, studiable by psychology, and the significance or intentionality of that configuration, conferred by the metaphysical self. Thought... will have the right mathematical multiplicity to depict the facts; but its multiplicity gives it only the *possibility* of depicting; that it actually does depict depends on the meaning of its elements, and that is given by the extra-psychological will giving those elements a use, an application.[10]

I do not believe it can be made intelligible how something that is not *in* the world (the metaphysical I or will) can *give* a thought-element 'a use, an application'. It seems to me that the cleanest and most plausible interpretation of the *Tractatus* is to say that *nothing* gives a thought-element its meaning. No meaning is given to a thought-element. It means a certain object, refers to that object, by virtue of its intrinsic nature. Its meaning is not *conferred* on it by anything, either by a human being or by a metaphysical I. It is not like a physical sign that has a use bestowed on it. It is actually inappropriate to speak of a thought-element as having a 'use'. Nor does a configuration of thought-elements have a 'use'. The configuration does not have its 'significance' conferred on it. The configuration depicts what it depicts without any outside help. In contrast a physical sentence, which in itself is 'dead', is endowed with life when a human being *uses* it to 'express' a thought. A physical sentence or other propositional sign takes on a sense when a sense is thought *into* it (3.11). But perhaps a psychologically more accurate account of the imagery we tend to have here is to say that the physical sentence does not 'take on a sense' or even that it 'has a sense' — but rather that the sentence is merely the perceptible clothing of *the real thing* that has sense, namely, the thought.

According to my interpretation, the *Tractatus* was heavily influenced by the notion that spoken and written sentences are the *clothing* of thoughts. This becomes explicit when, in speaking of sentences that are not 'completely analysed', Wittgenstein says:

> Language disguises thought. So much so, that from the outward form of the clothing it is impossible to infer the form of the thought beneath it, because the outward form of the clothing is not designed to reveal the form of the body, but for entirely different purposes. (4.002)

In his later writings Wittgenstein was constantly trying to formulate, and to criticize, the notion that our thinking is hidden within the words of language. A remark in *Zettel* presents as exact a formulation of this notion as one could wish for:

> Ever and again comes the thought that what we see of a sign is only the outside of something within, in which the real operations of sense and meaning go on. (*Z* 140)

Another way of phrasing this idea is to say that words and sentences have meaning and sense, but only *indirectly*. Their meaning and sense is *derivative*, i.e. derived from the mental elements and the mental thoughts which have sense and meaning *in themselves*.

It is highly interesting that Russell, in an essay of 1919 called 'On Propositions: What They Are and How They Mean', written while he was still somewhat influenced by the conversations he had with Wittgenstein before the First World War, raised the following question:

> Can the relation called 'meaning' be a direct relation between the word as a physical occurrence and the object itself, or must the relation pass through a 'mental' intermediary, which could be called the 'idea' of the object.[11]

It is noteworthy that in the *Investigations*, in a series of paragraphs containing frequent references to the *Tractatus*, Wittgenstein makes a remark that resembles Russell's question:

> The sentence and the word, with which logic deals, ought to be something pure and clear-cut. And we rack our brains over the nature of the *real* sign. — Is it perhaps the *idea* of the sign? or the idea at the present moment? (*PI* 105)

In my opinion Wittgenstein is referring here to a problem that confused and vexed him when he was working on the *Tractatus*. According to my interpretation he did conclude that the relation of a 'name' to an 'object' was *not* 'direct', but had to 'pass through a "mental" intermediary', which was a 'psychical constituent' of a thought. This thought-element referred to the object 'directly'. It could appropriately be called the 'idea' of the object.

In his essay of 1919 Russell adopted the same position. He declared that there are two kinds of propositions, image-propositions and word-propositions.[12] He says:

> A word-proposition, apart from niceties, 'means' the corresponding

image-proposition, and an image-proposition has an objective reference dependent upon the meanings of its constituent images.[13]

The truth or falsity of a proposition, according to Russell, depends upon its relation to a fact other than itself. This fact he calls the 'objective' of the proposition.[14] Both word-propositions and image-propositions 'refer to' their objectives. But the relation of referring is different in the two cases. The image-proposition, it seems, refers to its objective directly, without an intermediary; whereas the word-proposition refers to its objective via the image-proposition which it 'means'.[15] Russell provides the following illustration of an image-proposition:

> The simplest possible schema of correspondence between proposition and objective is afforded by such cases as visual memory-images. I call up a picture of a room that I know, and in my picture the window is to the left of the fire. I give to this picture that sort of belief which we call 'memory'. When the room was present to sense, the window was, in fact, to the left of the fire. In this case, I have a complex image, which we may analyse, for our purposes, into (a) the image of the window, (b) the image of the fire, (c) the relation that (a) is to the left of (b). The objective consists of the window and the fire with the very same relation between them. In such a case, the objective of a proposition consists of the meanings of its constituent images related (or not related, as the case may be) by the same relation as that which holds between the constituent images in the proposition.[16]

This passage presents a theory that has a superficial resemblance to the picture theory of the *Tractatus*. The image-proposition would be a picture consisting of elements related to one another in a definite way. The fact that the elements are so related depicts the things as related in the same way (2.15).

It is evident, however, that this image-proposition would not be an elementary proposition in the sense of the *Tractatus*. For an elementary proposition would consist solely of elements, each of which deputizes for a simple object. The image of the window, which is a component of Russell's complex image, is supposed to refer to or mean *the window*. But a simple object of the *Tractatus* is something that is unchangeable, enduring, indestructible (2.0271). This cannot be said of a window! Since a window is not 'a simple object', then a mental image of a window could not be an ultimate constituent of a thought.

It is most unlikely that Wittgenstein could have believed that the 'psychical constituents' of thoughts were mental images. In the first place, our mental images are images of people, trees, gardens, buildings — things which, on the *Tractatus* view, are 'complex' things. In the second place, if Wittgenstein had believed that mental images are the elements of thoughts, he would not have written to Russell, 'I don't know *what* the constituents of a thought are.' I have referred to Russell's notion of 'image-propositions' merely as an illustration of the always prevalent philosophical conception that an ordinary word-sentence derives its sense from a thought in a mental medium — from an 'internal representation' composed of elements that *intrinsically* mean simple objects — and that consequently an arrangement of such elements in a thought would *intrinsically* depict an elementary state of affairs. In my interpretation of the *Tractatus*, Wittgenstein held this general conception but would not have agreed with Russell that the ultimate components of thoughts are mental images. Wittgenstein was convinced that a thought must be composed of mental elements, but he arrived at no decision as to the nature of those elements. Indeed, he seems to have concluded that to attempt to decide this matter did not belong to his *logical* investigation of the nature of thinking and language, but would be an undertaking for empirical psychology.

The view of the *Tractatus* that I am presenting helps one to understand the striking claim that 'A proposition *shows* its sense.' (4.022) This claim will be studied in detail in the next chapter. Here I wish to indicate how it may be connected with the conception that a spoken or written sentence derives its sense from a thought. It seems implausible that our everyday sentences always *show* their sense. Often they are open to different interpretations. Their meaning can be ambiguous. If we are searching for something that is *incapable* of different inter-pretations, it seems that we will not find it in structures of physical signs. Meaning, sense, understanding, do not seem to have a firm enough ground there.

But if we consider *thoughts*, composed of 'psychical con-stituents', this problem appears to fall away. If a thought is a structure of mental elements, each element having an inherent meaning, then an arrangement of thought-elements will intrin-sically depict one and only one situation in the world. A thought is not open to different interpretations. When it is projected into a physical sentence it *is the meaning* of the sentence. It is in the *thought* that our understanding finds a firm footing. The thought is something that not only does not *require* interpretation but *cannot* be interpreted. It is where interpretation ends. In *The Blue Book* Wittgenstein describes this idea as follows: 'What one wishes to say is: "Every sign is capable of interpretation, but the meaning mustn't be capable of interpretation. It is the last interpretation."' (*BB*, p. 34) I think he was describing an idea that was embedded in the *Tractatus*. That which truly *shows* its sense is a *Gedanke*, not a *Satz*.

It is interesting to observe that a view similar to what I have called the 'hidden' philosophy of mind and language of the *Tractatus* is put forward in a recent book by John Searle. In his *Intentionality* Searle holds that many mental states or events, such as beliefs, desires, fears, hopes, and (presumably) thoughts, have the property of 'intentionality' — which means that they have the property of being 'directed at or about or of objects and states of affairs in the world'.[17] These mental states are 'representations' of the things or states of affairs they are about or of. A belief or desire is *intrinsically* a representation: it does not become a representation through being *used* by some agent as a representation.[18] In contrast, spoken and written sentences are not intrinsically representations: they do not have intrinsic intentionality. But they do have intentionality bestowed on them. Sounds and marks acquire *derivative* intentionality. They *become* representations by having the intentionality of mental states conferred on them.[19]

There is a striking resemblance between Searle's view of the relation between intentional mental states and sentences, and the conception of the *Tractatus* (according to my interpretation) of the relation between *Gedanken* and *Sätze*. This is not offered as any support for my interpretation, but only as a further illustration of how attractive such a position continues to be. (I will say something in criticism of Searle's view in chapter 5.)

----- CHAPTER 5 -----

Whether a Proposition Shows its Sense

In the *Investigations* there is a famous comparison of a rule with a sign-post:

> A rule stands there like a sign-post. — Does the sign-post leave no doubt open about the way I have to go? Does it show which direction I am to take when I have passed it; whether along the road or the footpath or cross-country? But where is it said which way I am to follow it; whether in the direction of its finger or (e.g.) in the opposite one? — And if there were, not a single sign-post, but a chain of adjacent ones or of chalk marks on the ground — is there only *one* way of interpreting them? (*PI* 85)

I wish to consider the doctrine of the *Tractatus* that 'A proposition *shows* its sense.' (4.022) So I will consider the remarks of *PI* 85, not as a comparison of a sign-post with a *rule*, but as a comparison of a sign-post with a proposition. A sign-post may not only be 'compared' with a proposition: it *is* a proposition. A motorist, who wants to drive to Dover, comes to an intersection where he can turn either left or right. There is a sign-post with the name 'Dover' on it, and an arrow pointing to the right. In the *Tractatus* this combination of the name and the arrow would certainly be deemed to be a propositional sign. The *Tractatus* says that a propositional sign could be composed of articles of furniture, such as tables and chairs: 'The spatial arrangement of these things will express the sense of the proposition.' (3.1431) Similarly, the spatial arrangement of the name 'Dover' and the arrow will *say* that Dover is to the right. It would be no different if a policeman standing there were to combine the words 'Dover is in *that* direction' with a pointing gesture.

The *Tractatus* makes some remarkable assertions about the

understanding of propositions. 'We understand the sense of a propositional sign without its having been explained to us.' (4.02) 'I understand a proposition without having had its sense explained to me.' (4.021) 'A proposition *shows* its sense.' (4.022).

It is clear that these assertions are completely general. They refer to *all* propositions, in *all* circumstances. It is declared not just that *sometimes* the sense of a sentence does not need to be explained, but that this is *never* required. Indeed, the view seems to be not just that the sense of a sentence does not need ever to be explained, but that the sense of a sentence *cannot* be explained. For it is stated that 'What *can* be shown, *cannot* be said.' (4.1212)

It might be thought that the last assertion does not apply to 4.022, for two reasons. First, 4.1212 is a comment on the statement that 'A proposition *shows* the logical form of reality' (4.121), rather than a comment on 4.022. Second, the second half of 4.022 states the following: 'A proposition *shows* how things stand *if* it is true. And it *says that* they do so stand.'

I think, however, that the correct interpretation is the following: The sense of a proposition '*p*' is that things stand in a certain way, and '*p*' says that they stand in that way. But *another* proposition '*q*' can neither show nor state the sense of '*p*'. If '*p*' and '*q*' showed and said the same thing they would be one and the same proposition (see 5.141). All propositions are alike in showing the logical form of reality, and all are alike in not stating what the logical form of reality is. This is something that cannot be said, cannot be expressed in language. But the *sense* of a proposition can be expressed and *is* expressed — by that proposition itself, and *only* by that proposition.

Although the *Tractatus* holds that there can be no explanation of the sense of a propositional sign, it also holds that the meaning of the component parts of the propositional sign *can* and indeed *must* be explained. 'The meanings of simple signs (words) must be explained to us if we are to understand them. But with propositions we make ourselves understood.' (4.026) The idea is that if anyone understands the constituent parts of a sentence, then he understands the sentence. Nothing more is required. In regard to any proposition, 'One understands it, if one understands its constituents.' (4.024) The imagery behind this conception appears in the remark that 'One name stands for one thing, another for another, and they are combined with one another. In this way the whole group — like a living picture — presents a state of affairs.' (4.0311) This imagery is most appropriate for an elementary sentence, which consists only of names. But the thesis that understanding the parts of a sentence is *sufficient* for understanding the sense of the sentence, seems to be completely general, applying both to elementary and non-elementary sentences. This thesis is at the heart of the picture theory.

The Dover road-sign is a propositional sign. It has two constituents: the name 'Dover' and the arrow pointing to the right. According to the *Tractatus*, understanding these two constituents is sufficient for understanding the sense of the sign. But paragraph 85 of the *Investigations* raises some questions about this. Does the sign-post show one whether to go by the road, or the footpath, or across open country?

The answer is: sometimes it does and sometimes it doesn't. A motorist driving his car would have no doubt that the sign tells him to take the *road* to the right. But suppose there was a state of war and the sign-post was put there to guide advancing foot-soldiers. They know it is dangerous to be on the roads where they would be exposed to attack by enemy aircraft. So they understand the sign to be telling them to go by the footpath or across open fields. On the other hand, suppose that the enemy aircraft have not been active for some days or weeks. The foot-soldiers might be in doubt as to how to interpret the sign-post. Does it tell them to take the road, or the path, or the open fields? As *PI* 85 says, a sign-post 'sometimes leaves room for doubt and sometimes not'. We can imagine that in these circumstances the military authorities might think it advisable to affix a supplementary *explanation* to the sign-post: e.g. the words 'Take the road', or 'Keep to the fields.'

We can imagine complications of a different sort. Suppose that it is possible to drive to Dover from the intersection either by going right or by going left. The highway administration has placed a sign-post there with an arrow pointing to the right, because that is the shortest route to Dover. On certain days, however, this route is closed for maintenance work. On those days the highway authorities direct motorists to take the route to the left, by placing an additional sign-post (*under* the original one) containing the name 'Dover' and an arrow pointing *left*. The motorists grow accustomed to going by the lower sign. It happens, however, that sometimes the wind blows the lower sign away, or that small boys remove it for fun. The motorists become confused when they see only the single original sign. The highway department then adopts the practice of supplementing the original sign (with its arrow pointing right) with another sign beneath it with an arrow pointing right, when it wants the motorists to turn right. When the department wants the motorists to turn left, *no* supplementary sign is affixed to the post. So the motorists become accustomed to interpreting a single arrow pointing right as telling them to turn *left*, and to interpreting double arrows pointing right as telling them to turn *right*. We could imagine still further complications.

The sign-post consisting of the name 'Dover' and an arrow pointing to the right, is a propositional sign. The *Tractatus* says: 'We understand the sense of a propositional sign without its having been explained to us.' (4.02) According to the picture theory of the *Tractatus* this is *always* true of *every* propositional sign. What paragraph 85 of the *Investigations* makes plain is that this is not so. *Sometimes* the sense of a propositional sign requires to be explained by another propositional sign: sometimes not. It depends on the circumstances. This is a refutation of the universal claim of the picture theory. But of course what is *not* meant in the *Investigations* is that the sense of *every* propositional sign needs to be explained. An explanation is not required 'unless *we* require it to prevent a misunderstanding' (*PI* 87). Usually the sense of road sign-posts does not need explanation. 'The sign-post is in order — if, *under normal circumstances*, it fulfils its purpose.' (*PI* 87, emphasis added) The imagined case in which a sign-post with an arrow to the right required for its explanation an additional sign-post with an arrow to the right, was not the *normal* case in which motorists find themselves. And the fact that in this imagined case the first propositional sign needed to be supplemented by a repetition of that propositional sign, in order to avert misunderstanding, does *not* imply that the second sign needed to be supplemented by a third one. The explanation could come to an end because, *as a matter of fact*, those motorists had no tendency to be perplexed by the meaning of the second sign. There *could* be circumstances in which the second sign did need to be supplemented by still another repetition of the sign in order to prevent misunderstanding. But that is not the case we imagined.

It seems to me to be likely that the *Tractatus* doctrine that every proposition *shows* its sense (4.002), and that in every case 'I understand a proposition without having had its sense explained to me' (4.021), seemed to Wittgenstein to be an *a priori* necessity, partly because he assumed that if in even *one* case a proposition needed to be explained by a second proposition, then an infinite regress of explanations would be required, and therefore *nothing* would be understood. Language would be impossible. Therefore, the only way to stop the regress is to prevent it from getting started: to hold that every propositional sign with a sense is *immediately* understood by anyone who understands its constituent parts. Otherwise there would be endless doubt about the sense of *any* sentence.

The difference between the *Tractatus* and the *Investigations* on this issue is very sharp, and is of immense importance. In the *Tractatus* Wittgenstein's thinking was focused on the *logical possibility* of doubt. If it were logically possible for a person who understood the constituent parts of a sentence to have a doubt as to the sense of the sentence, then all thought and language would be impossible. Doubt must not creep in anywhere; for if it did it would reappear in any attempt to remove the doubt. Doubt as to the sense of a propositional sign must be *logically* excluded!

The attitude of Wittgenstein in the *Investigations* is totally different. It makes no sense to suppose that a doubt as to the sense of a propositional sign could be *logically* excluded. Take the case of the Dover sign-post, which is a propositional sign. The ordinary British motorist knows the meaning of the name 'Dover', and is also familiar with the meaning of directional arrows on road sign-posts. Normally a motorist who saw at an intersection a sign consisting of the name 'Dover' and an arrow pointing to the right, would immediately understand the sense of this sign to be that the road to Dover was to the right. Suppose, however, that a particular motorist knows that the road to the right is sometimes blocked for repairs. He also knows of the local convention that when this is so a single arrow to the right indicates that he should turn *left*. He knows too that when the road to the right is open this is indicated by a second arrow pointing to the right, affixed below the first one. But he also knows that this second sign is a temporary affair, not securely fastened to the post, and so it is sometimes blown down by the wind. Thus, when he sees the single sign pointing to the right he is in doubt as to its sense. Does it mean he should turn right, or left?

This doubt is certainly conceivable, even though the motorist understands the constituent parts of the propositional sign. The important step taken by Wittgenstein in the *Investigations* is to distinguish between *conceivable* (logically possible) doubt and *actual* doubt. He says it is not the case that we are in doubt just because we can imagine or conceive of a doubt:

> I can easily conceive that someone is always in doubt before opening his front door whether an abyss does not yawn behind it, and that he makes sure about it before he steps through the door (and he might on some occasion prove to be right) — but that does not make me doubt in the same case. (*PI* 84)

> It may easily look as if every doubt merely *revealed* an existing gap in the foundations; so that secure understanding is only possible if we first doubt everything that *can* be doubted, and then remove all these doubts. (*PI* 87)

I think that Wittgenstein correctly diagnosed his position in the *Tractatus* as the view that any doubt as to the sense of a propositional sign would reveal an existing gap in the foundations. But in the *Tractatus* he thought that once any doubt was started it could not be stopped. Therefore he took the extraordinary measure of holding that one *could not* doubt the sense of a propositional sign *if* one understood the meaning of its constituent parts. Doubt was excluded at the beginning.

Let us consider 4.024 more closely. It says that one understands a proposition 'if one understands its constituents'. This is a puzzling assertion. How is one to interpret it? It would not be in keeping with the aims of the *Tractatus* to give it a psychological interpretation: e.g. to suppose it means that if the 'psychological states' of understanding the constituents occur, they will *cause* the 'psychological state' of understanding the proposition to occur. No. Remark 4.024 must be asserting that there is a *logical* connection between understanding the constituents and understanding the whole proposition. Presumably the logical connection would be one of *identity*. Understanding the constituents just *is* understanding the whole proposition. Wittgenstein says: 'Like Frege and Russell I conceive of a proposition as a function of the expressions contained in it.' (3.318)

Consider the following example. Suppose that I am about to go to the railway station to catch a train. A friend assures me that I do not have to hurry, for he is certain that the train will arrive late. I ask, 'What makes you so certain?' He replies, 'I feel certain in my hands.'

I would be astonished by this remark. I do not understand the sentence (proposition) 'I feel certain in my hands that the train will be late.' I understand all of the words that compose this sentence. They are familiar words. I am familiar with the phrase 'I am certain' — as, for example, in the sentence 'I am certain that the train will be late.' I am familiar with the phrase 'in my hands' — as, for example, in the sentence 'I held the vase in my hands', or in the sentence 'I feel pain in my hands.' I can even think of circumstances in which one might say, 'I feel certain *in my heart* that he is innocent.' But I am baffled by the combination of familiar words (the whole sentence) 'I feel certain in my hands that the train will be late.'

Is this a counter-example to the claim of 4.024, which says that one understands a sentence (a proposition) if one understands its constituents? Don't I understand the constituents of the problematic sentence, but fail to understand the sentence? Or are the words and phrases that compose this sentence not its actual constituents? If not, then what *are* its constituents?

At the level of a 'completely analysed' sentence the constituents would consist only of 'names'. The view of the *Tractatus* would presumably be that at that level; if we knew the meaning of the names, then we would know at once that a certain concatenation of names was either a meaningful sentence, or else was nonsense. If we take the assertion of 4.024 to be referring to completely analysed sentences, then it is impossible to construct a counter-example, since we don't know a single example of a 'name' or of a 'completely analysed' sentence. Taken in this way, the assertion of 4.024 is not an observation about sentences of ordinary language, but is instead an *a priori* conception about the imaginary language of completely analysed sentences.

Consider again the puzzling sentence 'I feel certain in my hands that the train will be late.' I should not wish to hold that this sentence is *necessarily* senseless. There is an inclination to think that we *know* the sentence is senseless *because* we understand it — we understand it so well that we see it could not make sense. In the *Investigations* Wittgenstein warns against this way of thinking. He says, 'When a sentence is called senseless, it is not as it were its sense that is senseless.' (*PI* 500) We are not to suppose that we have perceived a 'senseless sense'.

Instead of holding that the puzzling sentence is *necessarily* senseless, what is right to say is simply that I do not understand it. I have never encountered the combination of words 'I feel certain in my hands that so-and-so.' This combination is unfamiliar to me. I should have to ask the speaker how he uses this combination of words. In what circumstances does he speak of 'feeling certain in his hands' that so-and-so?

It is not impossible that this speaker should be able to give me a satisfactory explanation of the way he uses this phrase. He might tell me the following story. Normally his hands are weak and tremble a lot. He has noticed, however, that when he is inclined to the opinion that some future event will take place, sometimes this weakness and trembling goes away. He has further noticed that when this happens his opinion always turns out to be true. He has gradually come to have full confidence in an opinion of his when it is accompanied by this phenomenon. He calls this phenomenon 'feeling certain in my hands'. In the present case he started out with the tentative opinion that the train will be late. His hands became firm and strong. This convinced him that his opinion was correct. So he declared to me that he was certain that the train will be late. When I asked, 'What makes you so certain?', he replied, 'I feel certain in my hands.'

Although the story is bizarre, I would now understand his previously puzzling sentence 'I feel certain in my hands.' The important point is that I needed an *explanation* of that sentence. I did not understand *it*, although I understood its constituent words. I did not understand that *combination* of words. The explanation I received was an explanation of the whole sentence, not just of its constituents. I learned of the peculiar circumstances which gave rise to the employment of that sentence by this speaker. *That* is what brought about my understanding. It was not that I put together the component words and then perceived the sense emerge — as if the sentence were a mechanism that will work only if it has *these* parts and not those other ones (see *PI* 559).

The *Tractatus* conceives of the sense of a sentence as solely a function of the meaning of its constituent parts. This is an aspect of the picture-theory of sentence-meaning. But this is not how Wittgenstein views the matter in his later work. In the *Investigations* he gives the examples of the sentences 'The stove is in pain' and 'It is 5 o'clock on the sun.' (*PI* 350, 351) We understand the constituent parts of these sentences: but we do not understand the sentences. We have no idea of when to say that the stove is or isn't in pain, or that it is or isn't 5 o'clock on the sun.

There is an inclination to reply, 'But we *do* understand the sentence "The stove is in pain" — for we know that it is false.' Compare, however, the situation in which a nurse is reporting to a doctor on the condition of a patient. One of the things she says is 'The patient is not in pain.' She knows what to do, what to look for, in order to find out whether the patient is in pain. But the philosopher who says, 'The stove is not in pain', does not base his assertion on an observation of the stove. His assertion is *a priori*. What he is really saying is that *both* the sentence 'The stove is in pain' and its negation are lacking in sense. This is true; and it shows that the sense of a sentence is not solely a function of the meaning of its constituent parts. But here again we should not imagine that we perceive a 'senseless sense'. We have learned when to say, in a variety of circumstances, that a person or animal is or is not in pain. When we feel that the sentence 'The stove is in pain' is senseless, this is because we realize that the mastery we have acquired of the application of the word 'pain' to people and animals has in no way prepared us to apply this word to a stove.

And this is not just a matter of *saying the word*. Our word 'pain' is connected with natural *expressions* of pain; and also with responses of concern, comforting, treating the one who is in pain, calling the doctor, and so on. What would be an 'expression of pain' by a stove? How would one 'comfort' a stove? We don't know. Clearly, to seriously apply the word 'pain' to a stove would be to *extend* its familiar use. But along what lines would that extension be made? We don't know. Feeling that the sentence is senseless amounts to the realization that we have no idea of how it might be employed.

This point is especially clear in regard to the sentence 'It is 5 o'clock on the sun.' Most of us know that the earth has been divided into time-zones. This is a system, and a technique, for determining the local time at places on the earth. Knowing the local time in Chicago we can compute the local time in Portugal. The sentence 'It is 5 o'clock in Portugal' makes sense, even if false. The language of earth time-zones provides a place for it: but it provides no place for 'It is 5 o'clock on the sun.' Perhaps the new science of space exploration has created a system within which one can compute the local time on the sun. If it exists, this is a new language. To understand the question 'What time is it on the sun?', one would have to learn that language. This is an excellent illustration of Wittgenstein's general remark: 'To understand a sentence means, to understand a language. To understand a language means, to master a technique.' (*PI* 199)

Let us turn to the assumption of the *Tractatus* that there is such a thing as *the general form* of propositions. This general form is 'what all propositions, by their nature, have in common with one another' (5.47). 'The general propositional form is the essence of a proposition.' (5.471) 'To give the essence of a proposition means to give the essence of description, and thus the essence of the world.' (5.4711)

According to the *Tractatus*, 'The totality of propositions is language.' (4.001) There are different natural languages; but the differences between them are, in a sense, superficial. For in all of them propositions are expressed, and all of these have a common nature. This common nature is whatever is necessary and sufficient for something to be a proposition. What this essential nature of propositions comes down to is: a proposition is a picture of a possible state of affairs.

This idea comes across pretty clearly in the following remarks:

> It now seems possible to give the most general propositional form: that is, to give a description of the propositions of *any* sign-language *whatsoever* in such a way that every possible sense can be expressed by a symbol satisfying the description, and every symbol satisfying the description can express a sense, provided that the meanings of the names are suitably chosen.
>
> It is clear that *only* what is essential to the most general propositional form may be included in its description — for otherwise it would not be the most general form.
>
> The existence of a general propositional form is proved by this, that there cannot be a proposition whose form could not have been foreseen (i.e. constructed). The general form of a proposition is: this is how things are. (4.5)

I think there is a feeling of being 'let down' by this account of 'the general form' of all propositions. To say that the general form is *this is how things are* seems to come to no more than saying that every proposition, every meaningful sentence, is *a picture*. But we have already been told this, e.g. in 4.01 and 4.06.

Perhaps we expected an exciting new revelation about the nature of language. We didn't get that. Nevertheless, 4.5 is interesting. It contains the astonishing remark that 'there cannot be a proposition whose form could not have been foreseen.' That this is so is offered as a *proof* that there is *a general form* of propositions. But the proof, and what is proved, come to the same thing — namely to the view that language is homogeneous, uniform, everywhere the same. Every possible proposition can be foreseen, because they are all alike. All of them are just pictures of this or that situation in logical space. In knowing the nature of one proposition we know the nature of every proposition. For all of them are the *same kind* of thing.

The conception that a proposition says, 'This is how things are', is especially appropriate for an *elementary* proposition. For it is composed solely of 'names' — one name deputizing for one object, another name for another object — and the combination of names says, 'This is how things are' with those objects. But if this is what an elementary proposition does, then it is what *every* proposition does — for every non-elementary proposition is constructed out of elementary ones. This point is made explicit in the first comment on 4.5:

> Suppose that I am given *all* elementary propositions: then I can simply ask, what propositions can I construct out of them? And that is *all* propositions, and *that* fixes their boundary. (4.51)

Both 4.5 and 6 state the general form of a proposition. It is interesting to compare them: 4.5 states the general form in the simple words 'This is how things are.' In 6 the general form of proposition is given in a frightening-looking formula. But the meaning of this formula is less formidable than it appears. It is the formula for applying the operation of repeated negation to a set of elementary propositions in such a way as to obtain every truth-function of those propositions. As Wittenstein puts it, what the formula says 'is just that every proposition is a result of successive applications to elementary propositions of the operation' of repeated negation (6.001).

Thus 6 provides a technical method for generating every proposition out of elementary propositions. This method ensures that every proposition has a complete truth-functional analysis into elementary propositions (3.25). It also ensures that the pictorial quality of saying 'This is how things are', which is the general form of elementary propositions, is present in *all* propositions. Thus 4.5 and 6, despite their strikingly different ways of presenting the general form of propositions, come to the same thing.

In this chapter we have been concerned with the claim of the *Tractatus* that the sense of a sentence *cannot be explained*. I wish to relate this claim to the view of the *Tractatus* that there is a general form of all propositions. If all propositions have a common nature, then there is a clear sense in which this common nature could not be explained to anyone. For the explanation could be given only in a proposition — which a person would already have to understand in order to understand the explanation. As Wittgenstein put it in the *Notebooks*:

> What can be said can only be said by means of a proposition, and so nothing that is necessary for the understanding of *all* propositions can be said. (*NB*, p. 25)

If there were a person who had no comprehension of what it is to *say something*, then you could not tell him what this is *by saying something*! If, on the other hand, the person does understand some propositions, then he does already have a grasp of the common nature of propositions — which is everywhere the same. He cannot be *informed* of something he already knows.

The conception that there is a single common nature of all propositions is, I think, what underlies these famous assertions:

> A proposition cannot present logical form: it is mirrored in it. What mirrors itself in language, cannot be presented in language. What expresses *itself* in language, *we cannot* express in language. (4.12)

This is a rigorous consequence of the conception that there is *one* general form of all propositions. Thus, no proposition can explain the kind of sense that all propositions have. (If it should be objected that Wittgenstein does explain this in the *Tractatus*, the answer is that the philosophical propositions of the *Tractatus* are not genuine propositions: for they are put forward as *a priori* insights, and there is no picture, or proposition, that is true *a priori* (2.225).) Not only cannot the logical form of all propositions be explained, but also (as said earlier in this chapter) the sense of an individual proposition cannot be explained by another proposition. For the sense of an individual proposition just is a certain possible situation in logical space: any proposition that pictures *that* would be the *same* proposition.

One of the great differences between the *Tractatus* and the *Investigations* is that in the latter Wittgenstein flatly rejects his former assumption that there is a general form of propositions. In remarks that are obviously autobiographical, he says:

> Here we come up against the great question that lies behind all these considerations. — For someone might object to me: 'You take the easy way out! You talk about all sorts of language-games, but have nowhere said what the essence of a language-game, and

hence of language, is: what is common to all these activities, and what makes them into language or parts of language. So you let yourself off the very part of the investigation that once gave you yourself most headache, namely, the *general form of propositions and of language.*'

And that is true. — Instead of producing something common to all that we call language, I am saying that these phenomena have no one thing in common which makes us use the same word for all — but that they are *related* to one another in many different ways. And it is because of this relationship, or these relationships, that we call them all 'language'. (*PI* 65)

In another autobiographical remark, he says: 'We see that what we call "sentence" and "language" is not the formal unity that I imagined, but is the family of structures more or less related to one another.' (*PI* 108) Early in the *Investigations* Wittgenstein raises the question of *how many kinds* of meaningful sentences, of propositions, are there? In sharp contrast with the *Tractatus*, where he had held that all sentences with sense were of one and the same kind, he says:

There are *countless* kinds: countless different kinds of use of what we call 'signs', 'words', 'sentences'. And this multiplicity is not something fixed, given once for all; but new types of language, new language-games, as we can say, come into existence, and others become obsolete and get forgotten. (*PI* 23)

If not all propositions possess the same form, if there are many different kinds of ways in which meaningful, indicative sentences are used, then there appears to be no logical obstacle to being able to *explain* to a person the sense of a familiar sentence which is being used in a way that is unfamiliar to him. And in fact this is frequently done. It is done by describing the particular system of language in which the sentence is employed. For example, a child has learned to tell time by a clock. He can tell whether it is or isn't 5 o'clock. He lives in London. One day he is asked, 'What time is it in New York?' He laughs and replies, 'It's the *same* time as here.' When told that this wrong he is astounded. He thought he understood the question, but now he doesn't. Then the system of time-zones and the technique for computing local times is explained to him. This explanation does not teach him the meaning of a word that was previously unknown to him. He had previously understood the words 'It is 5 o'clock'; and also he knew what New York City is and where it is located. But he did not understand the sentence 'It is 5 o'clock in New York City.' The explanation he received was an explanation of the sense of this *whole* sentence, not of the meaning of some part of it. The explanation taught him the use of a *system* of propositions: it introduced him to a form of language that was unknown to him, and which he could not have *foreseen*. Without that explanation the propositions of this system did not and could not *show* him their sense.

The thesis that a proposition *shows* its sense is bound up with the thesis that a proposition is a *picture*. Consider these remarks:

> A proposition is a picture of reality. (4.01)
> We see this from the fact that we understand the sense of a propositional sign without its having been explained to us. (4.02)

In the decimal numbering of the *Tractatus*, 4.02 is the first remark after 4.01 that is equal to 4.01 in importance: so I take 4.02 to be a continuation of the thought of 4.01. What Wittgenstein was thinking, apparently, is that any ordinary picture *shows* its sense, i.e. its sense does not need to be explained. And since the sense of a sentence likewise needs no explanation, we see that a sentence too is a picture.

But of course the view is not that a picture presents some situation or other: the view is that it presents a picture of one, specific situation.

> A proposition makes a situation known to us, and so it must be *essentially* connected with the situation. And the connection is precisely that it is its logical picture. (4.03)

Every picture is a logical picture. (2.182) So any picture whatever is essentially connected with one and only one situation. The same idea is conveyed by the remark that a proposition determines one and only one place in logical space. (3.4, 3.42) The view about pictures seems to be that any picture is *essentially unambiguous*. This interpretation is confirmed by 5.5423, where there occurs a drawing of a cube. Wittgenstein remarks that the figure can be seen in two different ways; and he explains that as a case of our seeing 'two different facts'. (5.5423) That is, we see two different pictures — not one picture in two different ways.

In the *Investigations*, beginning at paragraph 139, there is a brilliant criticism of the idea of the *Tractatus* that a picture is essentially unambiguous. It can hardly be doubted that Wittgenstein was consciously aiming at the *Tractatus*: for *PI* 139 belongs to a sequence of paragraphs (starting at *PI* 134) in which Wittgenstein is explicitly attacking the thesis of the *Tractatus* that there is 'a general form of all propositions'.

In *PI* 139 the question at issue is what it is to *understand* a word. More specifically, the question is: what 'comes before one's mind' when one understands a word? Wittgenstein chooses the example of a person's hearing the word 'cube', and supposes that what comes before this person's mind is a *picture* of a cube, that is, a drawing of a cube. Someone is then imagined to declare that if the person pointed at a triangular prism and called it 'a cube', this application of the word 'cube' would not 'fit' the picture that he has before his mind. Only *a cube* would *fit* that picture. Whereupon Wittgenstein replies that it is easy to imagine a method of projection according to which a triangular prism *does* fit the picture of a cube. Therefore, this is an example of a picture that is *not* 'essentially unambiguous'. This picture does not pick out one and only one situation.

Suppose there is a storeroom containing various geometrical objects, such as spheres, cubes, rectangular solids, triangular prisms, and so on. A person A hands to his helper B a drawing of a cube, and says: 'Bring one of those from the storeroom.' B brings back a triangular prism. A is surprised: it had never occurred to him that anything other than a *cube* could fit that drawing. But B justifies his response to the order by explaining to A a method of projection according to which a drawing of a cube can be projected as a drawing of a triangular prism. A and B responded differently to the same drawing on paper. They might also have responded differently if the same drawing came before their minds, when they heard the word 'cube'. As Wittgenstein says, 'the same thing can come before our minds when we hear the word', but nevertheless we may apply the word differently (*PI* 140).

The argument now takes an even more subtle twist. Suppose it is admitted that a picture, by itself, does not unambiguously specify one and only one application of a word or a sentence. But if not only a picture but also *a method of projection* comes before our mind, when we hear a word or sentence, then surely one and only one application of the picture is possible! (*PI* 141)

I think this move is connected with something in the *Tractatus*. Speaking of the nature of pictures, the *Tractatus* says:

> The form of picturing is the possibility that the things are related to

one another in the same way as are the elements of the picture. (2.151)

That is how a picture is linked to reality; it reaches right out to it. (2.1511)

It is laid against reality like a measuring-stick. (2.1512)

Only the end-points of the graduating lines *touch* the object that is to be measured. (2.15121)

The conception of 'the picturing relationship' (*die abbildende Beziehung*), not to be confused with 'the form of picturing' (*die Form der Abbildung*), is introduced:

According to this conception the picturing relationship, which makes the picture into a picture, also belongs to the picture. (2.1513)

The picturing relationship consists of the correlations of the elements of the picture with the things. (2.1514)

These correlations are, as it were, the feelers of the picture's elements, with which the picture touches reality. (2.1515)

The idea expressed in 2.1513 is that the picturing relationship *belongs to the picture.* Is this the same idea that is expressed in the *Investigations*, when it conceived that not merely a picture but also a method of projection might come before our minds, when we hear a word or sentence? Is the notion of 'the picturing relationship' in the *Tractatus* the same as the notion of 'the method of projection' in *PI* 141? I think so. In *PI* 141 it is suggested that the method of projection might come before our minds: it might, for example, be 'a picture of two cubes connected by lines of projection'. When in *Tractatus* 2.1515 Wittgenstein spoke of the correlations between the picture-elements and the things in reality as being 'as it were, the feelers of the picture-elements, with which the picture touches reality', it looks as if he was conceiving of these *feelers* as *lines of projection.*

If so, then Wittgenstein's immediate criticism of the idea that if the picture of the cube were combined with a picture of the method of projection, then this would guarantee an unambiguous application of the word 'cube', is at the same time a criticism of the *Tractatus*. The *Tractatus* seems to assume that *if* a picture carries its own method of projection, then it is *impossible* for the picture to be ambiguous: it would pick out one and only one place in logical space.

It appears that according to the *Tractatus* a proposition *is* a picture that contains its method of projection. 'A proposition is a propositional sign in its projective relation to the world.' (3.12) 'To a proposition belongs everything that belongs to the projection.' (3.13) These remarks certainly seem to imply that a proposition contains its method of projection.

In *Investigations* paragraph 141 Wittgenstein concedes that when one hears the word 'cube' (or the order 'Bring me a cube') there might come before one's mind not only the picture of a cube but also the method of projection: for example, one might picture in one's mind two cubes connected by lines of projection. Surely this would be as good a case as one could desire of having before one's mind *both* a picture of a cube *and* the method of projection!

Wittgenstein's simple but crushing criticism, in *PI* 141, is that two people who had this same thing before their minds, *might apply it differently*! It will help to see this if we go back to the two people A and B. A wants B to go to the storeroom and fetch him a cube. He isn't sure whether B understands the word 'cube': so he draws for B on a paper a picture of a cube. But A is aware that there can be different methods of projection. So to make doubly sure that B will bring back the right thing, A draws the method of projection: that is, he connects the picture of the first cube by lines of projection to a picture of a second cube. But despite this precaution, B might not bring back a cube. He might bring a triangular prism, or two cubes connected by wires, or two triangular prisms connected by wires!

The doctrine of the *Tractatus* that a proposition *shows* its sense does appear to involve the conception that the method of projection is *a part of* the proposition. The proposition is a propositional sign *plus* the method of projection. Conceived of in this way, it would seem that a proposition must be absolutely unambiguous. The method of projection is a *bridge* between the propositional sign and reality. This bridge connects the propositional sign with one and only one situation.

This image of a method of projection, as 'a bridge' between a propositional sign and reality, is not mine but is Wittgenstein's. It appears in some remarks he wrote, probably in 1936. In these remarks he is explicitly referring to the *Tractatus*. This makes it likely that the image of a method of projection as a 'bridge' is an image that actually influenced him in the writing of the *Tractatus*.

In his remarks here he fastens on this image, and makes a striking criticism of it:

> If the method of projection is a bridge, then it is one which is not built, as long as the application is not made. (*PG*, p. 213)

According to the *Tractatus* everything necessary to make a picture say something *specific*, to make it depict unambiguously one particular state of affairs, is already *in* the picture itself. For its method of projection is supposed to be part of the picture: therefore, in grasping the sense of the propositional-picture, one has already correlated it with reality in one's mind!

But the retort of *PI* 141 is that if two people both had before their minds the same propositional-picture, including the same method of projection, they could still make different applications to reality (they could bring back different objects from the storeroom). In terms of the image of the method of projection as a 'bridge', the bridge is not a *completed* structure *until it reaches the other side* – which means that a method of projection 'hangs in the air', like any other interpretation (*PI* 198), until it is grounded in an *application*.

When Wittgenstein wrote the *Tractatus* he had the conception that a proposition is *necessarily* unambiguous. This seemed to be guaranteed if the propositional sign was combined with a method of projection. Early in his second philosophical career Wittgenstein realized that this was not so. A method of projection, whether expressed in a sentence, diagram, or any other sign, *could* be variously understood. This was a simple insight, but a deep one. It demolished the doctrine that a proposition *shows* its sense, and with it the picture theory of propositions.

In chapter 4 I argued for the view that in the *Tractatus* a *thought*, composed of 'psychical constituents', is *intrinsically* a picture — intrinsically a representation of a specific state of affairs. I suggested that perhaps that which 'shows its sense' is a thought, rather than a spoken or written sentence. In the present chapter I have talked so far only of sign-posts and sentences, and have employed Wittgenstein's later insight that even when one of these is combined with a method of projection it does not 'show' its sense, since a method of projection, just as much as a sentence, *can* be variously interpreted.

But what about *thoughts*? At the end of chapter 4 I mentioned Searle's conception that there are 'mental states', such as beliefs, desires, intentions, that are *about* something. According to Searle, the belief that it will snow is 'intrinsically' a representation of a possible state of affairs, namely, that it will snow. The belief does not *become* a representation of that state of affairs by virtue of being *used* by someone to represent it. In contrast the utterance 'It will snow' is not intrinsically a representation but is made into a representation through being used to report or express the mental state of believing it will snow. The representative content of the utterance is *derived* from the representative content of the belief. Searle's remarks about beliefs would have an exact parallel in remarks about thoughts.

Searle's view makes it look as if when one reports one's belief what happens is that one *translates* one's belief into a sentence. It is as if the belief were an object (or state or process) before one's mind, which one then puts into words. But how does one *learn* to do this? Could it be that some of us have an incorrect understanding of the technique of translating beliefs into words, and therefore *always* report our beliefs incorrectly?

This problem is one that applies to the whole range of psychological concepts — to sensation, desire, intention, imagination, memory, as well as to belief and thought. Searle's view seems to involve what Wittgenstein in his later works calls 'the idea of the private object'. It is the idea that my thought, or intention, or belief, or imagining, is something that no one else can perceive, and which I describe in words. In the *Investigations* Wittgenstein says:

> The great difficulty here is not to represent the matter as if there were something one *couldn't* do. As if there really were an object, from which I derive its description, but I were unable to show it to anyone. (*PI* 374)

Searle's notion appears to be that I have *this* (a certain 'mental state') and I know that *this* is called 'the belief that it will snow'. But how do I know that *this* is called *that*? Who could have taught me? Or did I make up this language for myself? But then, how can another person *understand* me?

Searle's view seems to be that each of us 'knows only from his own case' what it means to 'believe' something or to 'intend' something. On this view it would be impossible for one person to know what another person meant by those words. A consequence of this is that the words would have no *common meaning*. Thus, it would have no sense to say that anyone's use of those words was either 'right' or 'wrong'. Wittgenstein makes this point, in reference to 'sensation', in *PI* 258. (I expound it in relation to *rules* in chapter 9.)

Searle is right in saying that the belief that it will snow is 'intrinsically' the belief that it will snow — *if* this just means that a belief with a different content would be a different belief. But in *this* sense the uttered statement 'It will snow' is also 'intrinsically' the statement that it will snow: a statement with a different content would be a different statement.

Searle holds that the belief has *priority* over the statement — as if the belief might be there in one's mind, and one might *know* what it was, before one knew how to express it in words. On this conception, employing psychological language would require one to take account of which descriptions *match* which mental states. But if this comparison were carried out by each of us 'privately', it would be meaningless to say that the same words, uttered by two people, did or did not refer to the 'same' mental state.

This objection to Searle's view is also an objection to the conception, which I attributed to the *Tractatus* in chapter 4, that what truly *shows* its sense is a *thought* rather than a sentence. Wittgenstein's intensive criticism, in the *Investigations*, of 'the idea of the private object', applies to a theme that is embedded in his first book.

——— CHAPTER 6 ———

Two Kinds of Logical Analysis

I have been arguing against the universal claim of the *Tractatus* that we understand the sense of a sentence (a propositional sign) without having its sense explained to us (4.02). I turn now to a related topic: the connection in the *Tractatus* of the notion of *analysis* with the understanding of sentences. The *Tractatus* says, on the one hand, that 'Language disguises thought' (4.002); but, on the other hand, that 'All the sentences of our everyday language are actually, just as they are, in perfect logical order.' (5.5563) These two assertions *appear* to be in conflict.

If I am at the railway station waiting for a train, someone might say to me, 'The train will probably be late.' That is a sentence of our everyday language. Does this sentence 'disguise thought'? If so, how can it, nevertheless, be in 'perfect logical order', just as it is? It is a requirement of perfect logical order that sense must be definite, exact (3.23). 'A proposition must determine reality one way or the other: yes or no.' (4.023) But the remark that 'The train will probably be late' seems pretty vague. How late is 'late'? Will the remark be true if the train is only two minutes late? Or will it be true only if the train is at least ten minutes late? And how does one *measure* the lateness of a train? Is there some point on the train that one compares with some point on the station platform? Surely a better candidate for a 'yes or no' proposition would be a statement such as the following: 'This train will be exactly four minutes and 19 seconds late when the first point of the locomotive is abreast of the first point of the platform.' Even so, would there not have to be a decision as to which *clock* is to be used?

We recall from chapter 3 how Wittgenstein had struggled with the problem of the vague sentence. In the *Notebooks* he wondered whether the sentence 'The book is lying on the table' really has 'a completely clear sense'. His response was: 'But the sense must be clear, for after all we mean *something* by the sentence, and as much as we *certainly* mean must surely be clear,' (*NB*, p. 67) And he went on to say: 'It seems clear that what we *mean* must always be "sharp".' (*NB*, p. 68) 'It is clear that I *know* what I *mean* by the vague sentence.' (*NB*, p. 70)

In the *Investigations* Wittgenstein is obviously referring to those worries and convictions when he says: 'It seems clear that where there is sense there must be perfect order. — So there must be perfect order even in the vaguest sentence.' (*PI* 98) 'An indefinite sense — that would really not be a sense *at all*.' (*PI* 99) The ideal of exact sense, we think, 'must be in reality; for we think we already see it there.' (*PI* 101) In order for me to *mean* something, there must be exactness; there must be clear and strict rules, even though they do not actually meet the eye. 'The strict and clear rules of the logical structure of propositions appear to us as something in the background — hidden in the medium of the understanding. I already see them (even though through a medium): for I understand the sign, I mean something by it.' (*PI* 103)

I believe that these recollections by Wittgenstein of his previous ideas indicate how the vagueness of the remarks and statements of daily speech were to be reconciled with the demand for perfect logical order. The vagueness is merely *on the surface*. The clear and sharp thought is produced by a process in 'the medium of the understanding'. This process is *logical analysis*. The *Tractatus* says: 'There is one and only one complete analysis of a proposition.' (3.25) In its completely analysed form a proposition is an elementary proposition — a concatenation of names (4.22). Here there is perfect logical order, precise sense, no vagueness. But the original vague proposition and the elementary proposition that is derived from it by analysis, are logically equivalent. Therefore, they are one and the same proposition! (5.141) The surface vagueness of the remark 'The train will probably be late' is actually misleading. It has sense, and sense must be precise. Its sense *is* the sense of the elementary propositions to which it is equivalent, and which is arrived at by logical analysis.

This process of logical analysis goes on continually when we converse with one another in daily life. The analysis may never be articulated in words. For the most part it goes on unconsciously.

One is usually not aware of it. Normally one could not give an explicit account of it.

Man possesses the ability to construct language capable of expressing every sense, without having any idea how each word has meaning or what its meaning is — just as people speak without knowing how the individual sounds are produced. (4.002)

I think that in the conception of the *Tractatus* it is necessary to distinguish between *two* different procedures of logical analysis. One procedure is what every one of us supposedly engages in when we *mean* or *understand* something. This analysis is rarely if ever put into words. But it is *implicit* in one's understanding of everyday language.

The other procedure of logical analysis is the activity of philosophers and logicians. Philosophers become puzzled by and worry over concepts, such as causality, time, knowledge, truth, memory, and so on. The *Tractatus* says:

The aim of philosophy is the logical clarification of thoughts. Philosophy is not a body of doctrine but an activity. A philosophical work consists essentially of elucidations. The result of philosophy is not 'philosophical propositions', but the clarification of propositions. Philosophy should make clear and give sharp boundaries to thoughts which otherwise are, as it were, cloudy and indistinct. (4.112)

I understand this to mean that a philosopher-logician tries to *display* the meaning of a *philosophically* puzzling expression in a perspicuous notation. An example would be Russell's Theory of Definite Descriptions. The *Tractatus* says: 'Russell's merit is to have shown that the apparent logical form of a proposition need not be its real one.' (4.0031) The difference in logical form between two apparently similar expressions might be displayed either by rewording them in ordinary language, or by making use of an artificial sign-language 'that is governed by *logical* grammar — by logical syntax' (3.325). This activity of logical clarification might not go so far as to terminate in the 'complete analysis' of a proposition. It need go only far enough to clear up the confusion between it and an apparently similar proposition.

'Philosophy should make clear and give sharp boundaries to thoughts which otherwise are, as it were, cloudy and indistinct.' I understand this *not* to mean that the thoughts expressed in the sentences of everyday language are cloudy and indistinct. If it meant this it would be in contradiction with the assertion of 5.5563 that 'All the sentences of our everyday language are actually, just as they are, in perfect logical order.' I take Wittgenstein to have meant that only when doing philosophy do we tend to misapprehend the true logical form of an expression. (But it should be remembered that non-philosophers become immersed in philosophy at the drop of a hat!)

The two procedures of logical analysis envisaged by the *Tractatus* differ in the following ways. The first procedure is one that every human being necessarily engages in when employing the sentences of everyday language. This activity goes on mainly unconsciously, and it is not articulated in words or signs. It is an 'inner process'. It is bound up with *meaning* something by a sign. Indeed, this process *is* meaning and understanding. It achieves a complete analysis, for only in its completely analysed form is a thought in perfect logical order. This inner process of complete analysis is extremely swift, perhaps almost instantaneous.

In contrast the activity of a philosopher-logician who wants to show that two misleadingly similar expressions differ in their logical form, is a slow process. It proceeds haltingly. It is carried on consciously. It is visible — for it attempts to display differences of logical grammar in visible signs. It does not *accompany* ordinary speech. It is subject to error. And it may never achieve a *complete* analysis of a sentence of everyday language.

What was Wittgenstein's attitude, in his later philosophical thought, to these two conceptions of logical analysis? He regarded the procedure of analysis, carried out by a philosopher-logician, as *one* philosophical method that could sometimes produce good results. Speaking of misunderstandings about the use of words, caused by 'certain analogies between the forms of expressions in different regions of language', he says that 'Some of them can be removed by substituting one form of expression for another; this may be called an "analysis" of our forms of expression, for the process is sometimes like one of taking a thing apart.' (*PI* 90) He certainly did not think, however, that this kind of analysis was very fruitful, and he hardly ever used it. He thought that there was not *one* method in philosophy, but different methods (*PI* 133). Among the various methods he employed were

1 Giving descriptions of the circumstances in which a philosophically puzzling expression is actually used in everyday language
2 Inventing simple language-games as objects of comparison
3 Imagining fictitious natural history
4 Giving a 'psychologically exact account' of the philosophical temptation to use a certain expression (*PI* 254).

His attitude towards the other conception of logical analysis, the inner mental process that we are supposed to be constantly engaged in whenever we mean or understand something, was totally different. His persistent criticism of this conception plays a major role throughout the writings of his second period.

Before presenting this criticism (in the next chapter) I want to make clear, if it isn't already clear, a connection between the conception that meaning and understanding require an inner process of logical analysis, and the assertion that *every* meaningful sentence is a *picture*. The latter assertion of the *Tractatus* (4.01) can strike one as surprising. Wittgenstein thought that some sentences do clearly appear to us as pictures. 'It is obvious that we perceive a sentence of the form "*aRb*" as a picture. Here the sign is obviously a likeness of what is signified.' (4.012) An example would be 'Tom is taller than Jerry.' Do we perceive this as a picture? I won't try to answer the question.

What is interesting is that Wittgenstein thought that although some sentences do strike us as pictures, many of them do not. He says: 'At first sight a sentence — as it stands on the printed page, for example — does not seem to be a picture of the reality with which it is concerned.' (4.011) But he holds that this is a misleading impression. The ordinary sentences that we read, write, and speak, actually *are* pictures. 4.011 continues:

> But no more does musical notation at first sight seem to be a picture of music, nor our phonetic notation (the alphabet) to be a picture of our speech. And yet these sign-languages prove to be pictures, even in the ordinary sense, of what they represent.

The *Tractatus* expands on these comparisons:

> A gramophone record, the musical thought, the written notes, the sound waves, all stand to one another in that internal relation of depicting that holds between language and the world. They all have a common logical structure. (4.014)

What is the logical structure that is common to these diverse things? The *Tractatus* gives the following answer:

> There is a general rule by means of which the musician can obtain the symphony from the score, and which makes it possible to derive the symphony from the groove on the gramophone record, and, using the first rule, to derive the score again. Therein consists the inner similarity between these apparently entirely different forms. And that rule is the law of projection which projects the symphony into the language of musical notation. It is the rule for translating this language into the language of gramophone records. (4.0141)

These remarks are immensely interesting. There seem, however, to be differences between the 'rules' that Wittgenstein is talking about. The rule, or law of projection, for translating sounds into musical notation, or for translating notes into sounds, is a convention created by human beings. Different sounds are to correspond to different notes. But the relation between the grooves of the gramophone record and the sounds produced by the machine is not a relationship established by convention. Differences in the width and depth of the grooves result in different sounds: but here the law of projection is a law of nature, a causal law. The law of projection for translating sounds into musical notation is, in contrast, a human convention. The law of projection by which differences in the grooves produce differences in sounds, is not a human convention. It seems to me, therefore, that there is some confusion in 4.0141. Wittgenstein speaks as if there was *one* 'general rule' or 'law of projection' present in these examples — whereas two very different types of 'rule' or 'law' are involved.

It is a thesis of the *Tractatus* that every meaningful sentence is a picture of a possible state of affairs. The comparisons between gramophone records, musical thoughts, musical notation, and sound waves, are supposed to be illustrations of the picturing relation that holds between language and the world. Since the relation between language and the world is conventional, it would seem that the relation between musical notation and musical sounds is a better illustration of the relation of language to the world than is the relation between the grooves of a record and the sounds produced when the record is played. Both illustrations involve a 'system of differences': but in one case the system is purely conventional, in the other case the system rests on correlations found in nature.

The relation between musical notation and musical sounds is an excellent illustration of a system of differences. For the differences in a score there should be differences in the sounds produced by the musician who is guided by the score. The score, and the sounds to be produced, have the same 'multiplicity'. According to the *Tractatus* this is a necessary feature of the relation of language to the world. 'In a sentence there must be exactly as much to be distinguished as in the situation that it presents. The two must have the same logical (mathematical) multiplicity.' (4.04)

According to the *Tractatus* the requirement of same multiplicity will certainly be satisfied at the level of elementary propositions. For these propositions consist solely of names, and each name corresponds to one simple object. But, as said in chapter 5, the conception that the requirement is satisfied at the elementary level is not based on any observation of how things actually are at that level. It is an *a priori* conception: that is how things *must* be at the foundations.

A bar of a score is a picture of a musical phrase, and the entire score of a sonata is, or could be, a picture of the entire sonata that is played. Let us suppose that a note in a score is the 'name' of a musical sound, and that the names in the score have the same multiplicity as the sounds of the sonata. 'One name stands for one thing, another for another thing, and they are combined with one another.' (4.0311) The fact that the names are combined in a certain way depicts the musical sounds as being combined in the same way (see 2.15). The example of the relation of musical notation to musical sounds seems to really satisfy the conception of the picture-theory of language.

But we note at once that the relation of score to music does *not* have *the right direction of correspondence*. If a state of affairs that is depicted by a picture in language (a proposition) does not exist, then the proposition is false. But if a musician, following a score, plays different sounds than those indicated by the score, then the score is not incorrect — his playing is incorrect! Thus, the analogy between musical notation and musical sounds on the one hand, and language and the world on the other hand, breaks down at a crucial point.

The examples provided in 4.014 and 4.0141 do nothing to support the thesis of the *Tractatus* that every meaningful sentence is a picture. Let us consider some examples of sentences of everyday language in order to determine whether they are pictures of possible states of affairs. In doing this we should try to repress any urge to think that they *must* be pictures.

One example is the remark 'The train will probably be late', made to me by someone as I await the train at the station. Another example: an acquaintance presses me to accompany him to a book sale, on the ground that we might find many bargains there. I decline, saying 'I have more books than I know what to do with.' Another example: a friend has a bad headache. I persuade him to take aspirin. Some hours later I inquire of his wife how he is. She says: 'Shortly after he took the aspirin his headache went away.' Another example: I have been reading a novel, but throw it down in irritation. I am asked, 'What's the matter?' I reply: 'This novel is boring.'

We want to know whether the ordinary sentences of these examples are *pictures*. The conception of a picture, in the *Tractatus*, carries the precise requirement that a picture and what it depicts must have the same multiplicity. This means that when both the picture and the state of affairs depicted are analysed into elements, then the number of elements in the two will be the same (4.04). So we need to inquire whether the requirement of same multiplicity is satisfied in our examples. Is the sentence 'This novel is boring' already an elementary sentence? Or does it have a truth-functional analysis into elementary sentences? Is the word 'boring' a *name*, or does it stand for a complex? If the latter, what is the definition of the complex? ('The contraction of a symbol for a complex into a simple symbol can be expressed in a definition.' (3.24)) In the 'aspirin' example, is the word 'headache' an indefinable primitive term, or does it stand for a definable complex? The same question can be asked, in the 'train' example, about the word 'late'; and in the 'books' example, about the phrase 'more books than I know what to do with'. And so on.

These questions may give one a feeling of bewilderment. On reflection, however, we realize that whether a train will be said to have arrived 'late' will depend on what people expect and what needs are involved. In a situation of war, where large numbers of troops are being moved to the front by train to meet an imminent attack, a train arriving ten minutes behind schedule might be regarded as 'late', and the military dispatcher might be reprimanded. But in a remote frontier community, where life is leisurely, a train scheduled for Wednesday might be regarded as 'pretty much on time' if it arrived on Friday. Different circumstances create different standards of exactness. If definitions of 'late' were produced they would differ in the two cases.

If asked whether 'having more books than one knows what to do with' is definable or indefinable, I should have no idea what to say. But someone might propose an ingenious and witty definition which I would enjoy and find appropriate. Nor do I know whether a headache is something simple or something complex; but this is because I do not know to what system of ideas, to what language-game, I should relate this question in order to give it sense. In a household medical book there might be a classification of disagreeable sensations according to their typical physical causes. It might provide definitions of different types of headache, together with suggestions for treatment. But there could be a different system of classification: for example, a manual of psychotherapy might define various types of headache as manifestations of different unconscious emotional disturbances. The possibility of more than one system of classification shows that the question of whether the word 'headache' refers to something simple or something complex, has no clear sense when asked in this absolute way. In the example 'This novel is boring', is the quality of being boring simple, or complex? It is difficult to grasp the question when it is stated like that. Novels can be boring in different ways: the plot is so complicated that the reader cannot follow it and loses interest; the writing is laden with clichés; the characters have no depth; the story is too sentimental; the author is preaching; and so on. What is boring in novels is not just *one* thing. But it does not follow that 'boring' refers to a definable complex.

We are trying to come to grips with the question of whether the sentences of everyday language are 'pictures'. According to the *Tractatus* a sentence is a picture only if it possesses the same logical multiplicity as does the situation it describes. But the true multiplicity of the situation, and of the sentence that describes it, may not present itself on the surface: it may be hidden, and can only be revealed by logical analysis.

To *what* is the logical analysis to be applied? Is it to be applied to the *fact*, for example, that the train is late? Or to what one *means* when one says, 'The train is late'? Are there *two* things to be analysed, or just one? As I understand it, there are two things to be analysed, but *both* are analysed in *one* analysis. One starts out by analysing what one *means* in saying, for example, 'The train is late.' In the *Notebooks* Wittgenstein says: 'All I want is only for *my meaning* to be completely analysed!' (*NB*, p. 63) Also: 'It seems clear that what we *mean* must always be "sharp".' (*NB*, p. 68) What one *means* is the 'thought' or the 'proposition' that one expresses. It is this that is to be completely analysed. But at the same time one is analysing the state of affairs which the proposition pictures. The *Tractatus* says: 'A proposition is a model of reality, as we conceive it (*so wie wir sie uns denken*).' (4.01) The *Notebooks* say: 'The sense of the proposition must appear in the proposition as divided into its simple components . . . When the sense of the proposition is completely expressed in the proposition itself, the proposition is always divided into its *simple* components . . . and these are objects in the original sense.' (*NB*, p. 63)

A complete articulation of one's thought, one's proposition, is at the same time a complete articulation of the situation described, as one conceives it to be. In this complete articulation there will be names deputizing for simple objects. 'If there is a final sense and a proposition expressing it completely, then there are also names for simple objects.' (*NB*, p. 64) The complete analysis of what one *means* by a sentence, results in an exact correlation between simple signs and simple objects. Thus, it is automatically guaranteed that one's thought, and the situation in the world *as one conceives it to be*, will have the same logical multiplicity. The view of the *Tractatus*, as expounded in the *Investigations*, is that there must be perfect order in the vaguest sentence — for I *understand* the sentence, I *mean* something by it (*PI*, e.g. 98, 99, 101, 103).

The idea of the *Tractatus* is that a sentence, for example 'This novel is boring', considered by itself, in isolation from any context of utterance, is vague or ambiguous. Different speakers, who made that remark about the same novel, might mean different things. I might make this remark about this novel on different occasions, and mean something different each time. But on a particular occasion when I use this sentence, I mean *something*, and something *definite*. When my *meaning* is completely analysed it will be exhibited as a logical picture.

Is there any reason to believe this to be so? Consider the occasion when I exclaimed, 'This novel is boring.' I am asked, 'What do you mean by that? In what way is it boring?' I reflect, and then answer: 'The author preaches too much.' I have stated my meaning more precisely. But are we any closer to seeing that my statement is a logical picture? In order to be a picture it must divide into an exact number of components. How many components does my statement have? Is 'preaches', or 'preaches-too-much', a simple indivisible component, or does it stand for a complex? Perhaps different authors 'preach' in different ways. If I were to describe the particular way in which this author 'preaches', would this bring us nearer to the goal of determining the exact number of components of my statement? What reason is there to think so? The exact multiplicity of a proposition is displayed only when it is analysed into an elementary proposition consisting of a definite and countable number of simple signs. But we are dogged by the uncertainty as to whether a given word stands for something simple or something complex. If I reflect on what I mean in saying that the author 'preaches', will this reflection tell me whether by the word 'preaches' I mean something simple or something complex? If I consider what I mean in saying that the edge of this table is straight, will this inform me whether by 'straight' I mean a simple property or a complex one?

The unyielding nature of these questions is due to the assumption of the *Tractatus* that the distinction between 'simple' and 'complex' has an absolute sense. If one is thinking in terms of a particular calculus of geometry in which 'straight' is a defined term, then what one means by 'straight' is something complex. It is only in relation to some calculus, or to some system of classification, that it has sense to ask whether a word means something simple or something complex. In one and the same area of thought and language, it is possible to devise more than one calculus or system of ideas. And in many areas *no* system of defined and undefined terms has been devised. (When I said that the novel is boring, I had no conception of a calculus in which 'boring' is either a defined term or a primitive term.) Where there is no calculus, a sentence cannot be said to be either 'elementary' or 'non-elementary'. Where there is more than one calculus the same sentence might be elementary in one and not in the other. Or a sentence might be analysable in both but have a *different* analysis in each of the two systems. The assertion that 'There is one and only one complete analysis of a proposition' (3.25) expresses the assumption that there is *a* calculus *at hand* for the whole of language and thought. Presumably the primitive terms in this *one* calculus would be the *names*.

Wittgenstein later sharply criticized this assumption. In remarks, probably written in 1936, he says:

If one wants to use the designation 'elementary proposition', as I did in the *Tractatus Logico-Philosophicus*, and also as Russell used 'atomic proposition', one can call the sentence 'here there is a red rose' an elementary proposition. That is to say, it does not contain a truth-function and it is not defined by an expression that contains one. But if it is to be said that a proposition is an elementary proposition only if its complete logical analysis shows that it is not composed out of other propositions by truth-functions, that presupposes that one has a conception of such an 'analysis'. Formerly, I myself spoke of a 'complete analysis' with the thought that philosophy had to give a definitive dissection of every proposition in order to set out clearly every connection and remove every possibility of misunderstanding. As if there was a calculus in which this dissection would be possible. There hovered before my mind something like the kind of definition Russell had given for the definite article. Similarly, I once thought that by means of visual impressions, etc., one would be able to define, say, the concept of a sphere, and thus exhibit once for all the connections of the concepts and the source of all misunderstandings, etc. At the bottom of all this there was a false and idealized picture of the employment of language. (*PG*, p. 211)

It is fundamental to the thesis of the *Tractatus* that every genuine proposition is a picture, that there should be at hand a system within which logical analysis can exhibit any proposition whatever as a truth-function of elementary propositions. For it is only at the level of complete analysis, where 'one name stands for one thing, another for another thing' (4.0311), that it can be determined whether a proposition has 'exactly as many distinguishable parts' as does the situation it describes (4.04). The realization that the notion of there being an available calculus within which 'complete analysis' could be carried out was an illusion, meant that an assumption basic to the picture-theory was destroyed. The outcome is not that it has been established that some propositions are *not* pictures. No. What this realization implies is that the contention that all genuine propositions are pictures does not have the clear sense it once seemed to have.

One may wonder how Wittgenstein could have been inspired with the conviction that *every* proposition is a picture. In *Zettel* he himself gives the best account of the source of this conviction. Speaking of this 'theory' of propositions he says that:

It is the characteristic thing about such a theory that it looks at a special clearly evident case and says: '*That* shows how things are everywhere; this case is the exemplar of *all* cases.' — 'Of course! It has to be like that' we say, and are satisfied. We have arrived at a form of presentation that is *obvious* to us. But it is as if we had now seen something lying *beneath* the surface.

The tendency to generalize a clear case seems to have a strict justification in logic. Here one seems *completely* justified in concluding: 'If one proposition is a picture, then any proposition must be a picture, for they must all be of the same nature.' For we are under the illusion that what is sublime, what is essential, about our investigation consists in grasping *one* all-embracing nature. (*Z* 444)

I take these remarks to be in part autobiographical, probably referring to the incident during the First World War when he read an account in a magazine of a lawsuit concerning an automobile accident. A model of the scene of the accident was presented to the court, the model being composed of miniature cars, houses, people, corresponding to the actual cars, houses, people. The model was here used as a proposition that described the possible state of affairs. This struck Wittgenstein as a revelation: here was disclosed the essential nature of propositions! It is significant that in the *Tractatus* he says: 'A proposition is a model of reality as we conceive it.' (4.01) This is a striking example of generalizing from *one* clear case. The model in the law court certainly was a proposition, and certainly it was composed of parts, each of which stood for a thing in reality. The constituents of the model, and the constituents of the state of affairs, had the same multiplicity. Different arrangements of the parts of the model would present different possible situations.

The only thing wrong was the assumption that an insight had been obtained into the nature of *all* propositions. Since most of our ordinary sentences do not *seem* to be pictures or models in this clear sense, the necessary conclusion was that their real nature is *hidden* and needs to be revealed by logical analysis. 'That is, as if our usual forms of expression were, essentially, unanalysed; as if there were something hidden in them that had to be brought to light.' (*PI* 91)

If a meaningful sentence of ordinary language does not seem to satisfy the requirement for being a picture, then its true nature is not disclosed, and can only be disclosed by an analysis that exhibits the sentence as a truth-function of elementary propositions. For an elementary proposition is a picture *par excellence*. As Wittgenstein said, in remarks of 1931, he had believed 'that it is the task of logical analysis to discover the elementary propositions' (*WWK*, p. 182). In the *Tractatus* he had believed that it was impossible to determine *a priori* the forms of elementary propositions. 'Yet I did think that the elementary propositions could be specified at a later date. Only in recent years have I broken away from that mistake.' (ibid.) What was the mistake?

> The wrong conception which I want to object to in this connection is the following, that we can hit upon something that we today cannot yet see, that we can *discover* something wholly new. That is a mistake. The truth of the matter is that we have already got everything, and we have got it actually *present*; we need not wait for anything. We make our moves in the realm of the grammar of our ordinary language, and this grammar is already there. Thus we have already got everything and need not wait for the future. (*WWK*, p. 183)

What might look like only a slight shift was actually a radical change in Wittgenstein's conception of philosophy. Logical analysis, as he had previously understood it, was no longer of great importance. No longer did he assume that if one of our ordinary sentences was not *prima facie* a picture, then a future analysis of it into elementary propositions would reveal its real pictorial nature. The new method is to take a sentence that puzzles us philosophically, and *remind* ourselves (*PI* 127) of the occasions and purposes of life, in which and for which it is actually used. The method is *descriptive*, not 'analytic'. The theme of the new outlook is 'Nothing is hidden' (*PI* 435): 'Everything lies open to view.' (*PI* 126)

CHAPTER 7

The Inner Process of Analysis

In chapter 6 I distinguished between two different types of logical analysis that seem to be assumed in the *Tractatus*. The first one apparently occurs in each of us, philosopher and non-philosopher alike, whenever we mean or understand something. The language we speak and hear in daily life disguises our thought (4.002); yet these sentences are in perfect logical order just as they are (5.5563). Thus it seems that any surface vagueness or ambiguity in the sentences we hear and utter is converted into exact thoughts by rapid mental processes. These processes frequently seem to take no time at all: for often I understand a remark or an order *immediately*. Perhaps there the understanding or meaning is not a 'process', but an instantaneous *event*. In any case, exact sense is produced *in* our thinking, when we speak and when we take in the words of other speakers.

In his later philosophical work Wittgenstein was greatly occupied with this conception. He says: 'We don't get away from the idea that the sense of a sentence accompanies the sentence; is there with it.' (Z 139) He speaks of the inclination to think of the meaning of a word as if it were 'an atmosphere which the word brings with it and carries into every sort of application' (*PI* 117). In his last writing, *On Certainty*, he says:

> There is always the danger of wanting to find an expression's meaning by studying the expression itself, and the frame of mind in which one uses it, instead of always thinking of the practice. That is why one repeats the expression to oneself so often, because it is as if one must see what one is looking for in the expression and in the feeling that one has. (*OC* 601)

In these remarks Wittgenstein is referring to the tendency we have, when doing philosophy, to fix our attention on a puzzling expression — trying to gather from it, or from what goes on in us when we hear it or say it, what its meaning is. Instead, we should be considering 'the practice' with the expression: that is, the circumstances, the occasions, in which it is used.

The *Tractatus* seems to assume that a process of thinking necessarily goes on whenever we speak. For we use a sentence as a projection of a possible situation; and 'thinking the sense' of the sentence is the method of projection (3.11). Of course it is true that *sometimes* a process of thinking occurs when one says something, understanding what one says: but sometimes *not*. In the *Investigations* Wittgenstein employs an example in regard to which one would naturally suppose that some complicated thinking must have taken place.

> A has written down the numbers 1, 5, 11, 19, 29; at this point B says he knows how to go on. What happened here? Various things may have happened; for example, while A was slowly putting one number after another, B was occupied with trying various algebraic formulae on the numbers which were written down. After A had written the number 19, B tried the formula $a_n = n^2 + n - 1$; and the next number confirmed his hypothesis. (*PI* 151)

Here B did a lot of thinking. But Wittgenstein continues his description of possibilities:

> Or again, B does not think of formulae. He watches A writing down his numbers, with a certain feeling of tension, and all sorts of vague thoughts go through his head. Finally he asks himself: 'What is the series of differences?' He finds the series 4, 6, 8, 10 and says: now I can go on.

In this variation there was less thinking; but still some. We continue:

> Or he watches and says 'Yes, I know *that* series' — and continues it, as he would have done if A had written down the series 1, 3, 5, 7, 9. — Or he says nothing at all and simply continues the series. Perhaps he had what may be called the sensation 'that's easy!'

In the latter two cases there was apparently no thinking at all; although B understood the series, and would have understood what he said, if he had said, 'I can continue the series.' In these two cases B did not *think* of the formula or of the series of differences.

Wittgenstein remarks: 'Don't think of understanding as a

"mental occurrence" at all! — For *that* is the way of speaking which confuses you.' (*PI* 154) After a similar remark in *Zettel*, he adds: 'So let us not think we *must* find a specific mental occurrence, because the verb "to understand" is there, and because one says: understanding is a mental activity.' (*Z* 446)

One might suppose that of course a lot must go on in one's mind when one understands a sentence. For one understands *each word* in the sentence; and each word can occur in numerous different connections with other words; this whole array of possibilities must be present to one's mind when one understands a word. In *Zettel* Wittgenstein says:

> It looks as if a sentence with e.g. the word 'ball' in it already contained the shadow of other uses of this word. That is, the *possibility* of forming those other sentences. — To whom does it look like that? And under what circumstances? (*Z* 138)

To whom does it look like that? It may have looked like that to Wittgenstein in the *Tractatus*, where the following is said: 'If I know an object I also know all its possible occurrences in states of affairs.' (2.0123) So when I understand a word for an object I must understand *all* possible occurrences of that word in sentences. It is not sufficient to have a merely piecemeal grasp of the word.

William James had a somewhat different conception 'of what passes through the mind' when we utter a familiar sentence, such as 'The pack of cards is on the table.'[1] In the first place, he says, 'even before we have opened our mouths to speak, the entire thought is present to our mind in the form of an intention to utter that sentence.'[2] He continues:

> Now I believe that in all cases where the words are *understood*, the total idea may be and usually is present not only before and after the phrase has been spoken, but also whilst each separate word is uttered. It is the overtone, halo, or fringe of the word, *as spoken in that sentence*. It is never absent; no word in an understood sentence comes to consciousness as a mere noise. We feel its meaning as it passes; and although our object differs from one moment to another as to its verbal kernel or nucleus, yet it is *similar* throughout the entire segment of the stream. The same object is known everywhere, now from the point of view, if we may so call it, of this word, now from the point of view of that. And in our feeling of each word there chimes an echo or foretaste of every other.[3]

Wittgenstein addressed himself directly to James's ideas. He took up James's notion that 'the entire thought is present to our mind' at the beginning of the sentence. In *Zettel* he says:

> I tell someone: 'I'm going to whistle you the theme . . .': it is my intention to whistle it, and I already know what I am going to whistle. It is my intention to whistle this theme: have I then already in some sense, whistled it in thought? (*Z* 2)

This is both a joke and a serious question. If the thought was already there, in what form was it there? Furthermore, if I start to say something, and am interrupted, but then later continue my sentence, why should this imply that my thought was completed before I started to speak?

> 'You were interrupted a while ago; do you still know what you were going to say?' — If I do know now, and say it — does that mean that I had already thought it before, only not said it? No. Unless you take the certainty with which I continue the interrupted sentence as a criterion of the thought's already having been completed at that time. — But, of course, the situation and the thoughts which I had contained all sorts of things to help the continuation of the sentence. (*PI* 633)

It does sometimes happen that before saying something aloud one says it first to oneself. A man who is about to address a public assembly might nervously rehearse his remarks in his mind before going to the rostrum. But in the give and take of quick conversation this does not occur. What led James to assume that one's total thought 'usually is present' before one speaks? Is it because he supposed that if this were *not* so then one would not know what one was going to say — as Wittgenstein here suggests (see also *Z* 1, 38)? But it is a fact that usually I know what I was going to say, and also a fact that usually I do not rehearse it in my mind before I start to say it. So *in what form* was the thought there before I spoke? I *remembered* what I was *going* to say — but 'remembered', in this use, does not imply that I had already thought or said to myself what I was going to say.

Do I infer, or read off, what I intended to say, from my recollection of what the circumstances were when I started to speak? But what I recall might be very fragmentary: for example, that we were speaking of bank failures, that as I started to say something my friend on the other side of the table was looking at me sarcastically, and that my remark was interrupted by the arrival of another person. How could I gather from these items what I intended to say?

'I was going to say. . . .' — You remember various details. But not even all of them together show your intention. It is as if a snapshot of a scene had been taken, but only a few scattered details of it were to be seen: here a hand, there a bit of a face, or a hat — the rest is dark. And now it is as if we knew quite certainly what the whole picture represented. As if I could read the darkness. (*PI* 635)

But I don't infer or read off from anything, what it was I intended to say. I know what I was going to say: but this 'knowledge' is not based on evidence.

'I know exactly what I was going to say!' And yet I did not say it. — And yet I don't read it off from some other occurrence which took place then and which I remember. Nor am I *interpreting* that situation and its antecedents. For I don't consider them and don't judge them. (*PI* 637)

Knowing what one was *going to say* could be considered a special case of knowing what one was *going to do*. Wittgenstein produces an acute reason for saying that this kind of knowledge cannot be an inference from some evidence or other:

If I say 'I was then going to do such-and-such', and if this statement is based on the thoughts, images, etc., which I remember, then someone else to whom I tell only these thoughts, images, etc., ought to be able to infer with as great certainty as mine that I was then going to do such-and-such. — But often he could not do so. Indeed, were I myself to infer my intention from this evidence, other people would be right to say that this conclusion was very uncertain. (*Z* 41)

It can strike one as very remarkable that there should be this phenomenon of being able to state what one was going to say or do, *not* based on evidence or observation. But it is an ordinary phenomenon. What is remarkable about it? As Wittgenstein says: 'Yes, every such use of language is remarkable, peculiar, if one is adjusted only to consider the description of physical objects.' (*Z* 40) It is only when we try to squeeze declarations of past intention into another use of language, and cannot do it, that they seem mysterious.

Suppose that some friends come to my house to have a game of cards. One of them asks, 'Where is the pack of cards?' I reply, 'The pack of cards is on the table.' According to James, not only was the entire thought present to my mind before I spoke — but also as I spoke this sentence, I 'felt the meaning of each word as it passed'; and also as I uttered each word of the sentence, I felt an 'echo' of the word that preceded it, and an anticipation or 'foretaste' of the next word to come.

One can be sure that nothing like this occurs in the normal flow of conversation. James thought rightly that there is a difference between saying a sentence and *understanding* it, and saying it and *not* understanding it. But he thought wrongly that in the first case, one must be experiencing or 'feeling' the *meaning* of each word as it is uttered. Perhaps he 'confirmed' his idea by slowly repeating the words 'The pack of cards is on the table' to himself again and again. But there the sentence would be 'idling', not doing work (*PI* 132). As Wittgenstein says: 'When I think in language, there aren't "meanings" going through my mind in addition to the verbal expressions; but the language itself is the vehicle of thinking.' (*PI* 329)

There is a strong philosophical temptation to assume that to utter a sentence, *understanding* it, demands an activity of *thinking* the sense of the sentence. But the examples of 'knowing what one was going to say' and 'knowing how to go on', with which Wittgenstein deals in *Investigations* and *Zettel*, show that these two phenomena do not *require* a background process of thinking. A person who has been interrupted *can* tell us what he was going to say, even though he had not said or thought it to himself. And a person who is asked to continue a numerical series *can* do so *without* having thought of the formula or law of the series, or without having continued the series in his mind. These phenomena help us to see that when we talk in conversation, even 'thoughtfully', there is no need to suppose that we *must* be thinking to ourselves the very thoughts that we utter aloud.

In the *Notebooks* Wittgenstein said that 'thinking is a kind of language.' (*NB*, p. 82) In the *Investigations* he addresses what seems to be the same idea:

> Is thinking a kind of speaking? One would like to say, it is what distinguishes thoughtful speech from thoughtless speech. — And so it seems to be an accompaniment of speech. A process, which may accompany something else, or can go on by itself. (*PI* 330)

In *The Blue Book* he says:

> But can't one at any rate speak and leave out the thinking? Certainly — but observe what sort of thing you are doing if you speak without thinking. Observe first of all that the process which we might call 'speaking and meaning what you speak' is not

necessarily distinguished from that of speaking thoughtlessly by what happens *at the time you speak*. What distinguishes the two may very well be what happens before or after you speak. (*BB*, p. 43)

What happened *before* you spoke might be that someone had asked you a question, to which what you said was an informative answer. What happened *after* you spoke might be that someone disagreed with what you said, and you then explained and defended your previous remark.

Wittgenstein often asks his reader to make 'experiments'.

Make the following experiment: say and mean a sentence, for example: 'It will probably rain tomorrow.' Now think the same thought again, mean what you just meant, but without saying anything (either aloud or to yourself). If thinking that it will rain tomorrow accompanied saying that it will rain tomorrow, then just do the first activity and leave out the second. — If thinking and speaking stood in the relation of the words and the melody of a song, we could leave out the speaking and do the thinking just as we can sing the tune without the words. (*BB*, p. 42)

Make the following experiment: *say* 'It's cold here' and *mean* 'It's warm here.' Can you do it? — And what are you doing as you do it? And is there only one way of doing it? (*PI* 510)

We began this chapter by considering the conception, apparently assumed in the *Tractatus*, that the surface vagueness of the sentences we utter and respond to every day is given precision by inner occurrences of meaning, understanding, thinking — which take place with extreme rapidity as we speak and listen. Vague signs are converted into refined symbols. A complete reduction of an ordinary sentence into a complicated arrangement of elementary propositions, must be achieved nearly instantaneously in order for the thought expressed, or understood, to be in perfect order. This conception is what Wittgenstein later called a *myth*. 'In philosophy one is in constant danger of producing a myth of symbolism, or of mental occurrences. Instead of simply saying what anyone knows and must admit.' (*Z* 211)

Wittgenstein says:

It disturbs us as it were, that the thought in a sentence is not wholly present at any one moment. We regard it as an object which we create and never wholly possess, for no sooner does one part appear than another vanishes. (*Z* 153)

Undoubtedly this was something that had disturbed *him*, as well as others. William James expresses this feeling of frustration:

> Let anyone try to cut a thought across in the middle and get a look at its section, and he will see how difficult the introspective observation of the transitive tracts is. The rush of the thought is so headlong that it almost always brings us up at the conclusion before we can arrest it. Or if our purpose is nimble enough and we do arrest it, it ceases forthwith to be itself. . . . The attempt at introspective analysis in these cases is in fact like seizing a spinning top to catch its motion, or trying to turn up the gas quickly enough to see how the darkness looks.[4]

Wittgenstein refers to this feeling of puzzlement as to how a sentence can manage to express a thought — for 'it all goes by so quickly and I should like to see it as it were laid open to view.' (*PI* 435) But he holds that here philosophy is on a wrong track, which leads to no result:

> Here it is easy to get into that dead-end in philosophy, where one believes that the difficulty of the task consists in our having to describe phenomena that are hard to get hold of, the present experience that slips quickly by, or something of the sort. Where we find ordinary language too crude. (*PI* 436)

Earlier in the *Investigations*, when referring to the *Tractatus* view that perfect order, strict and clear rules, must be present in our everyday language, Wittgenstein says:

> When we believe that we must find that order, must find the ideal, in our actual language, we become dissatisfied with what are ordinarily called 'sentences', 'words', 'signs'. The sentence, the word, that logic deals with, should be something pure and clear-cut. And we rack our brains over the nature of the *real* sign. — Is it perhaps the *idea* of the sign? or the idea at the present moment? (*PI* 105)

It is probable that Wittgenstein is talking about worries that beset *him* during the period of the composition of the *Tractatus*. He continues:

> Here it is difficult as it were to keep our heads up — to see that we must stick to the things of our everyday thinking, and not go astray and imagine that we have to describe extreme subtleties, which in turn we are quite unable to describe with the means at our disposal. We feel as if we had to repair a torn spider's web with our fingers. (*PI* 106)

Let us consider again Wittgenstein's advice to avoid the notion that understanding something is a 'mental' occurrence or process: for, he says, that way of thinking or speaking 'confuses' us. (*PI* 154) What is he getting at? This remark occurs in relation to the example of the person B having been shown the initial segment of a numerical series and asked to continue it. He does continue it correctly: so apparently he understood the series. One is inclined to ask: what happened there? The answer is 'Various things may have happened.' (*PI* 151) Wittgenstein mentions some possibilities: for example, B thought of various formulae and tried them out as hypotheses, finally hitting on one that fitted; or instead, B thought of the series of differences; or B just says 'I know that series' and continues it; or B does not say or think anything, but just continues the series.

Wittgenstein then asks: are these occurrences *the understanding*? On reflection, one says, no: because B *might* have thought of the right formula but not have understood it, or have misapplied it. Likewise for the series of differences. And in the cases where he continued the series correctly for a few places with a feeling of confidence, he *might* have gone wrong if asked to continue it further. So it seems that we have not hit upon the meaning of 'He understands.'

> We are trying to get hold of the mental occurrence of understanding which seems to be hidden behind those coarser and therefore more readily visible accompaniments. But we do not succeed; or, rather, it does not get as far as a real attempt. For even supposing I had found something that happened in all those cases of understanding — why should *it* be the understanding? (*PI* 153)

We begin by assuming that sudden understanding consists in something that occurs *when* one understands. But then we realize that *different* things may occur then, and that *none* of them can be identified with the understanding. So then we think that we have not been able to uncover the understanding itself. We may then say, 'It is just a particular mental occurrence — perhaps indefinable.' We say this out of confusion. And our stating the matter in this way only deepens our confusion. This is what Wittgenstein is getting at in *PI* 154.

But the initial confusion lay in the question 'What happens when a man suddenly understands?' For the assumption which lay behind that question was that *if* we could describe what happened at that moment then we should have found out the meaning of 'He understands.' But:

The question of what the expression means is not answered by such a description; and this misleads us into concluding that understanding is a specific, indefinable experience. (*PI* 322)

Then how should we proceed? The answer is: we should not ask what understanding *is*, or what happens when one understands something, but how the words 'He understands' are used (cf. *PI* 370). That is, we should consider in what sort of circumstances we say 'He understands.' (*PI* 155) For example: we don't say it just because he utters the right formula. But if the circumstances are that he has learned algebra, and has previously used such formulae correctly, then if he utters the formula, we say 'He understands.' (*PI* 179) Our remark is *justified* — even if he surprises us by continuing the series incorrectly.

The inclination to feel that suddenly understanding something is a definite mental event, an occurrence in one's mind at a particular moment, is difficult to resist. The same for *suddenly remembering* something, *suddenly deciding* to do such-and-such, and so on. Our language seems to force this impression on us. For we say: 'As he turned the key in the lock of his office door, he suddenly decided to sell his business.' This could be a true description of what happened. The decision, the *essential* thing, coincided in time with the turning of the key. It happened right then! So the decision *consisted in* what happened at that moment!

But let us not be overwhelmed by these remarks. What happened at that moment might be that he said or thought to himself, 'I will sell my business!' perhaps with a feeling of relief. But note that this 'thought' and the accompanying feeling *would have no sense* unless there were institutions of money and commerce, and unless this man owned a business. Without those surroundings, what happened at that moment could not have had that meaning. Wittgenstein employs a brilliant analogy:

A coronation is the picture of pomp and dignity. Cut one minute of this proceeding out of its surroundings: the crown is being placed on the head of the king in his coronation robes. — But in different surroundings gold is the cheapest of metals, its gleam is thought vulgar. There the fabric of the robe is cheap to produce. A crown is a parody of a respectable hat. And so on. (*PI* 584)

Consider the phenomenon of *suddenly remembering* something. Surely that is an occurrence at a moment! For example, you are listening to a lecture. When it comes to an end you reach in your pocket for your car keys — but they aren't there! You are in a panic. Various thoughts race through your mind. Did you drop them? Were they stolen? Suddenly, with immense relief, you remember that you left them in your raincoat in the cloakroom! But suppose you were living in a society where there were no cars or car keys. Then those 'thoughts' would have been nonsense; and so would have been your 'sudden remembering'.

Philosophers who read Wittgenstein superficially sometimes get the impression that he *denies* that inner, mental events take place when we come to a decision, or suddenly understand something, or suddenly remember, and so on. But that is a mistaken impression. All manner of thoughts, feelings, sensations, images, inner convictions, etc., are taken for granted in his descriptions. He calls attention, for example, to 'characteristic experiences' of pointing to the shape of something, as contrasted with pointing to its colour (*PI* 35); to 'characteristic sensations' of reading a sentence, as contrasted with pretending to read it (*PI* 159); to characteristic images, feelings, thoughts, that occur when one suddenly understands something (*PI* 151, 152).

What Wittgenstein does go on to say is that the meaning of 'He understands' has 'more in it' than any of the typical mental accompaniments of understanding (*PI* 152). The same with the other examples. Consider another case of sudden remembering. If a person finds his wallet missing and is frantically trying to remember where he put it, various images and thoughts will race through his mind. Suppose he suddenly remembers: what happened then? Perhaps he had an image of the drawer where he often leaves the wallet, and he thought 'That is where I left it!', with a feeling of relief. What Wittgenstein will say in this case too, is that the meaning of 'He remembered' has 'more in it' than any of those mental accompaniments, and more than *any other* event that might have occurred at the moment when the person suddenly remembered.

The point is difficult to grasp. It seems that the obvious meaning of 'He suddenly remembered' is that everything necessary and sufficient for his having remembered took place at that very moment *when* he remembered. This is a nice illustration of how ordinary language can mislead us in philosophy. Take the sentence 'Just at the moment he stepped out of the room he suddenly remembered where he had left his wallet.' That could be a true description of what occurred. A philosopher who is trying to clarify what 'sudden remembering' means, might fix his attention on this sentence. It would be an example of 'wanting to find an expression's meaning by studying the expression itself' (*OC* 601). This sentence does *say* that the sudden remembering occurred 'just as he stepped out of the room': so the occurrence of the sudden remembering is located at an exact moment. This makes it *seem* that everything necessary for that remembering to have occurred was present *right then*! We easily come to realize, however, that the occurrences which were mentioned (the image, the thought, the feeling of relief), do not have enough in them to satisfy the meaning of 'He remembered.'

The movement of thought we are then drawn to make is this: *something else* must have occurred *at that moment* — something that we have not yet discerned, something that is still *hidden* from us — and *it*, whatever it may be, *is* the remembering. We make the same movement with sudden understanding, a sudden decision, a sudden hope, and so on. This is where we are inclined to say, 'It is just a certain *mental* occurrence; it is something *inner*.' The recourse to the words 'mental' and 'inner' expresses our feeling that the important thing is as yet hidden from us. It must be lurking right there, but so far we have been unable to isolate it. But this movement in philosophical thinking both aggravates our confusion and bars the way to the right sort of investigation.

What would be the right sort of investigation? One in which we consider the presuppositions that surround the employment of the words 'He remembered.' For example, that he did have a wallet; and that he did leave it in the drawer. Without those presuppositions, what happened at that moment would be not an example of remembering, or even of *seeming* to remember, but perhaps a queer kind of delusion. Just as placing a crown on a king's head would be, in certain circumstances, not a scene of pomp and dignity but one of derision and ridicule.

There is much in the lives of human beings that is enigmatic — unforeseen and unforeseeable; much that is hidden. But the meaning of 'He remembered' is not hidden. The impression that it is, gives rise to philosophical and psychological *theories* of memory. The impression arises from a failure to reflect on the 'grammar' of the words 'He remembered' — the *circumstances* that are presupposed when those words are correctly used. Those circumstances will include things that were the case both *before* and *after* that moment when the person suddenly remembered. Adult speakers have mastered this grammar: they handle it with ease in daily life. But when we study the concept of memory philosophically, the superficial appearance of the words 'He suddenly remembered' misleads us into thinking that everything necessary for remembering is condensed into that moment. Thus we speculate about what that *inner* event might be, which is the remembering. What Wittgenstein tries to do is to get us to turn away from 'the picture of the inner event' (*PI* 305).

Let us go back to Wittgenstein's remark that 'When I think in language, there aren't "meanings" going through my mind in addition to the verbal expression: but the language itself is the vehicle of thinking.' (*PI* 329) If my companion and I are about to do some work in the garden and he asks, 'Where did you put the trencher?', I might promptly reply, 'I left it in the garage', without any play of thinking going on in my mind. But the case could be different. Perhaps the word 'trencher' was not very familiar to me. So before replying I thought to myself, 'What does "trencher" mean? It probably means that tool used for digging trenches.' And then I replied. In this case a 'meaning' did go through my mind. But this sort of thing does not always, or even usually, occur. And even in this case there were not 'meanings' going through my mind *in addition to* the words I said or thought to myself.

Readers of Wittgenstein sometimes get the impression that, according to him, thinking just *is* speaking. This wrong impression probably arises from his emphatic criticism of the idea that when we *understand* what we are saying, a process of thinking must be flowing along with our words. But he provides examples where thinking occurs without words:

> I might also, when busy with various measurements, act in such a way that an onlooker would say I had — without words — thought: if two magnitudes are equal to a third, they are equal to one another. (*PI* 330)

In *Zettel* he gives a magnificent example which I will quote in full:

> Let us imagine someone doing work that involves comparison, trial, choice. Say he is constructing an appliance out of various pieces of material with a given set of tools. Every now and then

there is the problem 'Should I use *this* piece?' — The piece is rejected, another is tried. Pieces are tentatively put together, then dismantled; he looks for one that fits, etc., etc. I now imagine that this whole procedure is filmed. The worker perhaps also produces sounds like 'hm' or 'ha!'. As it were sounds of hesitation, sudden finding, decision, satisfaction, dissatisfaction. But he does not utter a single word. Those sounds may be included in the film. I have the film shown me, and now I invent a self-conversation for the worker, which corresponds to his manner of work, its rhythm, his play of expression, his gestures and spontaneous noises. So I sometimes let him say 'No, that piece is too long, perhaps another will fit better.' — Or 'What am I to do now?' — 'Got it!' — Or 'That is perfect', etc.

If the worker can talk — would it be a falsification of what actually went on if he were to describe it precisely and were to say, for example, 'Then I thought: no, that won't do; I must try it another way', and so on — although he had neither spoken during the work nor imagined these words?

I want to say: may he not later give his wordless thoughts in words? And in such a way that we, who might see the work in progress, could accept this account? — And all the more, if we had often watched the man working, not just once? (*Z* 100)

This passage reminds us that human thinking, perplexity, trying and testing, decision, satisfaction — are often displayed in movements, gestures, facial expressions, spontaneous sounds — without words spoken aloud or silently. But to say that a person's thinking may be 'displayed' in this way, does *not* mean that in addition to and, as it were, *underneath* the gestures, movements, facial expressions, there is an activity of silent thinking in one's mind.

Let us return to the conception of the *Tractatus* that the appearance of vagueness in the sentences of ordinary language is deceptive: for we *understand* these sentences, and understanding must be precise. Our understanding of what looks like a vague sentence actually conceals a process of thinking that transforms vagueness into exactness. This process is logical analysis. It is a kind of computation. It employs a calculus that provides clear-cut truth conditions for an ordinary sentence. The problem of how we can understand vague sentences is thereby solved. Vagueness is only superficial. It does not exist in our *understanding* of everyday language.

In the *Investigations* this conception of the *Tractatus* is described as follows:

> The strict and clear rules of the logical structure of propositions appear to us as something in the background — hidden in the medium of the understanding. I already see them now (even though through a medium): for I certainly understand the sign, mean something by it. (*PI* 102)

Wittgenstein, in his second philosophy of mind and language, regarded his previous conception as a *myth*.

> In philosophy one is in constant danger of producing a myth of symbolism, or a myth of mental processes. Instead of simply saying what anyone knows and must admit. (*Z* 211)

Wittgenstein does not just *call* it a 'myth' and leave it at that. In his careful scrutiny of examples of someone's understanding or meaning something, of obeying an order, following a rule, remembering, deciding, knowing what one was about to say or do, and so on — he shows that it *is* a myth. Anyone who reflects on his examples, or similar ones, 'knows and must admit' that commonly, little if any thinking occurs, and that when it does occur it is fragmentary. When we *examine* what goes on when we speak and when we respond to the words of others, we find no support for the idea that we are constantly employing a calculus. It is useless for a philosopher to hold that this exact thinking takes place at a subterranean, unconscious level — as the *Tractatus* hints when it says that it is impossible to gather immediately from everyday language 'what the logic of language is' (4.002). For this begs the question. It is a way of protecting from refutation an assumption that has been put forward as a *requirement*. As the *Investigations* says, 'The more closely we examine actual language, the sharper becomes the conflict between it and our requirement.' (*PI* 107)

When we assemble Wittgenstein's reminders we see the following: that when a person responds to an order to continue a numerical series from an initial segment, in some cases there will be thinking (e.g. of the algebraic formula), in other cases not: that in some cases we will be justified in saying that he understands the series if he merely continues it in the right way, *without* thinking of what the right way is; that when we say something and *mean* it, or when we speak and *understand* what we say, there is usually no silent thinking of what we mean and understand, which occurs prior to or alongside the uttering of the words; that in conversation our remarks conform to the grammar of the words, without our *thinking of* that grammar; that when someone is constructing something, or playing a position in football, he may *act* skilfully and intelligently but without mentally thinking out what to do; that when a person *knows* what he was *about* to say or do, before he was interrupted, his knowledge is not based on an *inference* from anything in the original situation.

These and similar reflections puncture the charm of the notion that normal human competence in language, and in acting, is only *possible* because of rapid mental processes of computation. The conception of the *Tractatus*, and of much of current linguistics and semantics, that whatever understanding of language we have is based on the operation of a mental calculus, is seen to have no foundation in experience — is seen to be a mere *dream* of our language.

—— CHAPTER 8 ——

Language as Expressive Behaviour

According to the *Tractatus* the essential nature of propositions is to be pictures of reality (4.01). A picture either agrees or fails to agree with reality (2.21). 'It is laid against reality like a ruler.' (2.1512) 'Reality is compared with a proposition.' (4.05) 'A proposition can be true or false only in virtue of being a picture of reality.' (4.06)

I want to sketch the development in Wittgenstein's thinking, after his return to philosophical research in 1929, of a new idea about language, an idea that was a sharp break with the *Tractatus*. The new conception was that there are meaningful sentences of everyday language which are 'expressive', *in the sense* in which a gesture, an outcry, a frown or a laugh, can express, not a *thought*, but indifference, or fear, or displeasure or amusement.

In tracing this new direction in Wittgenstein's thinking it is necessary to begin with the *Philosophical Remarks*, a work he wrote in 1929 and 1930. It contains a striking emphasis on the connection between *verification* and *sense*. This appears in many remarks, for example the following. 'The sense of a question is the method of answering it.' (*PR*, p. 66) 'Tell me *how* you are searching and I will tell you *what* you are searching for.' (*PR*, p. 67) 'To understand the sense of a sentence, means to know how to decide whether it is true or false.' (*PR*, p. 77) 'It is not possible to believe something one cannot conceive of as verified in some way.' (*PR*, p. 89) 'Each sentence is the guide to a verification.' (*PR*, p. 174) 'How a proposition is verified is what it says.' (*PR*, p. 200)

This conception was presented to some members of the Vienna Circle in numerous discussions, as may be seen from the book *Ludwig Wittgenstein and the Vienna Circle*. This work is largely composed of notes taken by Friedrich Waismann, which record conversations between Wittgenstein on the one hand, and on the other principally Waismann and Moritz Schlick, although Rudolf Carnap and Herbert Feigl were often present. This record of discussions covers a period from December 1929 to December 1931. Wittgenstein did most of the talking and plainly was the dominant figure in these meetings. Here again appears his insistence on a conceptual connection between sense and verification. For example, Waismann attributes the following remarks to Wittgenstein. 'If I can never verify the sense of a proposition completely, then I cannot have meant anything by the proposition either.' (*WWK*, p. 47) 'In order to determine the sense of a proposition, I should have to know a very specific procedure for when to count the proposition as verified.' (ibid.) 'Only when I have answered a question can I know what I was asking about.' (*WWK*, p. 79)

It is scarcely doubtful that those discussions were influential in making the Verification Principle (the meaning of a proposition is its method of verification) emerge as a central doctrine of the Vienna Circle. The Verification Principle contributed to the behaviourism, or 'physicalism', of the Circle. First-person present-tense psychological sentences — by which a speaker attributes to himself sensations, thoughts, feelings, intentions, moods — present an obvious problem for the Verification Principle. These sentences could not be dismissed as meaningless; but if they were meaningful they had to be verifiable. Behaviourism rejected the notion that one could verify one's own first-person declarations by comparing them with one's own inner experiences or mental states. The only alternative in sight was to hold that each person can verify his own first-person psychological sentences by comparing them with his own behaviour and/or physical states.

It is interesting that there is in Wittgenstein's *Philosophical Remarks*, despite its emphatic verificationism, a comment that hints at a criticism of behaviourism:

> It isn't possible to believe something for which you cannot imagine some kind of verification.
> If I say I believe that someone is sad, it's as though I am seeing his behaviour through the medium of sadness, from the viewpoint of sadness. But could you say: 'It looks to me as if I'm sad, my head is drooping so'? (*PR*, pp. 89—90)

This comical question indicates that there is something wrong with the notion that I might look at my own posture or behaviour to find out whether I am sad. But the question also poses a problem: if I do not verify that I am sad by noting my behaviour, then how *do* I verify it? Although Wittgenstein seems to have been criticizing behaviourism in the remark just quoted, he was not relaxing his insistence on a necessary connection between sense and verification. Two pages later he says:

> 'I have no pain' means: if I compare the proposition 'I have pain' with reality, it turns out false — so I must be in a position to compare the proposition with what is in fact the case. And the possibility of such a comparison — even though the result may be negative — is what we mean by the expression. (*PR*, p. 92)

To speak of the possibility of comparing a proposition with reality is equivalent to speaking of the possibility of verifying it. The remark just quoted poses two problems. First, *how* does one compare the utterance 'I'm in pain' with reality? What is the procedure? Second, *if* one does compare it with reality, then it would seem that one could *make a mistake*, just as one can make a mistake in measuring the width of a rug. It would follow that one could think oneself to be in pain when one wasn't, or that one could be in pain but not know it. Both consequences seem absurd.

Upon his sudden return to philosophical research in 1929, Wittgenstein began to lecture in Cambridge, and to discuss, think, and write, with the remarkable intensity that was always characteristic of him. In the early 1930s his philosophical ideas were changing rapidly. G. E. Moore's account of the lectures of Wittgenstein, which Moore attended from 1930 to 1933, illustrates the wide range of the lecture topics, and also the swiftness of movement and change in Wittgenstein's thinking. This is particularly evident in the following passage:

> He began the discussion by raising a question, which he said was connected with Behaviourism, namely, the question 'When we say "he has a toothache" is it correct to say that his toothache is only his behaviour, whereas when I talk about my toothache I am not talking about my behaviour?'; but very soon he introduced a question expressed in different words, which is perhaps not merely a different formulation of the same question, viz. 'Is another person's toothache a "toothache" in the same sense as mine?' In trying to find an answer to this question or these questions, he said

first that it was clear and admitted that what verifies or is a criterion for 'I have a toothache' is quite different from what verifies or is a criterion for 'He has a toothache', and soon added that, since this is so, the *meanings* of 'I have a toothache' and 'He has a toothache' must be different. In this connection he said later, first, that the meaning of 'verification' is different when we speak of verifying 'I have' from what it is when we speak of verifying 'He has', and then, later still, that there is no such thing as a verification for 'I have', since the question 'How do you know that you have a toothache?' is nonsensical. He criticized two answers which might be given to this last question by people who do think it is not nonsensical, by saying (1) that the answer 'Because I feel it' won't do, because 'I feel it' means the same as 'I have it', and (2) that the answer 'I know it by inspection' also won't do, because it implies that I can 'look to see' whether I have it or not, whereas 'looking to see whether I have it or not' has no meaning.[1]

Moore's account illustrates not only the rapid evolution of Wittgenstein's thinking about psychological sentences, but also the tenacity with which he pursued any philosophical problem. It is of interest that Wittgenstein wrote in a notebook the following observation about himself: 'My talent for philosophy consists in continuing to be puzzled when others have let the puzzlement slip away.'

Moore's account proves that by 1932 there had emerged from Wittgenstein's thinking the 'discovery' that the concept of verification has no application to some first-person psychological sentences. One cannot 'verify' that oneself feels hot, or hungry, or wants to sit down. It is ironic that some members of the Vienna Circle continued to insist that a sentence is meaningless if there is no possibility of verifying it, long after the originator of the Verification Principle had abandoned it.

Wittgenstein's new insight into the logic of first-person psychological sentences must have been very difficult to achieve. For it is compelling to reason as follows: 'The sentence "I am in pain" obviously has sense; so it depicts a possible state of affairs; so it is either true or false; so it must be possible to determine which it is; therefore it must be possible to compare the sentence with reality.'

It took a powerful and determined mind to break through that net of reasoning. The breakthrough had momentous consequences in the subsequent development of Wittgenstein's thought.

Wittgenstein began to use the word *Äusserungen* to characterize psychological sentences in the first-person present tense. This word is not easily translated. The noun *Äusserung* is related to the preposition *ausser*, which can mean *out*: for example, *ausser dem House essen* (to dine out). *Äusserung* is also related to the adjective *äussere* (exterior, outer, outside); to the verb *äussern* (to utter, to express, to give utterance); and to the reflexive verb *sich äussern* (to express oneself). The noun *Äusserung* itself has a variety of meanings: announcement, pronouncement, utterance, expression, assertion, statement, observation, remark. Translators of and writers on Wittgenstein have employed several different English words for *Äusserung*, for example expression, manifestation, utterance, avowal. I favour the word 'expression', for the reason that Wittgenstein was presenting an *analogy* between first-person psychological sentences and the non-linguistic behaviour that we normally regard as *expressions* of pain, fear, hope, dismay, expectation, and so on.

Wittgenstein gave different formulations of the relation of first-person psychological sentences to non-linguistic expressions of sensation and feeling. In some notes for lectures, composed in English from about the beginning of 1935 to March 1936, he wrote: 'We teach the child to use the words "I have a toothache" to *replace* its moans.' (*NFL*, p. 295; emphasis added) A few pages later he writes: 'Roughly speaking: the expression "I have a toothache" *stands for* a moan but it does not mean "I moan".' (*NFL*, p. 301; emphasis added) But in the actual lectures, according to Rhees, Wittgenstein said that it 'is a substitute for moaning', and 'replaces moaning', instead of 'stands for' a moan (*NFL*, fn., p. 301). In *The Blue Book* (dictated to students in 1933—4), he says: 'The difference between the propositions "I have pain" and "He has pain" is not that of "L. W. has pain" and "Smith has pain." Rather, it corresponds to the difference between moaning and saying that someone moans.' (*BB*, p. 68) When Wittgenstein wrote out carefully what he wanted to say, it was *not* that the uttered sentence 'I'm in pain' *stands for* moaning, but instead that it *replaces* moaning. That is how he puts it in the *Investigations*:

> A child has hurt himself and he cries: and then adults talk to him and teach him exclamations and later sentences. They teach the child new pain-behaviour. 'So you are saying that the word "pain" really means crying?' — On the contrary, the verbal expression of pain replaces crying and does not describe it. (*PI* 244)

This way of looking at the first-person psychological sentences diverged sharply from the viewpoint of the *Tractatus*. There the view is that every spoken meaningful sentence expresses a *thought*. For a sentence is a logical picture of a possible situation (4.03), and any logical picture of a situation is a thought (3). In the new conception the first-person psychological sentences are not thoughts and do not express thoughts. They do express something; that is why they are called *Äusserungen*. They express sensations, emotions, feelings, moods, not thoughts. This is an important distinction. In the *Investigations* Wittgenstein says that our perplexities about the relation between behaviour and sensation, and our temptation to suppose that the language of sensation must be founded on inner ostensive definitions, will disappear

> only if we make a radical break with the idea that language always functions in *one* way, always serves the same purpose: to convey thoughts — which may be thoughts about houses, pains, good and evil, or whatever. (*PI* 304)

This is a direct collision with the *Tractatus*. A few paragraphs later Wittgenstein says:

> Misleading parallel: a cry, an expression of pain — a sentence, an expression of thought.
>   As if the purpose of the sentence were to let one person know how the other feels: only, so to speak, in his thinking apparatus and not in his stomach. (*PI* 317)

Still later, there is this comment:

> 'The purpose of language is to express thoughts.' — So presumably the purpose of every sentence is to express a thought. Then what thought is expressed, for example, by the sentence 'It's raining'? (*PI* 501)

It depends on the circumstances whether a person who looks out of the window and exclaims 'It's raining!' is expressing a thought. If a walk in the country had been planned, he might be expressing the thought 'We shall have to cancel the walk.' But in other circumstances he would not be expressing a thought, although he might be expressing pleasure or dismay.

The conception of the *Tractatus* that a meaningful sentence necessarily expresses a thought, exerts a fascination on philosophers. It is sometimes claimed that it is a rule of language that if a person A utters a sentence, '*p*' to a person B, then A should have the intention to get B to think that A thinks that *p*.[2]

Let us take an example. Suppose that you are driving a car and I am your passenger. Occasionally there are icy stretches on the road, and both of us are aware of this, and both of us realize that one should drive carefully over these icy patches. I say to you, 'I see an icy stretch just ahead.' My intention is to *warn* you — not to get you to *think* that I *think* there is an icy stretch ahead. The purpose of my utterance was not to transmit, or to evoke, *a thought* — but to get you to drive carefully — to get you to *act*.

Let us return to Wittgenstein's characterization of first-person psychological sentences as *Äusserungen* (expressions). In *Zettel* he presents a brief sketch for the treatment of psychological concepts. The first remark is: 'Psychological verbs characterized by the fact that the third person of the present is to be verified by observation, the first person not.' The next remark is: 'Sentences in the third person of the present: information (*Mitteilung*). In the first person present: expression (*Äusserung*).' Then is added in parenthesis: 'Not quite right.' Wittgenstein then says: 'The first person of the present *akin* to an expression.' (*Z* 472; emphasis added)

What Wittgenstein seems to be saying is that the verbal utterance, for example 'I'm in pain', is *like* a natural, non-verbal, expression of pain, such as a groan or grimace. The word 'akin' should prepare us to note differences as well as similarities. An obvious difference is that the utterance 'I'm in pain' is a *sentence*, whereas a groan or facial contortion is not.

Some philosophers have laboured over the question of whether Wittgenstein denied that verbal 'expressions' are true or false, that is, denied that they 'bear truth-values'.[3] Now it is obvious that if I say 'I have a headache', I can be saying something true — that is, telling the truth — or I can be saying something false — that is, lying or faking. It is worth noting that 'I have a headache' (said by me) has the same truth-value as 'He has a headache' (said about me). In contrast, if a person is groaning we do not say that his groaning is 'false', but instead that he is 'pretending', 'faking', or 'putting it on'. Nor do we say that his groaning is 'true', but instead that it is 'genuine'.

I know of no evidence that Wittgenstein ever held that the *Äusserungen* are not true or false. What we should expect him to say is that the words 'true' and 'false' are used differently, have a different grammar, from the grammar they have when applied to a statement such as 'I have a decayed tooth.' There is a passage in part II of *Investigations* where Wittgenstein is imagining that he is saying something to himself in his thoughts, and another person is guessing what it is. Wittgenstein asks, 'What is the criterion for his guessing *right?*' Surely it would only be, Wittgenstein's *admitting* that the other had guessed right. A person's admission, confession, that he was thinking or saying so-and-so to himself, would be an *expression*; and Wittgenstein remarks that the *truth* of the confession 'is guaranteed by the special criteria of *truthfulness*' (*PI*, p. 222). Here truth is guaranteed by truthfulness! This seems remarkable. Why should it seem remarkable? Because one compares it with a physical object statement: for example, I have just measured a table and declare 'This table is exactly 71 inches long.' I am speaking truthfully — but that does not guarantee that my measurement was accurate. The words 'true' and 'false' have as much application to the *expression* 'I feel ill' as to the *statement* 'I am six feet tall': but it is a different use of those words.

In *Zettel* Wittgenstein observes that it is 'misleading' to call a verbal 'expression' a *statement* or *assertion* (*Behauptung*). He says:

> To call the expression (*Äusserung*) of a sensation a *statement* is misleading, because 'testing', 'justification', 'confirmation', 'refutation' of a statement are connected with the word 'statement' in the language game. (*Z* 549)

Wittgenstein is not saying here that in ordinary language it is incorrect to call a verbal 'expression' a statement, but rather that this terminology leads us, as philosophers, to search for the justification, confirmation, and so on, of the *Äusserungen* — concepts that do not apply to them.

Did Wittgenstein deny that verbal expressions of sensation, emotion, mood, are *descriptions*? It seems that at first he had this inclination. In the 'Notes for Lectures' he said:

> You couldn't call moaning a description: But this shows how far the proposition 'I have a toothache' is from a description, and how far teaching the word 'toothache' is from teaching the word 'tooth'. (*NFL*, p. 320)

But in the *Investigations* his treatment of this matter is far more subtle:

Are the words 'I am afraid' a description of a state of mind? I say 'I am afraid'; someone else asks me: 'What was that? A cry of fear; or do you want to tell me how you feel; or is it a reflection on your present state?' — Could I always give him a clear answer? Could I never give him one? (*PI*, p. 187)

Wittgenstein then gives a series of examples in which the words 'I am afraid' would be uttered in different contexts, and in different tones of voice. In one case the utterance would be a cry of fear; in another, a confession; in another, a self-reproach; in another a description of one's mental state. Wittgenstein says:

A cry is not a description. But there are transitions. And the words 'I am afraid' may approximate more, or less, to a cry. They may come quite close to it, and also be *far* removed from it.

We surely do not always say someone is *complaining*, because he says he is in pain. So the words 'I am in pain' may be a complaint, and may be something else. But if 'I am afraid' is not always something like a cry of complaint, and yet sometimes is, then why should it *always* be a description of a state of mind? (*PI*, p. 189)

The question 'Why should it *always* be a description of a state of mind?' discloses Wittgenstein's target — namely, the philosophical urge to insist that the first-person psychological sentences *must* be descriptions (or reports) of inner mental states — and therefore must be justified, confirmed, verified, by the speaker's observation of himself.

When we remind ourselves of the different ways in which these sentences are used, we see that in one context the utterance 'I am afraid' is a cry for help; in another it is an expression of disgust with oneself; in another it is a justification for some action or omission; in another it is a description of one's mental state. Understanding this, we can reject the philosophical insistence that the utterance 'I am afraid' is *always* a description of a mental state, without having to maintain that it *never* is.

But it may be overly optimistic to say that we *can* reject this philosophical view. For it has a strong grip on us. Of utterances such as 'I'm afraid', 'I'm in pain', 'I hope he will get well', 'I intend to go to Vienna', we have a powerful inclination to say: 'They are *propositions*; and when I utter them they are assertions or statements about *myself*. And I *know* whether they are true or false. This knowledge *must* be based on my *observation* of myself.'

All of these remarks are either misleading, confusing, or nonsensical. It is misleading to call these first-person utterances 'propositions', just as it is to call them 'statements' or 'assertions'. For this classification invites us to assimilate them to such a proposition (assertion, statement) as 'Cambridge is 60 miles from London', which can be checked, and confirmed or disconfirmed, independently of its utterance by a particular speaker. To say 'I *know* I intend to go to Vienna' is confusing; for what is it supposed to mean? The prefix 'I *know*' does not seem to be doing any work here — except possibly to provide emphasis, in which case the whole sentence is equivalent to 'I *do* intend to go to Vienna'. However, at the same time the prefix 'I know' fosters the illusion that I am aware of something that informs me of my own intention. To say that I need to *observe* something in order to find out my own intention is nonsensical: for *what* would I observe, and what would it mean to wonder whether my observation was carried out correctly or incorrectly? Sometimes one says, 'I don't know whether I intend to go to Vienna': but this means that I haven't yet made up my mind, not that I haven't yet observed my intention.

It is true of course that sometimes reflection on one's own past actions, reactions, agitations, may yield insight; may make one aware, or more aware, of one's own fears, hopes, anxieties. But to the extent that a remark, such as 'I really dislike him', or 'I am afraid of her', has its origin in such reflection or recollection, to the same extent it diverges from the role of being a pure 'expression' of fear or dislike, and has more the character of a self-assessment.

In likening the utterance 'I'm in pain' to a cry of pain, Wittgenstein was not declaring that it *is* a cry of pain. He was pointing out a *similarity* that, once seen, helped him to be freed from the foregoing tangle of misleading, confusing, or nonsensical ideas. The similarity is not something that Wittgenstein invented; it is really there. It is nonsense to suppose that there might be sensation, or fear, or hope, or intention, without these ever being expressed in human behaviour. The first-person psychological sentences, the *Äusserungen*, are a part of that expressive behaviour. Why should it be thought strange that saying 'I hope he will come' may be an expression of hope — and not indirectly, through the mediation of a thought, but just as directly as wringing one's hands, or pacing back and forth, may be expressions of the hope that he will come? When adults teach a child to say 'It hurts',[4] instead of crying out when the sore place is touched, it is literally true that 'they teach the child new pain-behaviour' (*PI* 244) — behaviour that is expressive of pain in the same direct way as is the cry that it replaces.

Though it may be conceded that the first-person psychological utterances are a part of expressive behaviour, one may want to insist that nevertheless they are *radically* different from non-verbal expressive behaviour. Of course they are different. But why '*radically*'? Behind this emphasis is the persisting urge to view them as 'statements' or 'propositions', and to hold that they are put forward as 'corresponding with reality'. The next move is to say that each person *knows* whether his first-person psychological utterances correspond with reality or not, and therefore he actually *compares* them with reality, or compares reality with them. In repeating these obsessive claims I mean to indicate how fiercely unyielding they are.

The *Tractatus* makes the universal claims that 'Reality is compared with a proposition' (4.05), that propositions are pictures (4.01), and that pictures agree with reality or fail to agree (2.21). Since they are universal, these claims must be assumed to apply to the first-person psychological utterances — for these certainly are meaningful sentences. Let us agree to call them 'propositions'. I want to tackle, from a different angle, the assumption that they are compared, or can be compared with reality.

First-person psychological utterances are, from the standpoint of ordinary school grammar, subject-predicate sentences. The pronoun 'I' is the grammatical subject, and 'am in pain', 'am angry', 'intend to go to Vienna', are grammatical predicates. Wittgenstein brought to light what is perhaps by now a familiar point, that I do not 'identify my sensation by criteria' (*PI* 290). I do not employ any criteria for determining whether what I have is a headache, or a pain in the chest, or an itching sensation. But when I apply these predicates to other persons I do employ behavioural criteria. Wittgenstein says:

> I infer that he needs to go to the doctor from observation of his behaviour; but I do *not* make this inference in my own case from observation of my behaviour. Or rather, I do this too sometimes, but not in analogous cases. (*Z* 539)

For example, I have observed from his behaviour that he feels breathless when walking, and infer that he needs to go to the doctor. I have noticed that I often feel breathless when walking: this could be called an observation of my behaviour. I infer that I should go to the doctor. The cases are not analogous: for I do not observe from my behaviour that I feel breathless!

The point that I do not apply predicates of sensation to myself, in accordance with criteria, holds for many other psychological predicates. For example, I do not determine on the basis of any criteria that I intend to go for a walk. And consider this case:

> What is the criterion for the sameness of two images? — What is the criterion for the redness of an image? For me, when it is someone else's image: what he says and does. For myself, when it is my image: nothing. And what goes for 'red' also goes for 'same'. (*PI* 377)

The *Tractatus* says that a picture, and therefore a proposition, 'is laid against reality like a ruler' (2.1512). Measurement by a ruler is a criterion of length. The Verification Principle is neither stated nor obviously implied in the *Tractatus*. But the analogy between a proposition and a ruler *suggests* that one does not understand a proposition unless one knows how to compare it with reality — just as one does not understand the use of a ruler if one does not know how to measure with it. Thus there seems to be an assumption in the *Tractatus* that all meaningful sentences are employed in accordance with criteria. This is not so in a multitude of cases when one applies a psychological predicate to oneself. This undermines the notion that the first-person psychological utterances are compared with reality — for usually their predicates are not employed in that way.

Let us turn from the predicates to the grammatical subject, the pronoun 'I'. Wittgenstein makes some startling observations about the use of this word. In *The Blue Book* he says that 'In "I have pain", "I" is not a demonstrative pronoun.' (*BB*, p. 68) This would seem to be a paradoxical remark. In ordinary school grammar 'I' is classified as a demonstrative pronoun. What can Wittgenstein mean?

Let us ask, what does one *do* with a demonstrative? What is its function? The answer is that the words 'this', 'that', 'he', 'she' are used to refer to, indicate, pick out, someone or something. Which person or thing a demonstrative picks out is shown by a pointing gesture, or by a previously given name or description, or by the context of previous or subsequent remarks. Wittgenstein's point in saying that the 'I' in 'I'm in pain' is not a demonstrative pronoun, would presumably be that the 'I' is not used there to refer to, or to designate, or to pick out one particular person among others. That this is his meaning is indicated by a remark in the *Investigations*:

> 'But at any rate when you say "I am in pain", you want to draw the attention of others to a particular person.' — The answer might be: no, I want to draw their attention to *myself*. (*PI* 405)

There is of course no logical significance in the fact that in English we have the two words 'I' and 'myself' (or in German, *Ich* and *mich selbst*) instead of the one word 'I'. There is no difference in meaning between 'Roger, Alfred, and myself were in the room', and 'Roger, Alfred, and I were in the room.' If there is a use of 'I' in which it does not refer to 'a particular person', this would also be true of 'myself' or 'me' when those words replace 'I'. That Wittgenstein's meaning is that the 'I' in 'I'm in pain' does not refer to, or pick out, a particular person, is confirmed by the following paragraph:

> 'When I say "I am in pain", I do not point to a person, who is in pain, since in a certain sense I don't know at all *who* is in pain.' And this can be justified. For the main point is: I did not say that such-and-such a person is in pain, but 'I am. . . .' Now in saying this I don't name any person. Just as I don't name anyone when I *groan* with pain, though someone else sees who is in pain from the groaning. What does it mean to know *who* is in pain? It means, for example, to know which man in this room is in pain: for instance, the one who is sitting there, or the one who is standing in that corner, the tall one over there with the blond hair, and so on. — What am I getting at? At this, that there are many different criteria for the '*identity*' of a person.
>
> Now which of them determines my saying that '*I*' am in pain? None. (*PI* 404)

Wittgenstein's point is perhaps blunted by his remark that when I say 'I'm in pain', I don't 'name' (*nenne*) any person. For it is also the case that when I say 'He is in pain' (pointing) I don't *name* any person. I think the point is better put like this: in exclaiming 'I'm in pain', I am not *identifying, designating, referring to*, a particular person.

It is possible that a person suffering from amnesia should not remember his name, or any of his past history, or anything at all about himself. He would, literally, not know *who* he is. Yet this would not deprive his utterance 'I'm in pain' of meaning. It might be objected that I can say of someone 'He's in pain' without knowing *who* he is. This is true, in a sense. But I could *point* to him. I would mean that the person at whom I am pointing is in pain. In this sense I *do* know who is in pain. If it is objected that the man with amnesia could point to himself when he says 'I'm in pain', the answer is that this would be an idle employment of the pointing gesture. Wittgenstein imagines someone saying:

> But surely the word 'I' in the mouth of a man refers to the man who says it; it points to himself, and very often a man who says it actually points to himself with his finger. (*BB*, p. 67)

Wittgenstein's reply is:

> But it was quite superfluous to point to himself. He might just as well only have raised his hand. It would be wrong to say that when someone points to the sun with his hand, he is pointing both to the sun and himself because it is *he* who points; on the other hand, he may by pointing attract attention both to the sun and to himself.
>
> The word 'I' does not mean the same as 'L. W.' even if I am L. W., nor does it mean the same as the expression 'the person who is now speaking'. But that doesn't mean: that 'L. W.' and 'I' mean different things. All it means is that these words are different instruments in our language. (*BB*, p. 67)

In saying 'I'm in pain' I may attract attention to myself; but so may I by crying out in pain. In neither case do I refer to, designate, or identify a particular person. If I supplemented my utterance 'I'm in pain' with the description 'The person in pain is the one who is saying "I'm in pain"', this description might fail to single out a particular person, since someone else nearby might also be exclaiming 'I'm in pain.' This other person might also be pointing to himself; so I would not distinguish one person from all others by pointing to myself and saying, 'The person in pain is the one who is pointing to himself.' In short, I might be unable to identify myself by any distinguishing feature whatever; yet this would in no way take away from the meaning of my utterance 'I'm in pain.' My use of the word 'I' here does not rely on or presuppose an ability to supplement the 'I' with a description, name, or pointing gesture. It is literally true, although at first sight paradoxical, that in this use 'I' is not a demonstrative pronoun. It is not even a pronoun; for it is not used as a replacement for a name or identifying description. In this use the word 'I' does not *refer* to anyone, not even to the person who utters it.

We have been dwelling on the inclination to suppose that one *compares* one's first-person psychological utterances (one's *Äusserungen*) with reality. The points made about the utterance 'I'm in pain' carry over to many other first-person psychological utterances.

We took such utterances to be divisible into grammatical predicate and grammatical subject. We saw that such predicates as 'am angry', 'am afraid', 'am expecting him at any moment', are not normally employed in accordance with any *criteria*. It seems wrong, therefore, to think that in the first-person employment of these predicates, one 'compares them with reality', or tries to determine whether they are in accord with how things are.

In respect to the grammatical subject, the 'I', we have seen that it is not normally used, in these first-person psychological utterances, to pick out, designate, or refer to, a particular person. In employing those sentences, we are not referring to a person, under some description or designation, and saying that *that* person is angry, or afraid, or expecting someone.

The consequence of all this is that the notion that one compares one's first-person psychological utterances with reality, does not have a leg to stand on. If one doesn't employ the predicates in accordance with any criteria, then one is not trying to determine whether the predicates fit either inner mental states or outer behaviour. If, in addition, one does not use the subject term, the word 'I', to refer to anyone or anything, then one is not trying to determine whether the predicate is true of some particular person or thing.

When we add together these points about the subject and the predicate, I cannot imagine a more decisive refutation of the notion that one somehow compares these sentences with how things are, and of the connected notions that one verifies, or perceives, or observes, or knows, that they are true, or false. The destruction of these notions helps us to appreciate the analogy that Wittgenstein draws between these first-person sentences, and the non-verbal, behavioural expressions of sensation, hope, fear, expectation, intention. Neither of them are, or can be, 'compared with the facts', by the person who expresses them. Yet both of them are informative to others. Both of them provide others with grounds for conclusions and predictions about the person who expressed them.

I think that Wittgenstein's realization, in the early 1930s, that the concept of verification has no *application* to 'I'm in pain' and similar 'expressions', played a big part in freeing him from the grip of his assumption in the *Tractatus* that language has a 'formal unity'. He now saw that there were quite ordinary sentences of everyday language, which certainly have sense, and are true (or false) — but which are not 'compared with reality'. This insight included the perception that the first-person and third-person psychological sentences are employed differently. The latter are often based on observation; the former not. The previous view, that all genuine propositions are structures which are essentially alike, was completely overthrown. The door was opened for Wittgenstein's intensive studies of the ways in which various sentences are actually *used*: for 'seeing differences' where before everything had seemed to be the same.

The notion that some of the sentences we utter are *Äusserungen* (expressions) rather than 'propositions', 'statements', or 'thoughts', was first applied by Wittgenstein to psychological sentences in the first person. As he puts it, when adults teach a child to replace his cries and screams when he has hurt himself, with words and sentences, they are teaching him *new pain-behaviour* (*PI* 244). The learned verbal expressions of pain, or fright, are no more due to thinking or reasoning than is the unlearned preverbal behaviour. Wittgenstein calls these verbal utterances *Äusserungen*, to indicate that they are *immediate expressions* of pain, fear, surprise, desire, and so on — and are not the result of thought.

Later, Wittgenstein began to apply this conception to sentences of other types: for example, to sentences that we use to refer to other persons. The sentence 'He is in pain' *can* be a detached statement of an observation. But also it can function in another way: it can be an expression of concern or anguish; it goes with the behaviour of trying to help or comfort an injured person. Wittgenstein remarks that 'it is a primitive reaction to tend, to treat, the part that hurts when someone else is in pain, and not merely when oneself is.' (*Z* 540) Obviously, there are natural reactions of shock, concern, distress, when we see that some person is badly hurt. Something of the same kind is observed in animals. In the *Zettel* passage just quoted, Wittgenstein asks himself what he means by saying that these reactions are 'primitive'? He answers:

> Surely that this way of behaving is *prelinguistic*: that a language-game is based *on it*, that it is the prototype of a way of thinking and not the result of thinking. (Z 541)

Wittgenstein is disagreeing with a 'rationalistic' explanation of this behaviour — for example, the explanation that we have a sympathetic reaction to an injured person 'because by analogy with our own case we believe that he too is experiencing pain' (Z 542). The actions of comforting or trying to help, that go with the words 'He is in pain', are no more a product of reasoning from analogy than is the similar behaviour in deer or birds.

> Being sure that someone is in pain, doubting whether he is, and so on, are so many natural, instinctive, kinds of relationship towards other human beings, and our language is merely an auxiliary to, and further extension of, this behaviour. Our language-game is an extension of primitive behaviour. (Z 545)

What does it mean to say that this language is an 'extension' of primitive behaviour? Well, first-person exclamations, such as 'It hurts' or 'I'm in pain', may just *replace* the instinctive behaviour of crying out, or of protecting and soothing the painful area. But the full language of pain adds something to this. One may say, 'It still hurts but not as much as it did yesterday.' Such a report goes beyond what could be conveyed by prelinguistic behaviour. And the third-person sentence 'He's in pain' is connected with exclamations and warnings such as 'Call a doctor!', 'Be careful how you move him!' These are extensions of primitive behaviour.

Even more unexpected is Wittgenstein's conception that our concepts of *causation* originate in primitive reactions. Philosophers often assume that concepts of causality originate in observations of uniform sequences of events. But this view is too intellectual. It implies that when one event is followed by another we remain in doubt whether the two events are related as cause and effect until we have satisfied ourselves by further observations that an event of the one kind is uniformly conjoined with an event of the other kind — whereupon we call the one *cause*, the other *effect*. On this view the *thought* of a universal regularity, and a *doubt* as to whether the regularity is satisfied by the events in question, is present at the very beginning of our employment of causal language.

In manuscript notes written in 1937 Wittgenstein presents an entirely different conception. Suppose a child runs into another child, knocking him down. The latter might react by jumping up and hitting the other one. He would be 'reacting to the cause' of his falling. Wittgenstein says: 'Calling something "the cause" is like pointing and saying: "He's to blame!"' (*C&E*, p. 410) The child would not be in doubt as to what made him fall. He would not wait to observe what happens in other cases. Nor could he be said to 'assume' that in similar cases the same thing occurs. Wittgenstein says:

> There is a reaction which can be called 'reacting to the cause'. – We also speak of 'tracing' the cause; a simple case would be, say, following a string to see who is pulling it. If I then find him – how do I know that he, his pulling, is the cause of the string's moving? Do I establish this by a series of experiments? (*C&E*, p. 416)

This 'reacting to the cause' can be called 'immediate'. This means, first, that there is no uncertainty, guessing, conjecturing, inferring, concluding. Second, calling it an 'immediate reaction' emphasizes the aspect of *action* – striking back, chasing away the cat that has hold of the string, pointing in anger at the one who broke the toy. Causal language, such as 'He knocked me down', 'The cat is pulling it', 'She broke it', is grafted on to these immediate reactions.

Later on the growing person will acquire a use of causal language into which enters doubt, hypothesis, testing, experiments, theory. Wittgenstein calls these 'second-order features' (*C&E*, p. 420). This is a sophisticated *addition* to the original primitive use of causal language. Wittgenstein says:

> The primitive form of the language-game is certainty, not uncertainty. For uncertainty could never lead to action. (*C&E*, p. 420)

> The basic form of the game must be one in which we act. (*C&E*, p. 421)

To suppose that wondering whether this caused that, or questioning in one's mind whether the two events are constantly conjoined, comes in advance of, or along with, the first occurrences of reacting to a cause, is putting the cart before the horse. The child who retaliates against the one who crashed into him, does not act because he 'thinks' that this caused his fall. No! He just acts! It is like brushing away an insect that is tickling one's skin. One does not make experiments to determine whether the tickling sensation is caused by the insect.

In saying that the primitive form of causal notions is 'certainty', Wittgenstein does not mean that the child 'thinks to himself' that 'it is certain' that the other one caused his fall, or that the child has a 'perception' or 'intuitive awareness' of the causal connection between his being crashed into and his falling down. No. Wittgenstein means that hitting back at the other child is an immediate reaction — not touched by uncertainty. This instinctive response is what he calls 'reacting to a cause'. The 'certainty' he is talking about is certainty *in action*.

Doesn't the child's response at least *presuppose* that he has *the concept* of causation? No. In the first place it is wrong to speak of *the* concept of causation, as if there were an *essence* of causation, a set of necessary and sufficient conditions, a hidden definition of causation that lies behind the differing uses of causal expressions. In the second place, these immediate reactions would be a *foundation* for the learning of causal language. Sentences, such as 'He knocked me down', 'He caused me to fall', would be linked to the instant reaction. Learning the meaning of these causal expressions would be rooted in such reactions and would not be presupposed by them — just as a child's crying out with pain when injured would be an occasion for its being taught to use the word 'pain' and would not presuppose that it has 'the concept' of pain.

A child's first learning of causal terms consists in learning to use them along with, or in place of, the unlearned reactions. Being *in doubt* about the cause of something, learning to investigate causes by trials and experiments, relying on evidence, would be a subsequent development.

Wittgenstein's conception that much of our language replaces and extends primitive behaviour, is a conspicuous feature of his post-*Tractatus* outlook. This conception is not present in the *Tractatus*. Instead, as I argued in chapter 1, the view there seems to be that a child has from the beginning a grasp of every logical possibility and every possible thought. Learning language is just learning to put these thoughts into words. We start out with a full-blown rationality.

Wittgenstein's new thinking is presented not only in *Zettel*, as we have seen, but also in *On Certainty*:

> I want to regard man here as an animal; as a primitive being, to which one grants instinct but not reasoning (*Raisonnement*). As a creature in a primitive state. . . . Language did not emerge from reasoning (*Raisonnement*). (*OC* 475)

It is not only that language is rooted in instinctive behaviour, but also that in innumerable situations of life we act with certainty, without seeking to justify the reliability of our memories or sense-perceptions. Wittgenstein says: 'Suppose someone were to ask: "Is it really right for us to rely on the evidence of our memory (or our senses) as we do?"' (*OC* 201) If we were truly 'rational', should we not obtain grounds for this reliance?

A child learns to respond to orders such as 'Hold out your hands', 'Wash your hands.' Shouldn't the child first assure himself that he *has* hands? But he doesn't: he just *acts*. Wittgenstein says:

> Why don't I satisfy myself that I still have two feet, when I want to get up from a chair? There is no why. I simply don't. That is how I act. (*OC* 148)

> Giving grounds, justifying the evidence, comes to an end; — but the end is not certain propositions striking us immediately as true, a kind of *seeing* on our part; but it is our *acting* which lies at the bottom of the language-game. (*OC* 204)

Something resembling the primitive reactions that underlie the first learning of words, pervades all human action and all use of language, even at sophisticated levels. This is manifested in the way in which people who have received instruction in some procedure (drawing a design, continuing a series of numbers, using a word, playing a game) will, when told to carry on from there, spontaneously go on in the *same* way. It would seem that from the initial instruction those people could branch out in an indefinitely large number of different directions. It is true that they *could*. But they don't! Nearly every one of them will go on in a way that the others will agree is the *same* way. This agreement in action is striking. It cannot be 'explained' by saying that they have 'intuitively grasped the rule', or 'internalized' it, or something of the sort. This confident going on in the same way, this acting with certainty, cannot be given a rational foundation. For without it there could not be language or reasoning. (I will return to this topic in chapter 9.)

If a previously normal person began to be in continual doubt about the use of ordinary words, not only could he no longer engage in the everyday employment of language, but also his behaviour would fall into disarray. Normally we *have no doubt* that a common word is used like *this*, or that a design or a series is to be continued like *that*. But usually we cannot 'justify' our certainty. Wittgenstein says:

Now I would like to regard this certainty, not as something akin to hastiness or superficiality, but as a form of life. (*OC* 358)

But that means that I want to conceive it as something that lies beyond being justified or unjustified; as it were, as something animal. (*OC* 359)

This natural certainty (or 'sureness') is too fundamental to be either 'justified' or 'unjustified'. It is presupposed by any use of language in which a justification might be framed.

Wittgenstein's realization that many ordinary sentences do not present 'propositions' or 'thoughts' that can be 'compared with reality', is an important correction of the *Tractatus*. But his conception that language does not emerge from reasoning but from natural forms of life is a more fundamental difference. According to the *Tractatus*, language is based on 'a kind of *seeing*' — on our *knowing* the possibilities of combination of the timeless simple objects. The change from this in Wittgenstein's later thought could hardly be more radical — for here the conception is that what lies at the bottom of language is 'our *acting*', not something's 'striking us as true'.

CHAPTER 9

Following a Rule

The *Investigations* contains an intensive study of the concept of 'following a rule'. Wittgenstein's thoughts on this topic are difficult to grasp. They can confuse readers; and they can produce misunderstandings. Part of what I want to do in this chapter is to consider some of these misunderstandings. I will turn first to Saul Kripke's recent book on Wittgenstein. Kripke says:

> Wittgenstein has invented a new form of scepticism. Personally I am inclined to regard it as the most radical and original sceptical problem that philosophy has seen to date.[1]

According to Kripke this new form of scepticism carries the astounding implication that 'there can be no such thing as meaning anything by any word.'[2] Kripke says: 'Wittgenstein's main problem is that it appears that he has shown *all* language . . . to be impossible, indeed unintelligible.'[3] If this were true it would be a matter of grave concern.

From what remarks did Kripke get the impression that Wittgenstein was endorsing a form of philosophical scepticism? Kripke alludes to *PI* 201 and quotes the opening words: 'This was our paradox: no course of action could be determined by a rule, because every course of action can be made out to accord with the rule.' Kripke says that the 'paradox' stated here 'may be regarded as a new form of philosophical scepticism'.[4]

It is surprising that Kripke should read Wittgenstein in this way, since Wittgenstein goes on to say, in the immediately following paragraph of 201, that this 'paradox' is a *misunderstanding*.

> It can be seen that there is misunderstanding here from the mere

fact that in the course of these thoughts (*in diesem Gedankengang*) we give one interpretation after another, as if each one contented us at least for a moment, until we thought of yet another standing behind it. What this shows is that there is a way of grasping a rule which is *not* an *interpretation*, but which is exhibited in what we call 'following the rule' and 'going against it' from case to case (*von Fall zu Fall*). (*PI* 201)

It is important to note that by 'an interpretation' of a rule, Wittgenstein means 'the substitution of one expression of a rule for another' (*PI* 201). He does not mean, by an 'interpretation', an *action* in accordance with the rule.

Wittgenstein was not *endorsing* the paradox that any way of *acting* agrees with a rule. He was instead saying that this paradox *would* be the consequence *if* the only way of understanding a rule was to provide an *interpretation* of it — that is, to replace one formulation of the rule with another formulation. He had already made this point explicit in a preceding paragraph:

> 'But how can a rule show me what I have to do at *this* point? Whatever I do is, on some interpretation, in accord with the rule.' — No, that should not be said, but rather: any interpretation hangs in the air along with what it interprets, and cannot give it any support. Interpretations by themselves do not determine meaning. (*PI* 198)

If an interpretation is not sufficient to fix the meaning of a rule, what more is required? Wittgenstein's answer is that what fixes the meaning of a rule is *our customary way of applying the rule in particular cases*. There is a way of *acting* that *we call* 'following the rule'. Indefinitely many other ways of acting are possible: but *we* do not call them 'following the rule'.

Who is this *we*? It is virtually all of us who have been given the same initial explanations and examples. It is *a fact* that everyone, almost without exception, will apply the rule in new cases, all *agreeing* that *this* is the right way to apply it. It is *conceivable* that someone might react to the explanations and examples in a different way — should take off in a different direction. That is what is striking about the pupil in *PI* 185, who surprises his teacher by going from 1000 to 1004, and who *believes* he is following the rule of adding 2. We need not suppose that he is less intelligent than the other pupils. His way of continuing from 1000 *could* have been *our* way of applying the rule 'add 2'. It *could* have been regarded by us as 'doing the same' as in the steps below

1000. But in fact it is a deviation from *our* way of continuing the series. He has to be corrected: *our* way enforced. We can say that he did not *understand* 'add 2'. But his *not understanding* was just his continuing the series in a way that *we* say is *not* 'the same way', and which he believed *was* 'the same way'.

Unless there was overwhelming agreement in applying a rule in new cases, the rule would have no fixed meaning. This is what Wittgenstein is getting at when he says:

> Hence 'following a rule' is a practice. And to *believe* one is following a rule is not following the rule. Hence one cannot follow a rule 'privately': otherwise believing he was following a rule would be the same as following it. (*PI* 202)

If there was no *we* — if there was no agreement among those who have had the same training, as to what are the correct steps in particular cases when following a rule — then there would be no *wrong* steps, or indeed any *right* ones. If there was no customary way of responding to sign-posts, there would be no 'going by a sign-post': 'a person goes by a sign-post only in so far as there exists a regular use of sign-posts, a custom.' (*PI* 198)

When Wittgenstein says that following a rule is a *practice*, I think he means that a person's actions cannot be in accord with a rule unless they are in conformity with a common way of acting that is displayed in the behaviour of nearly everyone who has had the same training. This means that the concept of following a rule implies the concept of a *community* of rule-followers. When Wittgenstein says, also in *PI* 202, that one cannot follow a rule 'privately', I think he means that the actions of a single individual, whether these actions are private or public, cannot *fix the meaning* of a rule. Wittgenstein relies, in *PI* 202, on a simple but powerful point, namely that the concept of a *rule* implies a distinction between *following* a rule and *believing* one is following a rule. A person can believe that he is following a rule but be *wrong*.

This distinction could *not* be made if the actions of a single individual could *fix the meaning* of a rule. The meaning of the rule would be exhibited in *whatever* this person did. If it *seemed to him* that he was 'doing the same thing' in following the rule as he had done previously, then he *would be* doing the same thing.

We easily see that this is an absurd consequence. This shows that the actions of a single individual, who believes that he is following a rule, must be *measured against* something other than his own actions. The point holds even if those actions are open to public view — as they were in the case of the pupil who went from 1000 to 1004, in the belief that he was following the order 'add 2'. Wittgenstein's point in *PI* 202 applies regardless of whether what a person does is 'inward' or 'outward' — regardless of whether what he does is 'in his mind' or is behaviour that is visible to others.

Some interpreters of Wittgenstein construe the word 'privately' in *PI* 202 in a different sense. Colin McGinn, for example, takes the word 'privately' to mean: 'within the sphere of consciousness in logical independence of behaviour'.[5] He thinks that 'privately' in *PI* 202 means 'inwardly', in contrast with 'outwardly' or 'publicly'.[6] According to McGinn, Wittgenstein did not mean that there cannot be such a thing as following a rule unless there is agreement within a community as to what actions are in accord with or in conflict with the rule: he meant only that you cannot follow a rule just in your own mind. I think this is a serious misreading of Wittgenstein, and will return to it later. On this important point Kripke understands Wittgenstein better than McGinn. Kripke sees that, on Wittgenstein's view, agreement within a community is essential for rule-following. Kripke says, for example:

> Almost all of us, after sufficient training, respond with roughly the same procedures to concrete addition problems. We respond unhesitatingly to such problems as '68 + 57', regarding our procedure as the only comprehensible one . . . , and we *agree* in the unhesitating responses we make. On Wittgenstein's conception, such agreement is essential for our game of ascribing rules and concepts to each other.[7]

Kripke also assesses correctly the relationship between *PI* 202 and the so-called 'private language argument' that begins at *PI* 243. The discussion leading up to *PI* 202 results in a conclusion of wide significance: any use of language at all presupposes a community in which there is agreement in the application of words and signs. From this alone it follows that the supposed 'private language of sensations' is not a language. Wittgenstein describes this putative language as follows:

> The individual words of this language are to refer to what can only be known to the person speaking; to his immediate private sensations. So another person cannot understand this language. (*PI* 243)

If there were such a language then its user would be following its rules 'privately', *in the sense of* this word in *PI* 202. Since the words of this language refer to what can be known only to its speaker, his application of those words could not be measured against their customary application by other speakers. It would be a case where there would be *no distinction* between *believing* one was following a rule and *following* a rule; between going on in the 'same' way and going on in a 'different' way; between the application of one of those words by the speaker *seeming to him* to be right and its *being right* (see *PI* 258).

But Wittgenstein does not leave this result to be simply deduced from the considerations that lead up to *PI* 202. Since virtually everyone has a strong, indeed overwhelming, inclination to think that his sensation-words refer to what can be known only to himself, Wittgenstein gives this inclination a thorough treatment on its own. As Kripke puts it:

> The 'private language argument' as applied to *sensations* is only a special case of much more general considerations about language previously argued; sensations have a crucial role as an (apparently) convincing *counter-example* to the general considerations previously stated. Wittgenstein therefore goes over the ground again in this special case, marshalling new specific considerations appropriate to it.[8]

Let us return to the crucially important view of Wittgenstein's that, in order for there to be rules, different people who have had approximately the same training must *agree* in their application of the rules to new cases. Now there is an inclination to ask, 'What is the *explanation* of this agreement?'; and to answer, 'Surely they agree *because* all of them are *guided* by the meaning of the rules.' But it should be clear by now that this proffered 'explanation' is no explanation. A rule is expressed by a sentence, or formula, or sign-post. But these things *can* be variously interpreted, as Wittgenstein frequently reminds us. Someone might interpret a NO ENTRY road sign as applying only to motorists, not to *cyclists*; and someone else might interpret it as applying even to *pedestrians*. A child might understand the instruction 'Always close the door after you enter the house' as *not* meaning to *keep* it closed. A novice in cooking might take the words of a recipe for a cake, 'Add two eggs', as meaning that the *whole* eggs, including their shells, should be added.

This is not to say that we are never guided by rules and recipes, but rather that their *meaning* is fixed by the customary agreement *in action* of those who have been given the ordinary explanations and examples. This teaching comes to an end, but the agreement *continues*! If this were not so – if in new situations half of us acted in one way and half in another – then the rules and recipes would have *no* meaning. Therefore, it is a mistake to say that we agree *because* we have absorbed the meaning of the rules. Instead, we should say that without this agreement the rules would be meaningless – would not be rules.

This agreement can strike us as mysterious. Is it mysterious? Isn't it a commonplace fact of human life? It strikes us as mysterious only when we conceive that from the same initial training some of us *could* have gone on in one way, some in another. The fact that we do go on to act in what we agree is the *same* way, then seems remarkable. As Wittgenstein says:

> The aspects of things that are most important for us are hidden because of their simplicity and familiarity. (One is unable to notice something – because it is always before one's eyes.) The real foundations of his enquiry do not strike a man at all. Unless *that* fact has some time struck him. – And this means: we fail to be struck by what, once seen, is most striking and most powerful. (*PI* 129)

The human agreement that is so fundamental for the concept of a rule, and for the possibility of any language, is an outstanding example of a 'form of life'. Can it be explained? Is there something, even more basic, that could be appealed to as an explanation? I should say, no. Such notions as those of 'following rules' or 'understanding the meaning of a word', which we are tempted to invoke as explanations, themselves presuppose what we seek to explain. This human agreement, this going on in the same way, is a particularly apt illustration of Wittgenstein's remark: 'What has to be accepted, the given, is – one could say – *forms of life*.' (*PI*, p. 226)

I wish to return to the question of why Kripke was *inclined* to think that Wittgenstein had endorsed a form of philosophical scepticism. Perhaps the best clue to this is a certain conception that was influencing Kripke. This is the conception that when one applies a rule, or a word, one is *guided*. For example, Kripke says the following: 'Normally, when we consider a mathematical rule such as addition, we think of ourselves as *guided* in our application of it to each new instance.'⁹

Now is this really true? A motorist driving through a large city that is unfamiliar to him, does look to the road-signs for guidance. If he comes to an intersection where there are no signs, he is bewildered: he doesn't know which way to turn. At last he does see a sign which tells him which way to go: he is relieved. In contrast, a motorist who is familiar with the city pays no attention to the signs: he knows his way: he doesn't need to be guided. When an adult person adds a column of figures in doing his accounts, which motorist does he more resemble? Surely the second one. When he adds 4 to 1016 he puts down 1020 without any hesitation. He doesn't feel any need for guidance; nor does he think he is guided. He just writes or says '1020', and goes on to the next sum. A child who was learning to add, might hesitate and feel uncertain. He might look to his teacher for guidance. But the adult doesn't look anywhere for guidance — not even to 'the mathematical rule of addition', whatever that is supposed to be. Nor does he dwell on the meaning of 'add 4'. He just adds 4.

We can now see that there is an ambiguity in Kripke's remark. *Who* is the 'we', of whom he says: 'Normally, when we consider a mathematical rule such as addition, we think of ourselves as *guided* in our application of it to each new instance'? This is certainly not true of us when we add numbers in connection with some practical concern of daily life. A person who is worried about his bank balance does not ponder the meaning of mathematical rules; nor does he think of himself as being *guided* as he adds the figures.

On the other hand, there is a good deal of truth in Kripke's remark if his 'we' applies only to people *when* they are engaged in *philosophical reflection* about rules. For there is something in this reflection which provokes the inclination to think, 'How can I follow a rule unless I am *guided*?' It is not easy to understand why there should be this inclination. But there is no doubt that it exists. Kripke expresses it, for his own case, in the following autobiographical remarks:

> Sometimes when I have contemplated the situation, I have had something of an eerie feeling. Even now as I write, I feel confident that there is something in my mind — the meaning I attach to the 'plus' sign — that *instructs* me what I ought to do in all future cases. I do not *predict* what I *will* do . . . but instruct myself what I ought to do to conform to the meaning. . . . But when I concentrate on

what is now in my mind, what instructions can be found there? How can I be said to be acting on the basis of these instructions when I act in the future? . . . What can there be in my mind that I make use of when I act in the future? It seems that the entire idea of meaning vanishes into thin air.[10]

The candour of Kripke's autobiographical remarks is admirable. Here Kripke is trying to do something which, according to Wittgenstein, it is necessary to do in philosophy, namely 'to give a psychologically exact account of the temptation to use a particular kind of expression' (*PI* 254). But as Wittgenstein also says:

Being unable — when we surrender ourselves to philosophical thought — to help saying such-and-such; being irresistibly inclined to say it — does not mean being forced into an *assumption*, or having an immediate perception or knowledge of a state of affairs. (*PI* 299)

Kripke acknowledges his temptation to feel that there is 'something in his mind' – the *meaning* of the 'plus' sign – that *instructs* him what to do in all future cases of addition. But how could this 'meaning-in-his-mind' *instruct* Kripke in that way unless that meaning had 'already taken' all of those future steps — unless they were *already there* in the *meaning* of the addition sign? In the *Investigations* 188 there is a comment addressed to the person who gave a pupil the order '+2' This person is imagined as thinking that all of the future steps of adding 2 were *settled* by what he meant when he gave the order. Wittgenstein's comment in *PI* 188 could be conceived of by us as addressed to the idea that Kripke expresses in saying:

Even now as I write, I feel confident that there is something in my mind — the meaning I attach to the 'plus' sign — that *instructs* me what I ought to do in all future cases.[11]

Wittgenstein's comment is:

Your idea was that meaning the order had in its own way already traversed all those steps: that when you meant it your mind as it were flew ahead and took all the steps before you physically arrived at this or that one.

Thus you were inclined to use such expressions as: 'The steps are *really* already taken, even before I take them in writing or orally or in thought.' And it seemed as if they were in some *unique* way predetermined, anticipated — as only meaning can anticipate reality. (*PI* 188)

I think we can now understand why Kripke was led to think that Wittgenstein was propounding a radical kind of scepticism. Kripke was under the philosophical impression that when we add numbers we are *guided*: we are guided by *the meaning* that we *attach* to the addition sign. That meaning *tells* us what we ought to do in all future cases of adding. But Wittgenstein's discussion disturbed Kripke's previous philosophical conception. He now felt that the meaning we 'attach' to the addition sign cannot do what it was supposed to do: it cannot guide our application of the sign in future cases. How could the meaning that is supposed to be in one's mind perform that service unless 'it already contained' the future steps? Kripke now realizes that this is an unintelligible idea.

What conclusion does he draw? He *might* have drawn the conclusion that his original philosophical impression that one is *guided* by the meaning of signs and words, was *wrong*. It is odd that Kripke does not draw this conclusion, just by itself. What he appears to further conclude is that if there is no meaning that has the magical property ascribed to it by his original philosophical impression, then there is *no meaning anything* by any sign or word! Kripke says:

> What can there be in my mind that I make use of when I act in the future? It seems that the entire idea of meaning vanishes into thin air.[12]

And Kripke appears to believe that this is the thrust of what he calls Wittgenstein's 'sceptical argument'. The radical conclusion of this argument, according to Kripke, is that 'there can be no such thing as meaning anything by any word.'[13]

It seems that Kripke reasoned as follows:

1 In order for a word to have meaning there must be something in one's mind that guides one's application of the word.
2 Wittgenstein has shown that there is nothing in one's mind that guides one's application of a word.
3 Therefore, Wittgenstein has shown that no word has any meaning.

But instead Kripke should have drawn the conclusion that the first premise of this reasoning is false. This premise states a philosophical conception of meaning. Wittgenstein attacks this philosophical conception. He does not argue that no word has any meaning, or that no one can mean anything by any word.

Perhaps the best clue to Kripke's misinterpretation of Wittgenstein is Kripke's remark that 'Normally, when we consider a mathematical rule . . . , we think of ourselves as *guided* in our application of it to each new instance.' As I noted previously, this remark is ambiguous. If it means that when we are doing philosophy we have the tendency to think this, then it is true. If it means that whenever in ordinary life we follow some rule, we think of ourselves as being *guided*, then it is false. If Kripke was confused as to what his remark meant, this would explain his impression that Wittgenstein had undermined the ordinary concept of following a rule. Whereas in fact Wittgenstein has only undermined a *philosophical opinion* as to what is involved in following a rule.

Let us turn to another point in Kripke's reading of Wittgenstein. This has to do with what Kripke regards as Wittgenstein's 'solution' of the 'sceptical paradox'. On Kripke's account, Wittgenstein continues to hold fast to the position that there is no 'condition in the world which constitutes my meaning addition by "plus" . . . there is no such fact, no such condition in either the "internal" or the "external" world.'[14] 'Wittgenstein holds, with the sceptic, that there is no fact as to whether I mean plus. . . .'[15] According to Kripke, although Wittgenstein retains this view, yet at the same time he does 'not wish to doubt or deny that when people speak of themselves and others as meaning something by their words, as following rules, they do so with perfect right.'[16]

How is this possible? How can it be *both* that 'there is no fact' as to whether a person meant something by a certain word or sign, and also it be *right to say* that the person meant such-and-such by that sign? To explain this Kripke draws a contrast between the *Tractatus* and Wittgenstein's later outlook. According to Kripke, the 'most basic idea' of the *Tractatus* is this: 'a declarative sentence gets its meaning by virtue of its *truth conditions*, by virtue of its correspondence to facts that must obtain if it is true.'[17] But this remark about the *Tractatus* contains a confusion. Kripke seems to be equating 'truth conditions' with 'correspondence with facts'. This is confirmed by other remarks of Kripke's. For example, he says: 'Now if we suppose that facts, or truth conditions, are of the essence of meaningful assertion. . . .'[18] Kripke is regarding the 'truth conditions' of propositions as meaning the same as their 'correspondence with facts'.

It is the case that in the *Tractatus* the sense of propositions is connected with their truth conditions: 'A proposition is the expression of its truth conditions.' (4.431) But truth conditions are not *facts*. Truth conditions are *possibilities* of truth or falsehood. Possibilities are not facts. The *Tractatus* emphasizes that the *sense* of a proposition is the *same* whether it is true or false. Only if it is true does it correspond with a fact. So the sense of propositions is not defined in terms of correspondence with facts, although it is defined in terms of truth conditions.[19]

According to Kripke the following important change took place in Wittgenstein's thinking: he abandoned 'truth conditions' in favour of 'assertability conditions' or 'justification conditions':

> Wittgenstein proposes a picture of language based, not on *truth conditions*, but on *assertability conditions* or *justification conditions*.[20]

We recall that 'Wittgenstein's sceptical conclusion', according to Kripke, is that 'no facts, no truth conditions, correspond to statements such as "Jones means addition by '+'."'[21] Kripke says,

> Now if we suppose that facts, or truth conditions, are of the essence of meaningful assertions, it will follow from the sceptical conclusion that assertions that anyone ever means anything are meaningless.[22]

Kripke thinks that Wittgenstein avoids this absurd outcome through 'the replacement of truth conditions by justification conditions'.[23]

> If we remain in the grip of the natural presupposition that meaningful declarative sentences must purport to correspond to facts; if this is our framework, we can only conclude that sentences attributing meaning and intention are themselves meaningless.[24]

According to Kripke, Wittgenstein's *solution* of 'the sceptical paradox' is the following:

> Wittgenstein finds a useful role in our lives for a 'language-game' that licenses, under certain conditions, assertions that someone 'means such-and-such' and that his present application of a word 'accords' with what he 'meant' in the past.[25]

> Wittgenstein's sceptical solution concedes to the sceptic that no 'truth conditions' or 'corresponding facts' in the world exist that make a statement like 'Jones, like many of us, means addition by "+"' true. Rather we should look at how such assertions are *used*.[26]

In order to appraise Kripke's interpretation, let us turn to the *Investigations*. In *PI* 136 Wittgenstein treats '"*p*" is true' as equivalent to '*p*'; and in *PI* 225 he says that the use of the word 'proposition' and the use of the word 'true' are 'interwoven'. So Wittgenstein does not disconnect the word 'true' from the words 'proposition', 'statement', or 'assertion'. The same for the word 'fact'. In ordinary speech the sentences 'The moon is full', 'It is true that the moon is full', 'It is a fact that the moon is full', are treated as logically equivalent to one another. There is no reason to think that Wittgenstein would wish to abolish these equivalences. When he criticizes, in *PI* 134, his attempt in *Tractatus* to define 'the general form of propositions' by the sentence 'This is how things are', he says that he might have said instead 'Such and such is the case', or 'This is the situation', or (one might add) 'This is the fact', or (as he adds in *PI* 136) 'This is true.'

Wittgenstein does constantly stress that when you are puzzled by the sense of a sentence, you should remind yourself of how the sentence is *used*. But this emphasis on observing the use does not mean that he withdraws from meaningful sentences the concepts of 'truth' and 'fact'. In *PI* 136 he does criticize the attempt to *explain* what a 'proposition' is by saying, 'A proposition is whatever can be true or false.' This 'explanation' is misleading because it makes it look as if *before* we know what a 'proposition' is we have an independent concept of truth and falsity, which we can use to determine what is or isn't a 'proposition'. But the situation is not like that. Our use of the word 'proposition' (or 'statement' or 'assertion') contains, *as a part of it*, the use of the words 'true' and 'false' — just as *check* is part of the concept of *the king* in chess.

Kripke says that in his second philosophy Wittgenstein replaced 'truth conditions' by 'justification conditions'. Is this correct? In the *Investigations* he does reject the idea of the *Tractatus* that there is 'a final analysis of our forms of language, and so a *single* completely resolved form of every expression' (*PI* 91). He stresses the fact that one and the same sentence is used, in different circumstances, to mean different things. In chapter 1 we considered the sentence 'He can walk.' In one set of circumstances it would mean 'He has learned to walk'; in another, 'He isn't tired'; in still another, 'He has permission to walk'; in yet another, 'His leg is healed'; and so on (see *PI* 183; *BB*, p. 114). And Wittgenstein warns us against the assumption that there is such a thing as 'the complete set of conditions' for a person's walking

(*BB*, p. 114). This implies that there are no *general* truth conditions for the sentence 'He can walk.' But it does not imply that when we are using this sentence in one of its many different possible senses, we are to avoid saying 'It is true that he can walk' or 'It is a fact that he can walk.' Wittgenstein does not cut away the notions of 'truth' and 'fact' from meaningful assertions.

In considering Kripke's impression that Wittgenstein replaced 'truth conditions' by 'justification conditions', we should bear in mind that of course there is a distinction between a person's being *justified* in saying or thinking that something is so and its *being* so. For example, there is an electrical failure in my flat and I phone the electricity company to tell them about it. I am told that they will send someone to take care of it. Within the hour a man turns up, carrying a bag of tools and wearing the badge of the electricity company. He says, 'I am from the electricity company.' I invite him in and explain what the trouble is. He says, 'I will take care of it.' I leave him and go back to my study. After a while he appears and tells me that he has to go to his lorry to fetch another tool. But he does not return. Later, I discover that I have been robbed. I call the electricity company, and they say that they had not yet sent a repair man. So here is a case where I was *justified* in thinking that the man who came was a repair man — but it turned out this wasn't true. Is Wittgenstein abolishing this distinction between justification and truth? Of course not.

Wittgenstein does often speak of one's 'having the right' to say something, or of being 'justified' in saying it. An example is in his study of the use of the expression 'Now I can go on' in the case, say, where someone has been shown the initial segment of a numerical series, and is asked to continue it. After some hesitation the pupil exclaims, 'Now I can go on!' Wittgenstein asks, 'What happened here?', and goes on to point out that *different* things might have happened (*PI* 151). One thing that might have happened is that the pupil thought of the algebraic formula of the series. Wittgenstein then remarks that the pupil's having thought of the formula, just by itself, would not give him 'the right to say' those words ('Now I can go on'). In order for him to have the *right* to say that, in order for him to be 'correctly using' those words, there would have to be such circumstances as that the pupil had learned algebra and had previously used such formulae (*PI* 179). Now it might be that even given those background circumstances, the pupil does not continue the series correctly. Would this mean that he did not have the right to say, 'Now I can go on'? Not necessarily. Perhaps he had a sudden spell of dizziness, or momentarily forgot how to apply the formula.

As a comparable case, Wittgenstein mentions this one:

Someone asks me 'Can you lift this weight?' I answer 'Yes'. Now he says 'Do it!' — and I can't. In what kind of circumstances would it count as a justification to say: 'When I answered "Yes" I *could* do it, only now I can't'? (*PI* 182)

What is Wittgenstein getting at? He is criticizing a simplistic philosophical idea about the meaning of the words 'Now I understand it', 'Now I know how to do it.' The idea is that these sentences are *reports* of the presence of a 'mental state' or 'mental occurrence'. If the mental state is there, the report is true; if not, false. Wittgenstein is here trying to overcome this philosophical picture, by showing that the criteria we use for saying 'He understands it' are more complicated 'than we are tempted to think' (*PI* 182). One aspect of this complicated grammar is a distinction between one's being *justified* in saying that a person understands something and its being *true* that he understands it. To call attention to this distinction is the reverse of abolishing it.

According to Kripke, Wittgenstein holds that there are no 'truth conditions' or 'corresponding facts' that make an assertion, such as 'Jones means addition by "+"' true. Instead, Wittgenstein's view is that 'we should look at how such assertions are *used*.'[27] Now in his treatment of philosophical problems about meaning, Wittgenstein does ask us to reflect on how we *use* sentences like 'He means (or "meant") such-and-such': but this certainly does not imply that Wittgenstein holds that it is never *true*, or never a *fact*, that a person meant such-and-such. Wittgenstein criticizes the philosophical idea that a person's meaning such-and-such consists in the occurrence of some 'mental event or state'. He tries to draw us away from this philosophical picture by getting us to think of the various criteria we use in everyday life for saying 'He means such-and-such.' If there ever was a question as to whether some person means addition by '+', we might settle it to our satisfaction by observing how he uses '+' in calculations; or we might settle it by asking him. These criteria for 'He means . . .' carry no implication about the presence of a 'mental event or state'.

Readers of Wittgenstein often get the impression that he *evades* the real issues. They want to know what it *is* for a person to *mean* something — and what *imagining* is, and *thinking*, and *remembering*, and *understanding*, etc. But Wittgenstein only speaks about how various expressions of language are used! So he doesn't go into the question of the *nature* of these things — of *what happens* when one means something, or understands it, etc. It occurs to me that perhaps Kripke feels this, and that this is what inclines him to think that Wittgenstein does not address himself to the *truth*, or the facts, but only to how words and sentences are *used*.

Wittgenstein was well aware of this possible response to his philosophical work. In the *Investigations* he says:

> One ought to ask, not what images are or what happens when one imagines something, but how the word 'imagining' is used. But that does not mean that I want to talk only about words. For the question as to the nature of imagining is as much about the word 'imagining' as my question is. And I am only saying that this question is not to be decided — neither for the person who does the imagining, nor for anyone else — by pointing; nor by the description of any occurrence. The first question also asks for a word to be explained; but it makes us expect a wrong kind of answer. (*PI* 370)

The question 'What is the nature of imagining?' could be expressed as the question 'What does the word "imagining" stand for?'; therefore it is asking for an explanation of the meaning of a word. But this question starts us off in the wrong direction. It leads us to think that one can answer it by inward pointing, or by describing something that occurs when one imagines something. But the question 'How is the word "imagining" used?' *is* about the meaning of the word; and it does *not* steer us into those dead-ends.

Describing what occurred when one imagined something, could mean just describing what one imagined. But *that* description could not remove this perplexity about the meaning of the word 'imagining'. Wittgenstein makes the same point with a different example:

> One would like to ask: 'What is it like — what happens — when one calculates in one's head?' — And in a particular case the answer may be: 'First I add 17 and 18, then I subtract 39. . . .' But that is not the answer to our question. What is called calculating in one's head is not explained by *such* an answer. (*PI* 369)

There can be a philosophical perplexity about the *meaning* of 'calculating in one's head'. If you asked someone, 'What went on, what took place, when you did that calculation in your head?', a straightforward answer would be an account of the steps he took in that calculation. But this reply would do nothing to diminish your perplexity about the notion of calculating in one's head.

What *would* remove this perplexity? A description of the circumstances in which *we say* (have 'a right to say', are 'justified' in saying) that someone has 'learned to calculate in his head'. What are these circumstances? First of all, that the person has learned to calculate orally or in writing: we know what in this case the teaching, correcting, testing, look like. In the second place, a person who has satisfied us that he is able to do calculations in this way, one day may give the right answer to a problem of calculation, but *without* doing the calculation in writing or orally. We ask him, 'How did you do it?', and he answers: 'I did it in my mind', or 'in my head.' (Perhaps he *points* to his head.) We accept this answer: but we would not accept it *if* he had been *unable* to learn to calculate in writing or orally.

The foregoing is a partial description of the circumstances in which we are prepared to say, 'He did it in his head.' This description shows that the sense of this sentence is connected with the ability to calculate outwardly. As Wittgenstein says:

> Ask yourself: would it be conceivable that someone learned to calculate in his head without ever calculating in writing or orally? — 'Learning it' will mean: it being brought about that one can do it. Only the question arises, what will count as a criterion for being able to do it? (*PI* 385)

One sometimes hears of people who are morons, but have extraordinary mathematical powers. They are unable to do quite easy calculations, but they can determine with great rapidity, 'in their heads', whether a large number is a prime number. There is a temptation to think that they obtain these astonishing solutions by 'incredibly swift mental calculations': 'for how else could they do it?' But this *cannot be said*: it goes against the grammar of 'calculating in the head', for these people cannot learn to calculate.

Normal people learn to calculate, and also learn to calculate in their heads. Does Wittgenstein deny, as Kripke would seem to think, that there are no 'truth conditions' or 'corresponding facts' for the statement 'He did the calculation in his head'? Of course not. If you have asserted 'He calculated the answer in his head', it would be redundant to add 'It is true that he did', or 'It is a fact that he did.' These additions would not help to remove anyone's perplexity about the meaning of the expression 'calculating in one's head'. But describing the circumstances that are presupposed when we apply this expression, does illuminate its meaning by linking it with the ordinary procedures of training someone to calculate orally or in writing.

Philosophical perplexity about 'the mind' and 'the mental' erupts in specific questions, such as 'What is it to *mean* something, or to *suddenly remember* something, or to *imagine* something, or to calculate a number *in one's head*, and so on?' Our first inclination is to ask, 'What happens, what takes place, in these cases?' When we pursue this question with one of these concepts, we find that different things take place, none of which gives us what we were seeking for. We are then drawn into the blind alley of concluding that the remembering, the calculating in one's head, and so on, are just particular mental states or mental events, whose nature and distinguishing characteristics we are unable to further specify. If, however, we follow Wittgenstein's lead and replace our original questions with the question 'What are the circumstances we presuppose when we *say* of someone, "He suddenly remembered where he had left his hat", or that "He calculated the number in his head"', then we obtain a fruitful answer: one that clarifies the puzzling concept.

In making this replacement Wittgenstein is not *evading* 'the real issue'. For the real issue is our perplexity about the meaning of an expression of everyday language. It is precisely to this that Wittgenstein addresses himself.

I wish to return to Wittgenstein's remark that *following a rule* is a *practice* (*PI* 202). The meaning of this remark is difficult to grasp. It is not surprising that there is a controversy about how to interpret it. As previously mentioned, Kripke takes Wittgenstein to be holding that there cannot be such a thing as following a rule unless there is a community whose members agree in their responses to a rule. But some readers of Wittgenstein, e.g. Colin McGinn, have sharply criticized Kripke for this interpretation. McGinn says the following:

> Let us re-examine 198—202 in which Wittgenstein is putting forward his positive view and opposing it to the view he rejects.

The most glaring feature of these sections in the present connection is that the words 'custom', 'practice' and 'use' are never qualified with 'social' or 'community' — and 'social custom/practice' is not *pleonastic*. Surely Wittgenstein would have inserted these qualifying adjectives if he really meant to maintain a social conception of rule-following, especially in view of the fact that the introduction of the community is taken to be a surprising result of signal importance — as sharply conflicting with what we antecedently expect. And if we look for a gloss on the use of 'custom' etc. we find . . . the insistence that rules must be followed on more than one *occasion* — i.e. the existence of rules depends upon 'regular use'. Wittgenstein does use 'custom' and 'practice' to suggest the idea of a multiplicity, but it is a multiplicity of *instances* of rule-following not of *persons* who follow the rules. And this is part and parcel of Wittgenstein's general thesis that meaning is use: a sign has meaning only in virtue of being (repeatedly) used in a certain way. *This thesis does not in itself carry any suggestion that meaning is inconceivable in social isolation.*[28]

I am saying only that Wittgenstein does not hold that the very notion of a rule of language must needs be explicated in social terms — that we cannot make sense of rule-following on the part of a given individual unless we relate that individual's behaviour to the behaviour of some community of rule-followers.[29]

And McGinn adds that 'it is well that Wittgenstein did not hold such a view, because it is clearly wrong.'[30]

McGinn is of course right in saying that an individual person can have a practice that is not a *common* practice. A man might have the practice of taking a warm bath every evening. This is something *he* regularly does: perhaps no other person follows this practice. According to McGinn the stress that Wittgenstein places on a *practice* does not imply a *common* practice, but at most something that an individual does habitually or 'as a rule'. Wittgenstein's conception that following a rule requires a practice only means, according to McGinn, that for an individual to follow a rule he must do the same thing *repeatedly*. I have already said that I agree with Kripke's 'social' interpretation. McGinn's 'individualistic' interpretation would do away with much of what is novel and important in Wittgenstein's post-*Tractatus* thinking.

Most of us, when thinking philosophically, tend to suppose that if a human infant grew up, by some strange chance, in complete isolation from any human society, this human being *could*, in his solitary existence, have many thoughts; and *could* devise a language, a system of signs, which he used to record observations, make predictions, set down rules of action for his own guidance. Wittgenstein rejects this natural assumption. His position does seem surprising, even shocking – as McGinn says, 'sharply conflicting with what we antecedently expect'. That this is, none the less, Wittgenstein's position is evident from many remarks. In the following I will bring together some of these remarks, although this will involve some repetition.

Let us go back to paragraph 1 of the *Investigations*. There Wittgenstein addresses himself to Augustine's account of how he thinks he *learned the names* of various things. Augustine presents the matter as if he understood that the adults around him *meant* to be indicating a certain object, and were *naming* it by the sound they uttered when they turned toward it. Augustine was apparently assuming that before he had learned *any* language he already knew what a *name* is, and what *meaning* something by a gesture is — and also that he made *observations* and drew *conclusions* about which things were *meant* by which *names*.

Wittgenstein criticizes this account in *PI* 32, saying that Augustine presents the matter as if he 'already had a language', and as if he 'could already *think*'. Wittgenstein is certainly holding that it makes no sense to attribute those concepts and that thinking to a child *before* it has learned any language. This rejection of Augustine's account is, *a fortiori*, a rejection of the assumption that a human being, who had lived a solitary existence from birth, *could* have any conception of what a *rule* is, or a system of *signs*, or a *language* — or *could* invent a system of signs that he employed according to rules.

In *PI* 198 Wittgenstein says that 'a person goes by a sign-post only in so far as there exists a regular use of sign-posts, a custom.' This surely implies that someone who had been always isolated from mankind could not be said to follow a sign-post. Only someone who had been a member of a community in which there was the *institution* of sign-posts, could be said to *take his direction* from a sign-post. In speaking of 'a regular use of sign-posts, a custom', Wittgenstein plainly is *not* talking about an isolated individual 'repeatedly' doing something.

In *PI* 206 Wittgenstein says:

> Following a rule is analogous to obeying an order. We are trained to do so; we react to an order in a particular way. But what if one

person reacts in one way and another in another to the order and the training? Which one is right?

The answer pretty clearly is that the one is right who reacts in the *normal* way. If there was *no* normal response to the training and the order, there would be no right or wrong response. Where there is no training and so no 'normal response' (as would be the case with an individual who was always isolated) it would have no sense to speak of a right or wrong response to a rule. The same point is implied in *PI* 201, where Wittgenstein is arguing that an action cannot be an example of following a rule unless there is a practice that 'is exhibited in what we call "following the rule" and "going against it" from case to case'. As I said earlier in this chapter, this reference to 'what we call . . .' is a reference to a community-agreement.

In many passages Wittgenstein stresses the point that a language can exist only if there is *agreement* between persons in their applications of the language.

> Disputes do not break out (among mathematicians, say) over the question whether a rule has been followed or not. People don't come to blows over it, for example. That is part of the framework on which the working of our language is based. (*PI* 240)

> There can be a dispute over what the correct result of a calculation is (say, a long addition). But such disputes are rare and of short duration. They can be decided, as we say, 'with certainty'.
> Mathematicians do not in general quarrel over the result of a calculation. (This is an important fact.) — If it were otherwise . . . then our concept of 'mathematical certainty' would not exist. (*PI*, p. 225)

These remarks about the importance of agreement can be misconstrued.

> 'So you are saying that human agreement decides what is true and what is false?' — It is what human beings *say* that is true and false; and they agree in the language they use. That is not agreement in opinions but in form of life. (*PI* 241)

In stating that *agreement* is part of the framework on which language is based, Wittgenstein plainly means agreement between different persons, not a solitary person's 'agreement with himself' — whatever that is supposed to mean. Different persons who have had the same initial training in arithmetic agree overwhelmingly that *this* is 'adding' and *that* is 'subtracting'. Without that kind of agreement there would be no such thing as calculating, not even calculating incorrectly.

It is the same with names of colours.

> Does it make sense to say that people generally agree in their judgements of colour? What would it be like for them not to? — One man would say a flower was red which another called blue, and so on. — But what right should we have to call these people's words 'red' and 'blue' *our* colour-words? (*PI*, p. 226)

Thus, it can be misleading to say that people 'generally agree' in their applications of colour-words — for that makes it look as if they *could* widely disagree. But overwhelming agreement is *internal* to the concept of employing names of colours: so much so that without it the words could not be called 'names of colours'. There can be disagreement — but it has to be *the exception*, not the rule.

Here we can see in a different light the significance of the remark: 'To understand a sentence means to understand a language. To understand a language means to master a technique.' (*PI* 199) One understands the sentence 'The sum of these numbers is 982' only if one understands the language of addition. One understands this language only if one has become competent in the technique of adding. One understands the sentence 'This cloth is purple' only if one has become competent in naming colours. For our present purpose, the important point is that there could not be these 'languages', or any 'techniques' of applying their terms, unless the different people who had received the same initial training went on to mostly agree in their particular judgements.

The fact that Wittgenstein constantly thinks of the different uses of words as analogous to different *games* shows that on his view it could not be right to attribute a language to a being who had always lived in isolation. In an apparently general remark about language-games, Wittgenstein says:

> But isn't the agreement of human beings essential to the game? Must not anybody who learns it first know the meaning of 'same', and doesn't this presuppose agreement? (*Z* 428)

In learning any technique (whether a technique of building a wall, of painting a house, of adding numbers, of making a cake, of playing a card-game) one must learn what *is called* 'doing the same' in that activity. On Wittgenstein's view, to say that a person is following a rule presupposes that there is in existence a regular way of acting which is taught and enforced — an established technique. Someone who had never encountered human society could not be said to be conforming to a technique — or even *intending* to do so.

> An intention is embedded in the situation, in human customs and institutions. If the technique of the game of chess did not exist, I could not intend to play a game of chess. (*PI* 337)

In his *Remarks on the Foundations of Mathematics*, Wittgenstein says something striking (and amusing) about the necessity for agreement between persons:

> Could there be arithmetic without agreement of those who calculate?
> Could a solitary man calculate? Could a solitary man follow a rule?
> Are these questions somewhat similar to this one: 'Can a solitary person carry on a trade?' (*RFM*, p. 349)

The point is that just as carrying on a trade presupposes a community, so does doing arithmetic and following a rule.

I think I have adduced a sufficient number of passages to show that for Wittgenstein the concept of a rule presupposes a community within which a common agreement in actions fixes the meaning of a rule. There is a strong inclination to think that this view is wrong. It goes against the 'intuitions' of philosophers. This can influence the way one reads Wittgenstein. One feels that he is too intelligent to hold such an obviously false view; and one tries to find a different meaning for his remarks about rules.

I will argue, very briefly, that Wittgenstein's view is correct. Suppose there was a human being who had lived from birth on an island in complete isolation from other people. Suppose that we were able to observe him from a distance. We might notice various uniformities in his behaviour. For example, he goes swimming every day. Would we have any justification for thinking that he is following a rule? Suppose that one day he did not go swimming: would we have any justification for thinking he had broken a rule? If a dog howls at night when and only when there is a full moon, should we conclude that the dog is following a rule? Regularity in behaviour, by itself, does not exhibit rule-following.

It is difficult to reflect on the example of a human being who is always isolated without, unwittingly, endowing him in imagination with thoughts and ideas that are rooted in the learning of a common language. One imagines that he might keep records, make predictions, devise sign-posts, form plans and carry them out, and so on. For example, McGinn conceives of an isolated human being, whom he names Romulus. McGinn raises the question of

> whether the very *notion* of grasping a rule requires sometime membership of a community of rule-followers. And it seems to me that it does not require this: I find it perfectly possible to imagine that Romulus, upon reaching the age of reason, hits upon the idea of distributing sign-posts around his island as an *aide-mémoire*. He wants to avoid the marshes, so he writes an arrow in the sand and undertakes to walk in the direction of its head when he comes across it in future; he follows his rule correctly in the future if he conforms his actions to his original intentions in respect of the arrow; and he may discover on occasion that he has followed his rule *in*correctly when, misremembering his original intention, he finds himself wallowing in the marsh (he mistakenly thought that his original intention was to follow the *tail* of the arrow). Nor do I see any conceptual obstacle to his introducing properly linguistic signs for his own use, e.g. to keep records of the weather: all he needs is a good reason to introduce the signs and the intelligence to operate with them. That he has never had contact with other rule-followers does not seem to me to put a logical wall between him and the activity of following rules.[31]

McGinn imagines that Romulus 'hits upon the idea' of employing directional signs to guide him. Now how are we to conceive of what went on when this 'idea' occurred to Romulus? Did he *say* to himself, 'In order to avoid the marsh I need signs to guide me'? But presumably Romulus has no language. So did he have that thought, without words? But whatever constellation of wordless images or feelings that Romulus had, by virtue of *what* would that constellation have the same meaning as the foregoing sentence? Why couldn't that constellation be translated into a sentence with a different meaning? Nothing could justify one translation rather than another.

Nor could that thought be displayed in the *behaviour* of Romulus. In human beings, as well as animals, surprise, fright, joy, and also thinking are often exhibited in behaviour. ('The dog thinks he is going to be taken for a walk'; 'The cat thinks there is a mouse in the rubbish bin.') In this way Romulus too could exhibit desire, fear, uncertainty, and primitive thinking. But nothing in his behaviour could display the thought 'In order to avoid the marsh I need signs to guide me.' This is like Wittgenstein's example:

> A dog believes his master is at the door. But can he also believe his master will come the day after tomorrow? (*PI*, p. 174)

Only a creature who had mastered the use of the words 'today', 'tomorrow', and 'the day after tomorrow' could have this belief. Only if Romulus had mastered the use of directional signs could he have the 'idea' of setting up sign-posts to guide him around his island.

McGinn says of Romulus:

> He writes an arrow in the sand and undertakes to walk in the direction of its head when he comes across it in future.[32]

What could Romulus do that would amount to his *undertaking* this? This reminds us of Wittgenstein's remark:

> It might be said: whoever gives himself a private explanation of a word, must inwardly *undertake* to use the word in such-and-such a way. And how does he undertake that? Shall I assume that he invents the technique of this employment of the word; or that he found it ready-made? (*PI* 262)

Romulus must be deemed to give himself a 'private' explanation of the use of this mark in the sand, since he is and always has been in complete isolation from any community of sign-users. And he must be deemed to give this explanation to himself 'inwardly', since he is alone *and* has no language in which he could give the explanation, even to himself, 'outwardly'. How does Romulus undertake to follow a sign in the future? As things are with us, a person can silently undertake to do something — for example, to paint his house. But this makes sense only because he understands the sense of the words 'painting my house'. Romulus could silently undertake to walk in the direction of the arrow-head, only if he understood the sense of the words 'walking in the direction of the arrow-head'.

It would seem that McGinn has magically endowed Romulus with the understanding of full-blown language. Either Romulus has to invent by himself the use of a sign, or he has an innate knowledge of what it is to follow a sign. In either case, what could show that Romulus was taking his direction from the shape he dug in the sand? A dog might dig a furrow in the sand and then gallop off in a certain direction. Even if the dog went from the furrow in the same direction every day, would this show that he was *taking his direction from* the furrow? Perhaps when the dog dug the furrow its intention was to go in the *opposite* direction — but thereafter it always *misremembered* its original intention!

One might admit that it is nonsense to talk this way about a *dog* — but feel that it is unfair to put Romulus on the same level. Why so? Romulus and the dog *are* on the same level in respect to understanding how to use a sign. Nothing in the behaviour of either would be an exhibition of being-guided-by-a-sign.

McGinn, appealing to his 'intuitions of logical possibility',[33] says it is a 'seeming possibility that God could have created a single rule-follower alone in the universe for all time'.[34] This is like saying that it is conceivable that God should suddenly give to a parrot the ability to say things to itself (*PI* 346). One feels that to deny this is to deny God's omnipotence. But that is not how it is. The question is whether the notion of a solitary rule-follower *makes sense*. God's omnipotence is irrelevant to that question.

Neither in the case of Romulus nor in that of the 'single rule-follower alone in the universe' could one even say that 'it *seems to him* that he is following a rule' — for this would be to grant him an understanding of the notion of following a rule.

In real life we have criteria for saying of someone that he is following a rule, or that he thinks he is following a rule. This is because the idea of a rule is embedded in an environment of teaching, testing, correcting — within a community where there is an agreement in acting in the way that is called 'following the rule'. To withdraw that environment is to withdraw the concept of following a rule.

Throughout his lengthy study in the *Investigations* of the concept of following a rule, Wittgenstein is dealing with a philosophical perplexity that is expressed in the question 'How is anyone *able* to follow a rule?' What is desired is an *explanation* of this ability. Now one might think that a satisfactory explanation is ready at hand, namely, one acquires this ability through *instruction*. In *PI* 208 there is a brief description of how one would teach a pupil to pick out the same shapes, same lengths, same colours; get him to continue an ornamental pattern, or a numerical series; give him

examples and exercises; encourage him, correct him; let him go
on, or hold him back; and so on.

But the *philosophical* puzzlement is not satisfied by this
reminder of what the teaching is like. There is a feeling that there
must be *more* to it than that, for the understanding goes deeper:
it reaches *beyond* all of the examples and exercises (*PI* 209). So
the problem remains: how does the pupil *know* how to continue a
pattern or a series by himself? (*PI* 211) What guides him, what
tells him, how to go on?

In the attempt to answer this question various inclinations,
more or less subtle, put in an appearance. Wittgenstein explores
them, one by one.

One of the strongest of these inclinations is to think that one is
guided by the 'meaning' of the rule. Kripke gave expression to
this idea in saying, in reference to addition, that 'something in his
mind — the meaning he attaches to the plus sign' *instructs* him
what to do in all future cases of adding. Wittgenstein brings out
the mythological character of this notion by describing it as the
idea that 'your mind as it were flew ahead and took all the steps
before you physically arrived at this or that one.' (*PI* 188) Another
criticism is put by the question: 'But if something of this sort
really were the case, how would it help me?' (*PI* 219) The point, I
think, is the same as the one about the sign-post in *PI* 85 ('Where
is it said which way I am to follow it?'); and also in the example of
a use of a table or chart in *PI* 86, where the table contains a
column of signs and a column of pictures of objects — but then it
is noted that the signs and the pictures could be correlated *in
different ways*. Going back to the question of *PI* 219: even if the
future steps were already taken in my mind, so that as it were all I
had to do was to *copy* them when I took the physical steps — still
there could be *different ways of copying*. Thus, the myth of the
steps being already taken in my mind could not, even if true,
solve the question of how I am able to follow a rule.

A second inclination is to appeal to *intuition*, to say 'At each
step in continuing a series or a pattern, I must have an intuition.'
The reply is short: 'And how do I know that it doesn't mislead
me? For if it can guide me right, it can also guide me wrong.' (*PI*
213)

A third inclination is to say that from the initial segment of a
series I *perceive* what continuing in *the same way* is, and so I
continue it in *the same way*. This idea is hinted at in the remark

'But isn't *the same* at least the same?' (*PI* 215) The reply indicated in *PI* 215 is that I cannot appeal to 'the same' in this abstract way. I need a criterion for what 'the same' is: but the criterion for doing the same is nothing other than following the rule. Hence, appealing to a perception of *the same* cannot *explain* how I am able to follow a rule. When considered apart from any particular rule, it makes no sense to ask whether in writing down the series 1, 3, 5, 7, 9, . . . one is doing the *same* thing each time, or something different (*PI* 226).

A fourth inclination is to think that one perceives, in a segment of a series, a finely drawn design, which only needs the addition of 'and so on' to reach to infinity (*PI* 229). In *Zettel* this is put as the idea that what one perceives in this way is not just the algebraic formula, which could be written, but something 'ethereal' for which the formula is only the *expression* (*Z* 276). But of course this is not the normal experience of someone who is expanding a numerical series in accordance with its algebraic formula. No one would entertain this idea — unless he was searching for an *explanation* of how one can continue the series in the right way.

A fifth inclination is to think that a rule or a pattern 'intimates' ('suggests', 'says') to me how I am to follow it. An inner voice tells me: 'Go *this* way.' (*PI* 222, 232) Wittgenstein makes clear how sharply this following an inner voice differs from following a rule. In so far as someone was heeding an inner voice, I could not require him to follow the rule or the pattern *as I do* (*PI* 232).

In treating these various attempts to explain how one can follow a rule, Wittgenstein is showing what following a rule *is* by showing what it is *not*. His handling of these pseudo-explanations is destructive — but at the same time illuminating! We see that there is *no* explanation of our ability to follow rules — other than the pedestrian but true explanation that we received a certain *training*.

Wittgenstein terminates this sequence of paragraphs on following a rule by connecting it with the attempt to explain how one is able to apply *a word* correctly:

> How is he to know what colour he is to pick out when he hears 'red'? — Quite simple: he is to take the colour whose image occurs to him when he hears the word. — But how is he to know which colour it is 'whose image occurs to him'? Is a further criterion needed for that? (*PI* 239)

This criticism is easy to grasp. The proffered explanation opens up an infinite regress of explanations. If one prevents the regress by saying, 'Well, he *just knows* what colour it is whose image occurs to him!', the reply is: 'If he can "just know" *that*, so can he "just know" that the colour of this book is red!'

The philosophical puzzlement over how one is able to follow a rule is repeated in the puzzlement over how one knows how to apply a word. In both cases the ability 'reaches beyond' the original teaching and examples. We go on, all agreeing, following rules and applying words in new cases — without guidance. Other than the past training, there is no explanation. It is an aspect of the form of life of human beings. It is our nature. To try to explain it is like trying to explain why dogs bark.

CHAPTER 10

Mind and Brain

We may say of a person that he 'has a big heart', or that he is 'warmhearted'. We should be astonished if someone thought we were talking about the size or temperature of a physical organ. For we were saying something about that *person* — that *he* is generous, or compassionate, or affectionate. We speak of someone as having 'a good brain', or 'an acute mind', or a 'dull', or 'superficial', or 'well-stocked' mind. Here again we are saying something about a person — that *he* does or can think acutely, or is dull witted, or thinks superficially, or is well informed.

In philosophy there is perplexity and confusion about *mind*. Some of this seems to stem from assuming that the noun 'mind' is the name of a *thing*. Descartes said explicitly that the mind is 'a thinking thing'. No doubt he would allow that when you speak of someone as 'having an acute mind', you are saying something about that person, namely, that he does or can think acutely. But on Descartes's view the statement 'He thinks acutely' would mean: 'He has a mind that thinks acutely.' The sentence 'He thinks acutely' has an acceptable sense, but a *derivative* one. In its *primary* sense the phrase 'thinks acutely' applies to that thing, or 'substance', the person's *mind*, and only in a secondary or derivative sense to the person himself.

Once it is assumed that a mind is an entity that thinks or has thoughts, the question arises as to *where it is located*? Descartes held that a mind is an immaterial or incorporeal thing and therefore it does not, strictly speaking, *have* a location. It has been generally assumed, however, that even if the mind of a human being does not have a spatial location, it stands in a close relation to a thing that does have a spatial location, namely, that person's brain. In the history of philosophy there have been many theories about the relationship between mind and brain. But it is fair to say that the two most popular theories are, first, that there is a *parallelism* between mind and brain (called 'psychophysical parallelism'); and, second, that the relationship is that of *identity* (called 'identity-theory').

According to the viewpoint of parallelism, for each thought, sensation, or feeling there is a corresponding event, process, or state in or of the brain (or central nervous system). For each difference in a thought or sensation, there is a matching difference in the corresponding brain-occurrence. It should be mentioned that even if a philosopher does not regard the word 'mind' as a term that designates a thing that thinks, he may still adopt the doctrine of parallelism. A thought, decision, or intention is conceived of as a non-material event or state, to which there corresponds a brain-event or brain-state.

Complications about *causality* enter into parallelism. Some proponents of parallelism hold that mental events or states have *no* part to play as *causes* of human behaviour. The burden of causality is carried solely by the corresponding brain-processes. On this view (called 'epiphenomenalism') if I decide to go for a walk, this decision is caused by the brain-process that corresponds to the decision. If I do go for a walk, that action is caused by neural processes: neither my decision nor my desire have anything to do with it.

In present-day philosophy of mind there is a movement away from parallelism towards identity-theory. Thinking of something, meaning something by a word or gesture, deciding to do something, remembering something — all of these *are* neural events or processes. On this view the human mind is, as Descartes held, 'a thinking thing': but, contrary to Descartes, the entity that thinks or has thoughts is not a non-material substance, but is the physical brain. It has a spatial location — inside the skull. The slogan of this view is: 'The mind is the brain.' One can speak of a *person* as thinking, remembering, deciding, and so on: but, as in the case of Descartes, such remarks have to be understood in a secondary or derivative sense. In the *primary* sense, thoughts, sensations, desires are occurrences in or states of a person's brain.

John Searle is one of the philosophers who thinks that the mental states of a person are states of the person's brain. In a recent book he says: 'If one knew the principles on which the brain worked one could infer that it was in a state of thirst or having a visual experience.'[1] Is saying that a brain is 'in a state of thirst' supposed to mean that it is *thirsty*? And what would *that* mean? The predicate 'thirsty' is applied by us to people and animals. Sometimes it is applied in an extended sense to plants — as when we say 'This plant is a thirsty one', meaning that it needs frequent watering. What would it mean to say that a brain is 'thirsty'?

The fact that to say 'My brain is thirsty' is a *comical* remark, is philosophically significant. It shows that the word 'thirsty' is being grossly misapplied. The same is true of the remark 'My brain is having a strange visual experience.' *People* have visual experiences, not brains.

A person who has just learned of some great good news may be filled with joy. His face, his gestures, his speech, radiate joy. He may even dance with joy. Is his brain joyful? Does *it* vibrate with joy? When we say that *he* is joyful, are we using language in a secondary and derivative sense? Is it his brain that is joyful, in the primary and fundamental sense of this word? The truth of course is that it is complete nonsense to apply the terms 'joyful', or 'thirsty', or 'visual experience' to a brain.

One of Wittgenstein's most profound insights, largely ignored in present-day philosophy, is that

> Only of a living human being and what resembles (behaves like) a living human being, can one say: it has sensations; it sees; is blind; hears; is deaf; is conscious or unconscious. (*PI* 281)

The application of these terms has its roots in the paradigm of a living human being. It is only in the expressive human face and eyes, in the gestures, posture, and actions of a human being, in human speech, that we can perceive in their fullest form, consciousness and thought, desire, decision, fear or anger. We apply some of these psychological terms to animals — but the further we go down in the animal scale, the greater the distance from the human paradigm, the more difficult it is to find a foothold for these terms.

A child playing with a doll will in imagination attribute thoughts and speech to the doll. It will be easier for the child to do this with a doll than with a piece of string. Why? Because a doll is an imitation of the human form.

In an interesting passage Wittgenstein considers the supposition that a *chair* might be thinking to itself:

The chair is thinking to itself: . . . Where? In one of its parts? Or outside its body; in the air around it? But then what is the difference between this chair's saying something to itself and another one's doing so, next to it? — But then how is it with a man: where does *he* say things to himself? How does it come about that this question seems senseless; and that no specification of a place is necessary except that just this man is speaking to himself? Whereas the question *where* the chair is talking to itself seems to demand an answer. — The reason is: we want to know *how* the chair is supposed to be like a human being; whether, for instance, the head is at the top of the back, and so on. (*PI* 361)

A child playing with a chair would find it easier to attribute thoughts to it in imagination, if it drew a face on the back of the chair.

One of the more startling conjectures of those who identify mind with brain is that if the brain of a human being could be removed from the body, kept alive in a chemical vat and stimulated with electrical impulses, that brain could have beliefs, desires, sensations, and intentions. John Searle says:

The brain is all we have for the purpose of representing the world to ourselves and everything we can use must be inside the brain. Each of our beliefs must be possible for a being who is a brain in a vat because each of us is precisely a brain in a vat; the vat is a skull and the 'messages' coming in are coming in by way of impacts on the nervous system.[2]

The world is represented to us in history books and maps, drawings and diagrams, newspapers, novels, paintings, plays and music. None of these is 'inside the brain'. Searle is so carried away by his philosophical picture that he has forgotten what *representations* are.

And what sense can there be in ascribing *beliefs* to a brain in a vat? Let us imagine a typical human scene. A family is about to sit down together for lunch, but it is discovered that there is no bread. One of the family volunteers to run out to a neighbouring bakery to fetch a loaf of bread. There is no difficulty in ascribing to *him* the belief that bread is needed and the intention to fetch it. No difficulty — for he is one person among others, participating with them in many activities, sharing a common language in which needs, desires, thoughts, beliefs, intentions, are expressed and are linked to consequences in behaviour. Because of this he can realize that bread is needed, declare his intention to get it, and act accordingly. Now with a *brain* all of this is stripped away: it is not a human being; it does not have a face or limbs; it cannot see, hear, speak; it cannot exhibit surprise, desire, intention, belief; it cannot look, move, gesture, act; it does not share a language with others. It makes as little sense to ascribe experiences, wishes, thoughts, beliefs, to a brain as to a mushroom.

Searle says that each of us *is* a brain in a vat, the vat being one's skull. Now if you *are* your brain then you are inside your own skull. You cannot walk or talk or see your friends. Searle says that you can receive 'messages'. But in that predicament, who wants messages?

Searle's idea is amusing — but at the same time one feels dismayed by the fact that an intelligent philosopher could assert such a view in all seriousness. It is a symptom of a grave disarray in the philosophy of mind.

The identity of mind with brain is endorsed by many psychologists as well as philosophers. For example, the well-known psychologist D. O. Hebb says:

> There are two theories of mind, speaking very generally. One is animistic, a theory that the body is inhabited by an entity — the mind or soul — that is quite different from it, having nothing in common with bodily processes. The second theory is physiological or mechanistic; it assumes that mind is a bodily process, an activity of the brain. Modern psychology works with this latter theory only.[3]

It is probable that thousands of college students are taught that mind is brain. But, fortunately, we do not have to choose between these 'two theories of mind'. The thing which perceives, thinks, imagines is neither a non-corporeal entity that 'inhabits' the body, nor a brain — but a living human being.

It is true that mankind commonly ascribes thoughts and desires to persons who have died, to God, and to immaterial spirits. But this is a *secondary* employment of these psychological concepts. To call it 'secondary' is *not* to disparage it. What is meant is a logical point. The employment of the psychological concepts that are taught and learned *first* is their application to living people. The primary use of these concepts could exist without this secondary use — but not the other way round.

What ideas produce the conception that mind is brain? It would be too much of an undertaking to try to give an account of all of the sources of this conception. But one notion that plays a prominent role is that whatever is 'mental' is 'inner'. David Armstrong is a prominent advocate of the view that 'the mind is simply the central nervous system, or, less accurately but more epigrammatically, the mind is simply the brain.'[4] Armstrong says:

> It is completely natural to speak of the mind as 'in' the body, and to speak of mental processes as 'inner' processes. Now 'in' is primarily a spatial word.[5]

A subsequent move is 'to identify these inner states with physico-chemical states of the brain'.[6]

Philosophers have got into the bad habit of referring to the instantiations of *all* psychological concepts as 'mental states'. Thus, thoughts, sensations, emotions, beliefs, intentions — even physical pains — are called 'mental states'. Our actual use of the expression 'mental state' is much narrower than that. A prolonged depression is called a mental state: but certainly not the pain of a twisted ankle; or the thought that it will probably rain this afternoon; or the intention to order seats for the opera.

Leaving this confusion aside, let us consider the notion that *all* thoughts, sensations, moods, impressions, intentions, and so on are 'inner'. A little reflection will show that this is not how we speak. A tickling sensation on one's wrist, produced by a fly, would not be called an 'inner' sensation; nor would the smarting of a slight cut on a finger. A physical pain deep in the chest might be called an 'inner' pain, and also a pain in the head caused by an infected ear: but many physical pains are not 'inner' pains.

Are all thoughts 'inner thoughts'? No. When we speak of 'inner thoughts' we mean thoughts that are not *disclosed*. If a person does not reveal his thoughts to me on a certain topic. I may say: 'I don't know what his inner thoughts on this subject are.' I would not say *that* of the thoughts he had frankly stated to me. I may have occasion to say of someone, 'I don't know what is going on in his mind': but in many cases not. I will say this of a person who is secretive about his intentions, but not of one who speaks of them openly and candidly.

People often do arithmetical calculations in their minds or, as we say, 'in their heads'. Are all calculations done in the head? Certainly not. Someone who laboriously worked out a compli-cated multiplication on paper, did not do it 'in his head'. This is not how this expression is used. One may be inclined to say: 'He must have done the calculation in his head *as well as* on paper. Surely he would not have been *able* to do it on paper unless he had done it in his head!' What a peculiar idea! In writing out the calculation, was he *copying* the calculation that he did in his head? Was the outward calculation *guided* by an inward calculation? Then what guided the inward calculation? To avoid an infinite regress one has to say that nothing guided *it*. But if one has to *stop*, why not stop with the calculation on paper? And the *explanation* of his being *able* to calculate would simply be that he learned it in school.

There are people who are unable to calculate in their heads. Most of us cannot do complex arithmetical calculations in that way. There is a philosophical temptation to think that calculating in one's head comes *first*, and that calculating on paper or aloud is derivative from it. But, as pointed out in chapter 9, the exact reverse is the case. We do not say of someone that he does calculations in his head, unless he has learned to calculate in writing or aloud. This is where the logical priority is.

'Calculating in one's head' is one of those expressions that seem to have been deliberately invented to mislead philosophers. It looks as if 'in one's head' must mean, in one's brain. So at least some calculations literally occur in the brain. But if we don't just look at the words but consider the circumstances in which they are used, we see that nothing is implied about an occurrence in the brain. We don't even understand the sentence 'He calculates in his brain', unless it just means that he calculates 'in his head'. And we don't say *this* of someone who has not learned to calculate 'outwardly'. To think that calculating in one's head means that calculations occur in the brain, is a nice illustration of Wittgenstein's remark:

> When we do philosophy we are like savages, primitive people, who hear the expressions of civilized men, misinterpret them, and then draw the queerest conclusions from their interpretations. (*PI* 194)

The conception that all thinking, all sensations, all motives, intentions, and so on are *inner* occurrences or states, receives no support from the actual use of the word 'inner'. Often we do think, reason, plan, 'in our minds'. But thinking in one's mind is only one *form* of thinking. Thinking that is openly expressed in conversation is not thinking 'in one's mind'. People often have inner motives and intentions: but motives that are frankly stated are not called 'inner motives'.

Does this philosophical conception have a deeper source than a misrepresentation of the use of the word 'inner'? I am sure that it has. There is the notion that thoughts, intentions, motives, are 'hidden'. Hidden from whom? Hidden from one another. The thoughts and intentions of other persons are hidden from me: but my own thoughts and intentions are not hidden from myself. Or put it like this: I can only *believe* that someone else is in pain, but I *know* it if I am. (*PI* 303) Or: I can only *surmise* what another's thoughts or motives are, but I *know* what mine are.

But isn't there just the same misunderstanding of the use of the word 'hidden' here that we have already encountered with the word 'inner'? Do I always say or think that another's thoughts, motives, feelings, are hidden from me? Certainly not. As Wittgenstein remarks:

> If I see someone writhing in pain with evident cause I do not think: all the same, his feelings are hidden from me. (*PI*, p. 223)

Still, there is a truth underlying the conception that another's thoughts, motives and feelings are 'hidden' from me — only it is badly expressed. What truth? Well, this — that I pay attention to another's words, facial expressions, behaviour, when I need to find out what he is thinking or feeling, as I do not pay attention to my own. Wittgenstein remarks that the sentence 'He alone knows what his motives are' is 'an expression of the fact that we ask *him* what his motives are' (*PI*, p. 224). I pay attention to what another says and does when I need to learn his thoughts and intentions: but I do not do this in my own case — at least not normally. I do not infer my beliefs and feelings from *my* words and facial expressions — whereas I often do this with other people.

This is a striking feature of the logical grammar of the psychological concepts. But it is badly expressed if we say that the thoughts and feelings of others are 'hidden' from oneself. For what is implied is that one's *own* thoughts are *not* hidden from oneself. Thus, the total thing one is trying to say is: I don't know what someone else is thinking, but I do know what I am thinking. Wittgenstein remarks that this is to get things exactly backwards. He says:

> I can know what someone else is thinking, not what I am thinking.
> It is correct to say 'I know what you are thinking', and wrong to say 'I know what I am thinking.'
> (A whole cloud of philosophy condensed into a drop of grammar.)
> (*PI*, p. 222)

Of course, one may say, 'I don't know what I think about that topic', where this just means: I have not formed any definite thought about it. But if I had previously arrived at a definite thought, it would be meaningless to say, 'I *know* what I think.' We can see this from the following consideration. Suppose I express a thought of mine by saying, 'I think that so-and-so.' It would be nonsense if another person asked, 'How do you know that you think that?' He would seem to be asking for my grounds or evidence that I think so-and-so. This would be like asking me for my evidence that I feel dizzy or have a pain. In my own case I do not have evidence. Whereas, if I have said of another person, 'He thinks that so-and-so', the question 'How do you know?' is in order. I could answer by citing something he said or did. I would be giving evidence. But there is no such thing as my 'giving my evidence' that *I* think so-and-so.

Another way of looking at it is this. I can have evidence that *you* think so-and-so; but the evidence may not be convincing, and so I can be in doubt. But when it comes to what *I* think, there is for me neither evidence *nor* the corresponding doubt. It is the latter point that inclines one to say, 'I *know* what I think.' But this is a misunderstanding of the grammar of 'know' — where doubt is *logically* excluded, so is knowledge.

Wittgenstein makes this point in connection with the notion of someone's saying something silently to himself:

> That what someone else says to himself is hidden from me belongs to the *concept* 'saying inwardly'. Only 'hidden' is the wrong word here; for if it is hidden from me, it ought to be obvious to him, *he* would have to *know* it. But he does not 'know' it; only the doubt which exists for me does not exist for him. (*PI*, pp. 220–1)

The tangle we get into here is partly due to our confusing the case where we *could* be in doubt about something but in fact are not in doubt, with the case where doubt would be *senseless*. Sometimes we use the words 'I know' to mean the same as 'I don't doubt'. But when I have a definite thought, there is for me neither 'doubting' nor 'knowing' what I think.

Let us apply these considerations to the conception that thinking, feeling, sensation are occurrences in or states of the brain. In philosophy there is a strong inclination to say that these psychological phenomena are 'inner' or 'hidden'. We recall Armstrong's remark that 'It is completely natural to speak of the mind as "in" the body, and to speak of mental processes as "inner" processes.' I have tried to show that it is a confusion to suppose that thinking, feeling, and so on are *in general* 'inner' or 'hidden'. But underneath this confusion there is the perception of a striking truth about the psychological concepts, namely, that each of us stands in a different relation to his own thinking and feeling than does anyone else. Every philosopher must have at least a dim awareness of this truth, since it is embedded in the grammar of the psychological language that he uses every day. A philosopher cannot be completely oblivious of this grammar, even if he forms incorrect opinions about its significance.

The assertion that sensation, thinking, emotion, and so on are 'inner' occurrences or states arises, I am arguing, from the awareness that you and I stand on a different level in regard to what *I* think or feel. Leaving aside the unconscious thoughts and feelings with which psychoanalysis deals, the fundamental difference is that *you* can have evidence for what I think and feel, in my words and expressive behaviour, whereas *I* cannot.

What is happening in today's philosophy of mind is truly extraordinary. The idea that thoughts and feelings are 'inner', in a metaphorical sense; has been transformed into what is believed to be a precise, hard-headed, scientific theory, namely, that thoughts and feelings are actually *in* the head. This seems to be building a philosophical position on a pun: what was first regarded as *metaphorically* 'inner' is now taken to be *literally* 'inner'.

This development has a surprising consequence. The original metaphorical use of the word 'inner' reflects the realization that you and I stand on a different logical level in regard to what *I* think and feel. But the view that thoughts and feelings are brain-processes *abolishes* this logical difference. If this view were true, you and I would stand on the *same* level in regard to what I think and feel. In order to ascertain my thoughts and feelings you *and* I would equally have to rely on advanced technology and scientific theory. This is a splendid illustration of how in philosophy it is possible to saw off the branch on which one is sitting!

The conception that psychological phenomena are 'hidden' is an intricate web of different notions. In addition to the idea that my thoughts and feelings are hidden from others but not from myself, there is the notion that, in another sense, they are even hidden *from me*. I paid attention to the latter idea in chapter 7. It is an idea that emerges when one tries to recall what actually occurred on some typical occasion of making a decision, or of recognizing someone, or of suddenly understanding something, and so on. When one tries to describe accurately what one is aware of as having taken place, all that one can put one's finger on is an utterance or gesture, or a sensation of relief, or some physical action, etc. We feel that there must be 'more to it' than these 'typical manifestations' of decision or recognition. We feel that we have not been able to *identify* what making a decision, or recognizing something, *is in itself*. The real nature of these phenomena seems to be hidden from everyone — from myself as well as from others. This feeling of frustration easily misleads philosophers and psychologists into thinking that future investigations in neurophysiology will reveal what is presently hidden.

Wittgenstein undermines this source of the idea that psychological phenomena are hidden by drawing on two of his most powerful conceptions. The first is that there is no 'essential nature' of deciding, or of recognizing, or of seeing, or thinking, or expecting, and so on. Instead, each of the psychological concepts covers 'a *family* of cases', cases that exhibit similarities and differences, but no formal unity. It is the same point he makes early in the *Philosophical Investigations* about the various phenomena that we call 'language', namely, 'that these phenomena have no one thing in common which makes us use the same word for all' (*PI* 65) (see chapter 5). Wittgenstein points out, for example, that the sentence 'I am expecting him' is sometimes used to mean just that one believes the person will come, although whether he will come or not does not occupy one's mind. But also it sometimes means 'I am *eagerly* awaiting him.' Wittgenstein goes on to say:

> We could imagine a language in which different verbs were consistently used in these cases. And similarly more than one verb where we speak of 'believing', 'hoping', and so on. Perhaps the concepts of such a language would be more suitable for understanding psychology than the concepts of our language. (*PI* 577)

The second conception that Wittgenstein brings to bear against the notion that the psychological phenomena are hidden from us, is connected with the first one. I am thinking of Wittgenstein's constant emphasis on the part that *the circumstances*, the surroundings, in which we say something, plays in determining the *meaning* of what is said. In some circumstances, the sentence 'I am afraid' is a *cry* of fear; in other circumstances, a description of one's state. In one case, saying 'I am in pain' is an *expression* of pain; in another, a calm report to a doctor. We recall Wittgenstein's parable of a coronation, which in certain surroundings is a scene of pomp and splendour, in other surroundings a spectacle of shame and ridicule. (*PI* 584)

When we are philosophically perplexed about the nature of belief, or remembering, or meaning something, our natural tendency is to search *inwardly* into our minds or brains. That is a dead-end. Wittgenstein teaches us to look *outwardly* — to *take note* of how a difference *in circumstances* changes *the meaning* of what we say and do. Giving an account of this role of circumstances is not easy. In everyday life we learn to use the psychological terms in various circumstances. But the needs of everyday life do not require us to learn to *describe* those circumstances. (See *Zettel* 114—16.) Therefore, 'we do not *command a clear view* of the use of our words.' (*PI* 122) To the degree, however, that we succeed in obtaining a clear view of our psychological language, to the same degree we see how misguided is the idea that our philosophical perplexities about memory, belief, meaning something, and so on, could be removed by neurophysiological discoveries.

One thing to the credit of the identity-theory is that it is a justified reaction against parallelism. In so far as parallelism conceives of psychological phenomena as 'immaterial' or 'incorporeal', these phenomena seem to be so insubstantial and elusive that it appears unintelligible how they could have any *influence* on human behaviour or human life and thought. It appears that it would not matter if the psychological phenomena did not even exist! As previously mentioned, some advocates of parallelism actually hold to the doctrine of 'epiphenomenalism', according to which the whole burden of causality, in human thought and action, is carried by events in the nervous system. The psychological phenomena in themselves have no causal powers.

But in everyday life we commonly speak of causal connections between psychological phenomena. For example: 'He decided to leave the meeting *because* he suddenly remembered his promise to come home early.' If we think of the decision and the sudden remembering as 'immaterial' occurrences, it will seem mysterious how there could be any relation of 'causality' between them. Parallelism, in its epiphenomenalist version, 'solves' this problem by postulating that the real causal connection was between the 'corresponding' brain-processes. Thus 'strictly speaking' one should have said: 'The brain-process corresponding to his decision was caused by the brain-process corresponding to his sudden remembering.'

Wittgenstein makes the following comment on parallelism:

> The prejudice in favour of psychophysical parallelism is a fruit of primitive interpretations of our concepts. For if one allows a causality between psychological phenomena which is not mediated physiologically, one thinks one is professing belief in vaporous (*nebelhaften*) mental entities. (*Z* 611)

I take it that by the 'prejudice' or 'bias' in favour of parallelism, he is referring to the assumption that for each psychological phenomenon (a memory, a thought, a feeling) there must be a corresponding neural phenomenon. This seems necessary because it is felt that the psychological phenomena in themselves are too nebulous, too intangible, too vaporous, to *do* anything! Therefore, they must be supplemented by neural events which have actual causal efficacy.

This picture, or image, of the psychological phenomena as being so 'intangible', so 'gaseous', that they cannot bring anything about, is completely false. All of us know in everyday life that a feeling of having been humiliated can cause a desire for revenge. Or that remembering a promise can move one to the physical action of carrying out the promise. The psychological phenomena are linked to human behaviour in countless ways. They are not insubstantial, vaporous, powerless.

This unrealistic image of the psychological concepts leads both to the dualism of parallelism and to the reaction against it of the monism of the identity-theory. One absurdity engenders another absurdity. Both arise from a 'primitive' interpretation of the psychological concepts. What is 'primitive' is the notion that these concepts refer to phenomena that are nebulous, lacking solidity: they are, so to speak, not 'real' but merely 'mental'.

If we have this philosophical picture, and if we also allow for causal connections between psychological phenomena (if we think, for example, that the feeling of having been humiliated might cause a desire for revenge) then it will look as if we were claiming that one vaporous something *caused* the occurrence of another vaporous something. To avoid this embarrassment we adopt parallelism and hold that the actual causal connection was between brain-processes. This sets the stage for the identity-theorist, who 'simplifies' matters by *identifying* the psychological phenomena with brain-processes.

The assumption of brain-states corresponding to psychological phenomena is particularly conspicuous in regard to *memory*. Psychologists and neuropsychologists overwhelmingly *take for granted* that remembering is due to physiological 'memory-traces'. Memory-traces are not discovered by neural surgeons in their investigations of the brain, as dentists discover cavities. Instead, memory-traces are postulated as a theoretical *requirement* for the causation of remembering.[7] Wittgenstein attacks the notion of there being such a requirement:

> I saw this man years ago: now I see him again. I recognize him, I remember his name. And why does there have to be a cause of this remembering in my nervous system? Why must something or other, whatever it may be, be stored up there *in any form*? Why *must* a trace have been left behind? Why should there not be a psychological regularity to which *no* physiological regularity corresponds? If this upsets our ideas (*unsere Begriffe*) of causality then it is time they were upset. (*Z* 610)

In speaking of 'a psychological regularity' Wittgenstein means the frequent, not universal, regularity of remembering events and people previously encountered. In speaking of 'our ideas of causality' I think he means philosophical assumptions about causality such as, for example, the assumption that there cannot be causality across 'temporal gaps'. Wittgenstein then provides a striking analogy:

> Imagine the following phenomenon. If I want someone to take note of a text that I recite to him, so that he can repeat it to me later, I have to give him paper and pencil; and while I am speaking he makes lines, marks, on the paper; if he has to reproduce the text later he follows those marks with his eyes and recites the text. But I am assuming that what he has jotted down is not *writing*, it is not connected by rules with the words of the text; yet without these jottings he is unable to reproduce the text; and if anything in it is altered, if part of it is destroyed, he gets stuck in his 'reading' or recites the text uncertainly or carelessly, or cannot find the words at all. — This *can* be imagined! (*Z* 612)

Not merely can this be imagined, but something like it actually occurs. Often when listening to a lecture, I have jotted down a single word here and there, or drawn lines between two such words, or put down question marks, exclamation marks, and so on. Anyone else who looked at those jottings would find them completely unintelligible. But if I wish to respond to the lecturer, or to disagree with some theme of his, I cannot do it unless I look at these jottings. They enable me to remember the gist of the lecture.

Wittgenstein continues *Zettel* 612 as follows:

> What I called 'jottings' would not be a *rendering* of the text, not so to speak a translation into another symbolism. The text would not be *stored up* in the jottings. And why should it be stored up in our nervous system? (*Z* 612)

The analogy that Wittgenstein intends may be the following. As I listen to the lecture there are innumerable events occurring in my nervous system. There are no systematic correlations between these and the text of the lecture I hear. The text is not *encoded* in these neural events, not *deposited* in my nervous system in any form whatever. Yet without the occurrence of those neural events I should not be able to remember the text. The *disanalogy* is that the neural events do not serve me as *reminders*, as do the jottings.

There is another idea that is an important source of mind-brain identity-theory. I have alluded to it already in mentioning the postulation of physiological 'memory-traces'. The idea is that if I perceived a certain happening last week, then I could not remember it this week unless my perception of it had been deposited in me in some form and had remained stored in me throughout the week. This idea has a wider application than to the conscious remembering of past perceptions. It is applied to intentions, desires, and promises. If yesterday I promised to write a letter today, and I do write it today *because* I had promised to, then the promise must have been 'stored' in me during the intervening time. Or consider the notion of acting from a previous intention. How could this occur unless the intention I previously formed remained 'present in me' until the time of my carrying out the intention? When I form the intention to do a certain thing a month from now I do not of course *dwell* on that intention during every moment of the month. But if I do act on the intention at the appropriate time, then the intention must have 'existed' during the entire interval. The only plausible account of the matter, according to an identity-theorist, is that the persisting intention is a continuous state or process in my nervous system. It remains there unless I give up the intention. If I do not give it up, and do act on it at the appropriate time, then the state or process, which *is* the intention, must have been there right up to the moment of acting on it.

If you are inclined to deny that the intention was a state that existed continuously throughout the month, a mind-brain identity-theorist (such as Armstrong) will accuse you of having a 'magical' conception of *causality*. He will say that apparently you believe that an event occurring a month ago could *cause* you to do something *now*, even though there was no bridging link between the two events.

This reasoning of the identity-theorist may strike us as dubious: but we can hardly leave it at that, for it appeals to many earnest philosophers and psychologists. To unravel this tangle of ideas is a difficult undertaking.[8] I will briefly mention two points. The first is that the intention, and the act of carrying out the intention, do not have the kind of 'logical independence' from one another that is regarded by many as the hallmark of a genuine 'causal' relation. Of course a particular intention may never be carried out. But to suppose it could be that *no* intentions were ever carried out, is as logically absurd as to suppose that all moves that have ever been made in playing chess may have been illegal moves.

The second point is that an intention is not a 'state' or 'process' in the sense in which a state or process could be continuously observed, or monitored, day and night, as can for example the motion of a wheel or the flow of a current through a wire. Brain-states and brain-processes *could* be continuously monitored in this way. Therefore, intentions are not 'states' in the sense in which brain-states are 'states', and so intentions cannot be sensibly identified with brain-states.

Some philosophers who wish to espouse a materialist theory of mind, feel uncomfortable about saying that a particular intention (or hope or fear) is 'identical' with a particular neural state or process. They are influenced, for one thing, by the consideration that different species of animals may have markedly different neurophysiological systems. Suppose a man and his dog encounter a lion. Both man and dog are afraid of the lion. But if the nervous system of the dog is very different from that of the man, then the neural state of the dog that is supposedly identical with its fear of the lion may be quite different from the 'corresponding' neural state of the man. If this is so, being afraid of a lion would not be always the same neural state.

These philosophers try to hold on to their materialist theory of mind by substituting the term 'realization' for the term 'identity'. What they say is that intentions, hopes, fears, and so on are 'realized' in the brain. I have never seen a coherent account of what their term 'realized' is supposed to mean. In everyday language we speak of the realization of hopes, desires, intentions. A lieutenant hopes to be promoted to captain. When we say, 'His hope was realized', what do we mean? Just that he was promoted to captain. When a philosopher says that the lieutenant's hope is 'realized' in his brain, does he mean that the lieutenant has been promoted 'in his brain'? One would hope not. The shift from the term 'identity' to the term 'realization' seems to open up the possibility that each time I want my breakfast, this desire is 'realized' by a *different* neural process — which would mean that the notion of *identifying* the desire with any brain-process would have to be abandoned.

Another idea that figures in both parallelism and identity-theory is that a thought has a 'structure' and that the correlated or identical neural state or process has the *same* structure. The neurologist, Ewald Hering, who believed in parallelism, said:

> The soul does not move unless, simultaneously, the brain moves. Whenever the same sensation or the same thought recurs, a certain physical process which belongs to this special sensation or thought is repeated; for both are inseparably connected. They are conditioned by and productive of each other. Accordingly, from the course of our sensations we can draw inferences concerning the simultaneous and corresponding course of processes in the brain. The resolution of our sensations into their various elements is at the same time an analysis of the involved interactions of the various elementary cerebral functions or irritations.[9]

The conception of parallelism seems to be the following: a thought or sensation is a structure of mental elements, the corresponding brain-process is a structure of neural elements, and these two processes are identical in structure. This is what the psychologist, Wolfgang Köhler, endorsed as 'the principle of psychophysical isomorphism'. According to him, 'the structural properties of experiences are at the same time the structural properties of their biological correlates.'[10] For each mental structure there is a matching brain-structure. If we knew the laws that link mental elements with neural elements, and the laws governing the possible combinations of elements, we could infer brain-processes from thoughts, and thoughts from brain-processes.

Those who favour the mind-brain identity-theory reject parallelism. But they too hold that thoughts and beliefs are 'structures'. Armstrong says that a belief is 'a complex structure in the mind'.[11] It is 'a structural state' composed of 'mental constituents'.[12]

Thus, both parallelism and identity-theory conceive of thoughts, beliefs, and so on as 'structures'. Parallelism holds that for a given belief there are *two* structures, one mental, one neural. Identity-theory holds that there is *one* structure, which is both mental and neural.

Is a belief a 'structure'? This is a puzzling question. In calling something a 'structure' we certainly mean that it is a complex composed of parts or elements. One of the impressive demonstrations of Wittgenstein's *Philosophical Investigations* is that nothing is either simple or complex in 'an absolute sense'.[13] Anything whatever can be regarded as 'simple' from some point of view; or as 'complex' from another point of view. And if we regard something as 'complex' we can make different decisions as to what are its 'constituent parts'. This point holds for beliefs, as well as for trees, or clouds, or chessboards.

Suppose that I want to buy an additional rug for my living room. The rug merchant asks, 'What colour is the rug that is at present in your living room?' I try to remember, and finally say: 'The rug now in my living room is orange.' Let us say that in uttering this sentence I expressed a belief.

If a belief is a structure of mental constituents, we have a right to ask — what are the constituents of the belief I expressed? How *do we count* the constituents? Well, we might decide to regard each word of my sentence as standing for a constituent of my belief — giving *nine* constituents to my belief. We might decide, however, that the two words 'living room' stand for only one constituent of my belief, since the living room is only one room. We might also decide that the two words 'the rug' stand for only one constituent. So we have now reduced the total number of constituents of the belief to *seven*. We might, however, decide that the whole phrase 'The rug now in my living room' stands for only one constituent, since it is the subject of the sentence; that the verb 'is' stands for another constituent, and the predicate 'orange' for another — thus obtaining *three* constituents of my belief. Suppose I think that orange colour is a complex of red and yellow — would that mean that the word 'orange' in my sentence stands for more than one constituent of my belief? Suppose I had responded to the merchant's question by uttering the single word 'Orange.' Would the same number of belief constituents have been present as when I said the full sentence? We can even imagine some philosopher declaring that the belief I expressed was 'an indivisible unity' — and so not a 'structure' at all.

The notion that a belief (or thought, or desire) is a 'structure', is too hazy to get hold of. So also is the notion of the 'mental constituents' of a belief. It is a philosophical image that is *empty* — in the sense that we don't know how to apply it to actual examples. In real life we know when to say that someone, by words or actions, expressed a belief: but we don't know anything about beliefs being 'structures' composed of 'mental constituents'. Both parallelism and identity-theory rely on a notion that is too nebulous to bear any weight.[14]

Wittgenstein makes, in *Zettel*, a highly provocative remark about the notion that thinking goes on in the head. He says that this is a dangerous idea for a philosopher to have: 'The idea of thinking as an occurrence in the head, in a completely enclosed space, gives him something occult.' (*Z* 605, 606)

Could it be that the conception of mind as brain — a view that is supposed to be 'scientifically oriented' — is actually nourished by the charm of *the occult*? I think so. Popular lectures and articles speak of the brain with peculiar awe. What a marvellous mechanism it is! Certainly the brain is marvellous — but so is the heart and the digestive system. Why should the brain attract special awe? Surely because it is conceived of as 'the organ of thinking'.

In our discourse with one another we make innumerable references to things and situations. We employ concepts, descriptions, representations. We express impressions, feelings, expectations, doubts, anxieties. The idea that all of these ingredients of thinking are packed into that narrow space inside the skull, fills one with amazement. It provides the thrill of the incomprehensible — just as *magic* does!

───── CHAPTER 11 ─────

Certainty

Wittgenstein's last notebooks, published under the title *On Certainty*, were written in the final year and a half of his life. They are rough notes, completely unrevised. They are his discussions with himself, with no anticipation of publication. There is much repetition; the same questions are returned to again and again; earlier remarks are sometimes later rejected. The sequence of remarks is far from orderly: to get a grip on Wittgenstein's thinking about a particular question one must move back and forth through hundreds of remarks. Many readers find the whole thing bewildering.

But these notes reward hard study. Not only are there individual comments of great beauty, but also lines of thought emerge that are not to be found elsewhere in Wittgenstein's writings. We are presented with a new and highly original treatment of the concepts of knowledge and certainty.

Present-day 'epistemology' has to a large extent taken its direction from Descartes's attempt to discover something of which he could be 'entirely certain'. The central ideas in his undertaking are 'the impossibility of imagining any doubt' and 'the impossibility of being mistaken'. In *On Certainty* Wittgenstein made an intensive study of these same ideas. It is of interest, therefore, to compare the thinking of Descartes and Wittgenstein on these notoriously difficult concepts.

METAPHYSICAL CERTAINTY

Descartes distinguishes between 'moral assurance' and 'meta-physical certainty'. In part IV of the *Discourse* he says that although we have a 'moral assurance' that we possess bodies, and that there are stars and an earth, we do not have 'metaphysical certainty' on these matters.[1] Apparently, to say that we have a 'moral assurance' that a belief is true is just to say that the truth of the belief is probable or highly probable. In the *Principles* Descartes says:

> As regards the conduct of our life, we are frequently obliged to follow opinions which are merely probable, because the opportunities for action would in most cases pass away before we could deliver ourselves from our doubts.[2]

But even the highest probability falls short of metaphysical certainty. For Descartes, something is 'metaphysically certain' if it is impossible to 'imagine the least ground of doubt'. In the *Discourse* he says that his procedure will be 'to reject as absolutely false everything as to which I could imagine the least ground of doubt, in order to see if afterwards there remained anything in my belief that was entirely certain.'[3] In *Meditation* II he says: 'I shall proceed by setting aside all that in which the least doubt could be supposed to exist, just as if I had discovered that it was absolutely false.'[4]

Let me anticipate by saying that on Descartes's view, if a person B is 'metaphysically certain' that a proposition q is true, the following four things are implied:

1 It is impossible for B to conceive of any ground for doubting that q is true.
2 It is impossible for B to be deceived or mistaken about the truth of q.
3 B knows that q is true.
4 q is true.

Among these four implications of metaphysical certainty there is one that might be called 'operational'. It is the one that Descartes uses as a measuring rod or criterion of metaphysical certainty: namely, whether it is possible or impossible to imagine (conceive, suppose) any doubt that the belief is true. When this test is applied to a belief, any doubt that emerges must not be arbitrary or capricious. It must be based on reasons: 'we need to have some reason for doubting.'[5] On applying this test, Descartes thinks he arrives at the result that

There is nothing in all that I formerly believed to be true, of which I cannot in some measure doubt, and that not merely through want of thought or through levity, but for reasons which are very powerful and maturely considered.[6]

But then he comes upon something that is apparently immune to any possible doubt, namely, that he himself exists:

I myself, am I not at least something? . . . But I was persuaded that there was nothing in all the world, that there was no heaven, no earth, that there were no minds, nor any bodies: was I not then likewise persuaded that I did not exist? Not at all; of a surety I myself did exist since I persuaded myself of something. But there is some deceiver or other, very powerful and very cunning, who ever employs his ingenuity in deceiving me. Then without doubt I exist also if he deceives me, and let him deceive me as much as he will, he can never cause me to be nothing so long as I think I am something. So that after having reflected well and carefully examined all things, we must come to the definite conclusion that this proposition: I am, I exist, is necessarily true each time that I pronounce it, or that I mentally conceive it.[7]

Descartes has finally arrived at something that is metaphysically certain. He says: 'I am, I exist, that is certain.'[8] He assumes that this certainty is equivalent to *knowledge*: 'I know that I exist, and I inquire what I am, I whom I know to exist.'[9] According to the *Principles* this 'first knowledge' is derived from the perception of a contradiction:

That we cannot doubt our existence without existing while we doubt; and this is the first knowledge that we obtain when we philosophize in an orderly way.

While we thus reject all that of which we can possibly doubt, and feign that it is false, it is easy to suppose that there is no God, nor heaven, nor bodies, and that we possess neither hands, nor feet, nor indeed any body; but we cannot in the same way conceive that we who doubt these things are not; for there is a contradiction in conceiving that what thinks does not at the same time as it thinks, exist. And hence this conclusion *I think, therefore I am*, is the first and most certain of all that occurs to one who philosophizes in an orderly way.[10]

Also in the *Discourse* it appears that this first certainty is derived from the perception of a contradiction: 'I saw from the very fact that I thought of doubting the truth of other things, it very evidently and certainly followed that I was.'[11] The contradiction would be: 'I doubt, but I do not exist.'

There is, however, a dramatic passage in *Meditation* III (*after* Descartes has achieved the supposed proof of his existence in *Meditation* II) which indicates that he has *not* established with certainty anything at all, not even his own existence! This passage occurs after Descartes has posed the question of whether he can take it 'as a general rule that all things which I perceive very clearly and very distinctly are true'.¹² As an objection to this 'general rule' he notes that in the past he has believed many things 'to be very certain and manifest, which yet I afterwards recognized as being dubious'.¹³ He thinks, however, that these errors occurred when he was presented by his senses with ideas of things external to him, and when he thought he perceived clearly ('although in truth I did not perceive it at all') that there were external objects from which these ideas proceeded and to which they were similar. When, however, he considers some other judgements of his, to which the assumption of external physical objects does not pertain, he is perplexed as to how these judgements could be open to any doubt. He expresses this perplexity in *Meditation* III as follows:

> But when I took anything very simple and easy in the sphere of arithmetic or geometry into consideration, e.g. that two and three together made five, and other things of that sort, were not these present to my mind so clearly as to enable me to affirm that they were true? Certainly if I judged that since such matters could be doubted, this would not have been so for any other reason than that it came into my mind that perhaps a God might have endowed me with such a nature that I may have been deceived even concerning things which seemed to me most manifest. But every time that this preconceived opinion of the sovereign power of a God presents itself to my thought, I am constrained to confess that it is easy for Him, if He wishes it, to cause me to err, even in matters in which I believe myself to have the best evidence. And, on the other hand, always when I direct my attention to things which I believe myself to perceive very clearly, I am so persuaded of their truth that I let myself break out into words such as these: let who will deceive me, he can never cause me to be nothing while I think that I am something, or some day cause it to be true that I have never been, it being true now that I am, or that two and three make more or less than five, or any such thing in which I see a manifest contradiction. And certainly, since I have no reason to believe that there is a God who is a deceiver, and as I have not yet satisfied myself that there is a God at all, the reason for doubt which depends on this opinion alone is very slight, and so to speak

metaphysical. But in order to be able altogether to remove it, I must inquire whether there is a God as soon as the occasion presents itself; and if I find that there is a God, I must also inquire whether He may be a deceiver; for without a knowledge of these two truths I do not see that I can ever be certain of anything.[14]

There are a number of striking things in this passage. One is the thought that God might have created him in such a manner that even his clearest and most distinct conceptions would be erroneous — even his judgement that 2 + 3 = 5. He says that he sees 'a manifest contradiction' (*repugnantiam agnosco manifestam*) in the supposition that this proposition of arithmetic is false. Yet the fact that he sees this supposition to be a contradiction does not prevent him from thinking that it could be true! (It should be noted that in various writings, from 1630 to 1649, Descartes emphatically maintained that God's power is so completely unlimited that He could if He wished make contradictions true!)[15] Descartes goes on to say, in the above passage, that since he has no reason to believe there is a God who is a deceiver, this reason for doubt is 'very slight, and so to speak metaphysical'. But we must remember that Descartes's whole aim is to arrive at 'metaphysical certainty': i.e. to discover judgements that are subject to *no doubt whatsoever*, not even 'metaphysical' doubt. The propositions of arithmetic and geometry do not, according to him, satisfy this requirement.

But what is most remarkable in this passage from *Meditation III* is that it poses a doubt about the judgement *I exist*. In *Meditation II* Descartes had declared that even if there is a powerful deceiver, 'let him deceive me as much as he will, he can never cause me to be nothing so long as I think that I am something.'[16] And immediately he drew the conclusion that the proposition *I exist* is necessarily true each time he pronounces or conceives it. In *Meditation III*, however, he 'breaks out' with the same words he used in *Meditation II*: 'Let who will deceive me, *he can never cause me to be nothing while I think that I am something.*'[17] He says that he sees 'a manifest contradiction' in the supposition that this could be brought about. *Yet*, Descartes continues, there is a reason for being in doubt as to whether this manifestly contradictory proposition might not be true, a reason that is slight and metaphysical, but nevertheless *a reason for doubt*! And this reason for doubt cannot be removed *until* he has found out whether there is a God, and whether He may be a deceiver: 'for without a knowledge of these two truths I do not see that I can ever be certain of anything.'

What can we make of this? It surely appears that Descartes is *withdrawing* his assertion of *Meditation* II that *it is certain* that he exists, and that he *knows* that he exists. In *Meditation* III he seems *not* to regard as certain beyond all question the proposition of *Principle* 1, 7 that 'we cannot doubt our existence without existing while we doubt', and also the proposition of *Discourse* IV that 'I saw from the very fact that I thought of doubting the truth of other things, it very evidently and certainly followed that I was.' He is saying in *Meditation* III that if there is a deceiving God, this God may be of such unlimited power that he can cause Descartes to be in error about things that Descartes perceives clearly and distinctly — such as that $2 + 3 = 5$, or *that he must exist whenever he thinks he exists*. In ending this passage by declaring that he must find out whether there is a God, and if so whether this God may be a deceiver, 'for without a knowledge of these two truths I do not see that I can ever be certain of anything', Descartes is implying that he is *not yet* certain of either the proposition *I exist*, or of the proposition *I think, therefore I exist*.

I do not see how one can avoid the conclusion that Descartes worked himself into a dreadful confusion in the *Meditations*. According to this passage early in *Meditation* III he has not, up to that point, established *anything* with metaphysical certainty — that is, beyond all conceivable doubt. He cannot know that *any* of his clear and distinct perceptions are true until he has *first proved* that God exists and is not a deceiver. And of course he cannot carry out any such proof without taking some of his clear and distinct perceptions to be true. Thus, Descartes is in the impossible predicament of trying to hoist himself by his own bootstraps.

OBJECTIVE CERTAINTY

In *On Certainty* Wittgenstein asks: What does it mean to say that 'the truth of a proposition is *certain*?' (*OC* 193) From the wording 'the truth of a proposition' it would seem that he is thinking of sentences such as: 'It is certain that the door is locked', where what is said to be certain is *that the door is locked*. This is to be contrasted with our saying of some person, 'He is certain that the door is locked.' Here we are not saying that it is certain that the door is locked, but rather that *this person* is certain that. . . . In the first case we are saying that *the truth of a proposition* is certain; in the second case that *a person* is certain.

What about the sentence 'I am certain that the door is locked'? At first sight this may seem to belong to the second case, i.e. to be attributing certainty to a person (the speaker) and not to the truth of a proposition. But this is a misleading appearance, as shown by the fact that it would be a contradiction, or nearly one, to say: 'I am certain that the door is locked, but it isn't certain that the door is locked.' It seems that to make an assertion of the form 'I am certain that *q*' is to say that the speaker is certain that *q* is true, *and also*, if not explicitly to *say*, at least to *imply*, that the truth of *q* is certain.

If we consider again an assertion of the form 'It is certain that *q*', we see that what is explicitly said is that the truth of a proposition is certain. Does this assertion imply that the speaker is certain? Surely it does. For if yesterday you said, 'It is certain that *q*', then today I would be justified in remarking to you that yesterday *you* were certain that *q*.

Thus, there is not as much difference between the meaning of the phrases 'I am certain' and 'It is certain' as one might first think. The phrase 'It is certain' says that the truth of a proposition is certain, and implies that the speaker is certain. The phrase 'I am certain' says that the speaker is certain, and implies that the truth of a proposition is certain. I think we can say that both phrases are 'expressions' of the certainty of the speaker. In addition, one of the phrases says explicitly that the truth of a proposition is certain; the other one implies that this is so.

Although in *OC* 193 Wittgenstein asks about the meaning of saying that the truth of *a proposition* is certain, it is clear that what he wants to explore is the concept of *a person's* being certain of something — as may be seen from the immediately following remark:

> With the word 'certain' we express complete conviction, the total absence of doubt, and thereby we seek to convince other people. That is *subjective* certainty.
>
> But when is something objectively certain? When a mistake is not possible. But what kind of possibility is that? Must not a mistake be *logically* excluded? (*OC* 194)

Here he is speaking of *certainty* as something that is attributed to a person, although this certainty is *about* the truth of some proposition. This human certainty is what is 'expressed' by sentences of the form 'It is certain that . . .', or 'I am certain that. . . .' Furthermore, Wittgenstein is suggesting that sentences of these forms are used to express two different *concepts* of certainty, which he labels 'subjective' and 'objective'. To be *subjectively* certain of something is simply to have no doubt about it. To be *objectively* certain of something is different. It means that we regard our being *mistaken* about something as being 'logically excluded' — or, one could say, as being 'logically impossible'. Another way to put it is to say that we regard our being mistaken as *inconceivable* (*OC* 54). Still another way of putting it is that when our certainty of something is *objective*, that means that for us *it makes no sense* to doubt that the something is so (*OC* 56).

Wittgenstein is calling attention to a real distinction. Sometimes we say such a thing as 'It is certain that he will come tomorrow', when we mean only that we have no doubt that he will arrive tomorrow — not that it is impossible or inconceivable that we should be mistaken about it. It is, however, this latter concept of certainty — objective certainty — that is Wittgenstein's primary concern.

We commonly regard simple calculations in arithmetic as certain. What is the basis for this certainty? Does it rest on the employment of a *rule*? 'Can it be seen from a *rule* in which circumstances a mistake in the employment of rules of calculation is logically excluded?' (*OC* 26) The answer is 'No!' Even if we had such a rule we could make an error in applying it (ibid.). For example, if you have subtracted *b* from *a* and obtained *c*, it is an *a priori* rule that this calculation is correct if *c* added to *b* gives *a*. But you could make a mistake in adding *c* and *b*, and so wrongly conclude that your subtraction was correct.

A different kind of rule — not *a priori* but a 'rule of thumb' — might be that a calculation that has been checked three times is correct. But the employment of this rule would presuppose that the checking was done 'in normal circumstances' (*OC* 27). You should not have done the checking carelessly, or in a hurry, or when feeling dizzy, or when looking at the figures upside down, and so on. This is the 'and so on' of *indefiniteness*. There is no 'complete list' of normal circumstances for checking a calculation. 'We recognize normal circumstances but cannot precisely describe them. At most, we can describe a range of abnormal ones.' (*OC* 27) We can describe how we satisfied ourselves in a particular case that a calculation was correct. But this description, even though it may mention a rule of calculation, will not mention a rule *of a kind* that would ensure that a *miscalculation* was logically excluded (*OC* 44, 46). On reflection we see that there could not be such a rule.

Wittgenstein is making the point that no rule could guarantee that an error in calculation was logically impossible. It is worth mentioning that this point undermines a part of Descartes's undertaking. Descartes wanted to adopt the rule that all of his clear and distinct judgements were true. He tried to *prove* this proposition in the *Meditations*. But even if he had succeeded in his proof he could not have reached the result that a mistake in judgement was impossible, for he could still make a mistake in deciding that a particular judgement was 'clear and distinct'. Descartes even acknowledged this, somewhat laconically, in the *Discourse*, when he said that 'there is some difficulty in ascertaining which are those [judgements] that we distinctly conceive.'[18]

Having observed that no *rule* can ensure the impossibility of error in calculation, does Wittgenstein conclude that in every multiplication or addition we may be in error? No. His suggestion is that for any person who is learning to multiply, some multiplications will become *fixed* (*feststehend*); others will not (*OC* 48). A school child will quickly reach the stage where $5 \times 5 = 25$ is 'fixed', i.e. removed from any possible doubt. It may take longer for $12 \times 12 = 144$ to attain that status for the pupil. When it does, that will mean that the idea of its being a possibly incorrect multiplication, one that needs to be checked, will cease to make sense for him. Among adults there can be differences in regard to *which* multiplications are removed from any possible doubt.

Let us turn to 'empirical' propositions. In philosophy the term 'empirical proposition' has commonly been taken to mean: a proposition the truth of which can be confirmed or disconfirmed by experience. Many philosophers have held that empirical propositions are, one and all, *hypotheses* that are subject to some degree of doubt. Any statement asserting or implying the existence of a particular physical thing has been held to be a hypothesis: for example, that there is a planet at such-and-such a distance from the sun, or that *this* is my hand. Not so, says Wittgenstein: the first is a hypothesis, but the second is not (*OC* 52). 'For it is not true that a mistake merely gets more and more impossible as we pass from the planet to my own hand. No: at some point it has ceased to be conceivable.' (*OC* 54) 'Doubt gradually loses its sense.' (*OC* 56) Wittgenstein is pointing out an analogy between propositions of arithmetic and empirical propositions. In each of these domains of language the truth of some propositions becomes fixed, unshakeable: the idea that one might be mistaken becomes inconceivable.

Wittgenstein imagines a philosopher saying: 'What right have I to not doubt the existence of my hands?' (*OC* 24) It occurs to me that what may lie behind this question, which might be put by a philosopher who thinks it is reasonable to doubt the existence of any physical thing, is the assumption that doubt is *justified* if there is no *rule* or *principle* which *guarantees* that a judgement about the existence of any physical thing is true — a rule that makes a mistake logically impossible.

But the case here is exactly the same as with arithmetical propositions and calculations. Of course there can be no *rule* that logically excludes the possibility of being mistaken in a judgement about a physical thing — since such a rule, if there were one, could itself be incorrectly employed. Nevertheless, there are particular propositions about physical things, in regard to which the idea that we could be wrong *has no meaning* for us. We do not understand *how* we could be mistaken.

Where doubt has 'lost its sense', where a mistake is not conceivable, is the proposition still to be called 'empirical'? In such a case it is not appropriate to say that the proposition 'can be confirmed or disconfirmed by experience'. I think the phrase 'contingent proposition' provides a more suitable terminology.

There are propositions that are 'contingent' in the sense that although they are true they *might not* have been true, yet in regard to which it is inconceivable for us that we might be mistaken in accepting them as true: for example, that the earth has existed for more than 100 years, or that this present writing of mine is in English and not in Chinese, or that I have never been to the moon. The earth *could* have come into existence less than 100 years ago (although it did not); it *could* have been that I was writing in Chinese now (although I am not); it *could* have been that I had travelled to the moon (although I have not). But for me the supposition that I am mistaken about any of these contingent propositions is unintelligible. In this sense, the possibility that I am mistaken is, for me, 'logically excluded'. Just as, for me, some propositions of arithmetic are fixed, unshakeable, so are some contingent propositions. As Wittgenstein says: 'There are cases where doubt is unreasonable, but others where it seems logically impossible. And there seems to be no clear boundary between them.' (*OC* 454)

OBJECTIVE CERTAINTY AND KNOWLEDGE

There are two points of agreement between Descartes's conception of 'metaphysical' certainty and Wittgenstein's conception of 'objective' certainty. Both conceptions have these two features: first, being certain of something, in either sense, entails the impossibility of being able to seriously entertain any doubt about it; second, this certainty entails the impossibility of one's being mistaken. Descartes's conception has the third feature that this certainty entails that one *knows* what one is certain of. But in Wittgenstein's conception this is rejected.

When Descartes arrived in *Meditation* II at the realization that it was nonsense for him to doubt his own existence, he proceeded directly to the assertion: 'I know that I exist.' He assumed that if there is something that would be nonsense for him to doubt, then this is something that he *knows*. Wittgenstein regards this as an erroneous assumption. He does not refer to Descartes, but he does criticize Moore for making that assumption. When Moore asserts that he *knows* that *this* is a hand, that he is a human being, that his body has existed continuously since his birth, etc., Wittgenstein interprets him as wanting to say that doubting those things *makes no sense*. If this is right, then an *expression of doubt*, such as 'I don't know whether I am a human being', makes no sense. In that case, the opposite assertion, 'I *know* that I'm a human being', *also* makes no sense (*OC* 58).

This point is frequently not understood. It has to do with how the expression 'I know' is actually used in everyday language. Of course that use is complex. But in general it is used to oppose someone's doubt or disbelief. One could say that 'I doubt it' and 'I know it' belong to the same domain of language — like 'up' and 'down', or 'left' and 'right'.

Let us consider some of the ways in which 'I know' is used. Sometimes it is used to *reassure* someone — as in 'Don't worry. I know that he will come.' One might even say this to oneself to calm one's own anxiety.

When another is uncertain of something, you may say, 'I know it is so, because ...' — and you proceed to offer *evidence* that it is so.

If someone has warned you that it is very cold outdoors (you are about to go out), your 'I know it' would inform him that you are already aware of it, the situation being that, as far as he knew, you were not aware of it. Here your words would *not* be a prelude to presenting evidence that it is cold outside: they serve to remove the other's doubt as to whether you are aware that it is cold out there.

If you have shown someone the result of a calculation (perhaps pertaining to the cost of a holiday trip), and he asks doubtfully, 'Are you *sure* this is correct?', your reply, 'I know it is', might mean that you have *made sure* it is correct, that you have carefully checked the figures.

If you exclaim, 'Now I know who did it!', that would mean that your own previous uncertainty has been removed.

One may have occasion to say, 'You believe it, but I *know* it!', where oneself has *witnessed* a particular happening or situation, whereas the other person is relying on a report of it that he heard or read. By this remark one would be contrasting the firmness of one's first-hand information with the insecurity of the other's second-hand belief.

These examples differ in various ways, and still different examples could be given. But in all of them 'I know' seems to be used in contrast with someone's (perhaps one's own) previous, present, or potential, disbelief, or doubt, or insecure belief.

This is why the words 'I know' *do not belong* in a case where being in doubt would not make sense, where doubt is logically excluded. For there, 'I know' has no *job* to do. Those words would not have their normal function. There is no actual or possible doubt for those words to oppose, overcome, put to rest, or to contrast with. If in full awareness of this, you still want to say, 'I know' (e.g. 'I know that I exist', or 'I know that I'm a human being'), then it may be that you are trying to make the conceptual point that in such a case doubt is logically excluded, and that therefore both 'I don't know' and 'I know' are out of place. But to express this conceptual point in this way is to guarantee the maximum amount of confusion, both for yourself and for others — for you are *using* 'I know' to say that 'I know' cannot be said!

Thus Descartes created confusion in moving to the assertion 'I know that I exist' from his insight that it was logically absurd for him to doubt his own existence. And Moore, instead of stating 'I know that I'm a human being', should have realized not only that his being uncertain whether he is a human being would be unintelligible but also, *because* of that fact, that he could not speak of *knowing* that he is a human being.

In the *Investigations* Wittgenstein puts very concisely this point about the way 'I know' is used: '"I know . . ." may mean "I do not doubt . . ." but does not mean that the words "I doubt . . ." are *senseless*, that doubt is logically excluded.' (*PI*, p. 221) In the volume entitled *Last Writings*, Wittgenstein says: 'I know how to ascertain that I have two coins in my pocket. But I cannot ascertain that I have two hands, because I cannot doubt it.'[19] He also comments on the philosophical tendency to bring in 'I know' where it does not belong:

> We say 'I know . . .' where there can be doubt, whereas philosophers say we know something precisely where there is no doubt, and thus where the words 'I know' are superfluous as an introduction to the statement.[20]

In remarking that philosophers say 'we know something precisely where there is no doubt', Wittgenstein clearly does not mean that philosophers say this merely when no one *in fact* has any doubt, but rather that they say this in cases where an expression of doubt would be nonsensical.

After these abundant warnings against saying that one 'knows' something in a case where a doubt about that something would not make sense, the reader of *On Certainty* will be perplexed on noting that Wittgenstein himself sometimes uses 'know' in precisely such cases. For example:

> I know, not just that the earth existed long before my birth, but also that it is a large body, that this has been established, that I and the rest of mankind have forebears, that there are books about all this, that such books don't lie, etc. (*OC* 288)

Here Wittgenstein is saying 'I know' in relation to examples that are the same as or similar to Moore's! A big difference, however, is that Wittgenstein does not *insist*, as Moore does, that he *knows* those things: for he goes on to say, in the same remark: 'And I know all this? I believe it.' (*OC* 288) (See also *OC* 234.) I am sure,

214 *Certainty*

however, that Wittgenstein does not regard 'I believe it' as a happier choice of words than 'I know it': nor would 'I am certain of it', or 'I am convinced of it', or 'I assume it', be any better. What he is wanting to say is that a doubt, e.g. as to whether the earth existed long before his birth, has for him *no sense*. He explains why this is so:

> If someone doubted whether the earth had existed a hundred years ago, I should not understand that for *this* reason: I would not know what this person would still allow to be counted as evidence, and what not. (*OC* 231)

This is a conceptual ('grammatical') observation. A person cannot be doubtful about this matter and *also* be employing our ordinary conceptions of evidence. When Wittgenstein says that he 'knows' or 'believes' that the earth existed long before his birth, he is applying this conceptual point to himself: *he* would not understand what to count as evidence, *if* he had this doubt about the age of the earth. Neither 'I know' nor 'I believe' are suitable expressions for stating this conceptual point. This is why Wittgenstein sometimes employs the metaphor 'It stands fast for me.' He suggests that Moore could have said this, instead of 'I know.' (*OC* 116) The examples he lists in *OC* 288 are examples of things that 'stand fast' for him. In saying that he 'knows' them to be true, he is not using 'know' as it is normally used in everyday language: for *there* one does not use it to make *conceptual* observations. In saying that he 'knows' or 'believes' that the earth existed long before his birth, he is trying to indicate that to doubt it would be destructive of his thinking about anything! The conceptual nature of this observation is clearer when he says: 'If I wanted to doubt the existence of the earth long before my birth, I should have to doubt all sorts of things that stand fast for me.' (*OC* 234)

OBJECTIVE CERTAINTY AND TRUTH

According to Wittgenstein, when one's 'certainty' of something is 'objective', it is inappropriate to say that one *knows* that the thing is true. I want now to ask a different question: if one's certainty of something is objective, does it follow that the something is *true*?

Descartes did hold that if one is 'metaphysically certain' of something, then it follows that the thing is true. If one has purified a judgement to the point where it is perfectly clear and distinct, then the judgement *must* be true. At the end of *Meditation* IV he says:

As often as I so restrain my will within the limits of my knowledge, that it forms no judgement except on matters which are clearly and distinctly represented to it by the understanding, I can never be deceived; for every clear and distinct perception is without doubt something, and hence cannot derive its origin from what is nothing, but must by necessity have God as its author — God, I say, who being supremely perfect, cannot be the cause of any error; and consequently we must conclude that such a judgement is true.[21]

So Descartes holds that when your judgement is so clear and distinct that you cannot conceive of any grounds for doubting its truth, then not only is it impossible that you should be *mistaken*, but also your judgement must be *true*.

Wittgenstein agrees that there are cases where a doubt would have no sense — where a mistake is logically excluded — but he does not accept the assumption that therefore one's judgement must be *true*. He says that in certain circumstances one cannot make a *mistake*, but that this does *not* mean that what one says cannot be *false* (*OC* 155). In part this is an observation about the special logical grammar of the concept of a *mistake*, of *being mistaken*. All of us are often mistaken about various things: you think you are driving north when you are driving south; you think you are on Piccadilly Street when you are on Regent Street: these would be mistakes. But if you thought you were in Trafalgar Square when you were on a Scottish moor, that would be, *not* a mistake, but a *mental disturbance* (*OC* 71). As Wittgenstein says: 'If I believe that I am sitting in my room when I am not, then I shall not be said to have *made a mistake*.' (*OC* 195)

It may be felt that this is a nice grammatical distinction, but that it is not in disagreement with Descartes, who held that when your judgement is free from any possible doubt, then you cannot be mistaken, or deceived, or mentally disturbed, or *wrong in any way*: you *know* that your judgement is true, and it *is* true. But it is exactly these assumptions that Wittgenstein is questioning. He says: 'I cannot possibly doubt that I was never in the stratosphere. Does that make me know it? Does it make it true?' (*OC* 222)

Wittgenstein seems to be saying that when a human being is objectively certain of something, when he cannot be in doubt about it, when he cannot conceive how it could be false — it does *not follow* that the thing is so. This interpretation is confirmed by the following remarks:

> To say of a man that, in Moore's sense, he *knows* something; that what he says is therefore unconditionally the truth, seems wrong to me. — It is the truth only in so far as it is an unshakeable (*unwankende*) foundation of his language-games. (*OC* 403)

> I want to say: it is not that on some points men know the truth with perfect certainty. But perfect certainty is only a matter of their attitude. (*OC* 404)

Being perfectly certain (i.e. objectively certain) of something — in the sense of regarding it as unintelligible that one might be wrong — is an attitude, a stance, that we take towards various matters; but this attitude does not necessarily carry *truth* in its wake.

UNHEARD-OF OCCURRENCES

In an attempt to draw more clearly the boundaries of the attitude of 'objective certainty', Wittgenstein tries to determine how this attitude would be affected by (imaginary) extraordinary events. For example, he might have occasion to tell someone in a letter, that he is now living in England:

> Even a proposition like this one, that I am now living in England, has these two sides: it is not a *mistake* — but on the other hand, what do I know of England? Can't my judgement go entirely wrong (*ganz fehl gehen*)?
>   Wouldn't it be possible that people came into my room and all declared the opposite? — even gave me 'proofs' of it, so that I suddenly stood there like a madman alone among people who were all normal, or a normal person alone among madmen? Couldn't I there come to doubt what to me now is at the furthest remove from doubt? (Könnten mir da nicht Zweifel an dem kommen, was mir jetzt das Unzweifelhafteste ist?) (*OC* 420)

One possibility he seems to be envisaging is that he might actually come to be in doubt as to whether he is living in England. Certainty might turn into doubt. In another remark he goes even further, by suggesting that some of his most certain judgements might turn out to be *false*:

> What if something *really unheard-of* happened? — If, say, I saw

houses gradually turning into steam without any apparent cause; if the cattle in the fields stood on their heads and laughed and spoke comprehensible words; if trees gradually changed into men and men into trees. Now, was I right when I said before all these things happened 'I know that that's a house', etc., or simply 'That's a house', etc.? (*OC* 513)

In asking whether he was *right* in making those statements, Wittgenstein seems to be suggesting a negative answer — that those weird happenings would prove his statements to be *not true*.

But *another* possibility, which he considers, is that the impact of such unheard-of occurrences might be to take away his ability to make any judgements at all. For example:

If I were contradicted on all sides and told that this person's name was not what I had always known it was (and I use 'know' here intentionally) then in that case the foundation of all judging would be taken away from me (*OC* 614).

But what could make me doubt whether this person here is N. N., whom I have known for years? Here a doubt would seem to drag everything with it and plunge it into chaos. (*OC* 613)

The same thought is expressed in this remark: 'If my name is *not* L. W., how can I rely on what is meant by "true" and "false"?' (*OC* 515) 'Not only do I never have the slightest doubt that I am called that, but there is no judgement I could be certain of if I started doubting that.' (*OC* 490)

When imagining unheard-of occurrences that would appear to challenge something of which one is objectively certain, the *first* possibility, sketched by Wittgenstein, is that the certainty would be replaced by doubt — or perhaps even by the conclusion that the thing of which one was certain is not (was not) true. The *second* possibility is that this challenge would produce such a shock to the framework within which one thinks, questions, doubts, makes sure, draws conclusions, etc., that one's capacity for thinking and making judgements might be undermined. There is still a *third* possibility, namely, that one would *stand fast* on one's certainty — refuse to be shaken — refuse to accept the seeming evidence against this certainty:

If something happened (such as someone telling me something) calculated to make me doubtful of my own name, there would certainly also be something that made the grounds of these doubts themselves seem doubtful, and I could therefore decide to retain my old belief. (*OC* 516)

Wittgenstein suggests that this posture of rejecting doubt, or refusing to consider anything as evidence to the contrary, involves something like an *act of will*. In regard to his own name he says that he *would refuse* to consider any argument meant to show that it isn't L. W. He then asks: 'And what does "I *would* refuse" mean? Is it the expression of an intention?' (*OC* 577) 'If someone says that he will recognize no experience as proof of the opposite, that is after all a *decision*.' (*OC* 368) Speaking of his 'knowledge' that *this* is his foot, he says that 'if anything happened that seemed to conflict with this knowledge I should have to regard *that* as deception.' (*OC* 361) He follows this up by saying: 'But doesn't this show that that knowledge is related to a decision?' (*OC* 362) He asks himself the question: 'What if you had to change your opinion even on these most fundamental things?'; and the answer seems to him to be: 'You don't *have* to change it. That is just what their being "fundamental" is.' (*OC* 512)

REVIEW

Wittgenstein is trying to describe the role that the concept of objective certainty has for human beings in the daily course of their lives. There are many propositions, some the same for all of us, some differing from one person to another – but all of them of the character that for us doubting them makes no sense; we consider it to be inconceivable that we might be mistaken. Some are propositions of mathematics; some are contingent propositions. All of them 'stand fast' for us. They are not subjected to inquiry, testing, verification. Instead, they belong to the framework within which the activities of questioning, checking, investigating, proving, take place. The sense in which these propositions are 'fundamental' for us is that they give shape, fix boundaries, for those areas where we can intelligibly doubt, inquire, obtain evidence, and come to know. Without them our thinking would be formless: indeed, would not *be* thinking.

In the normal course of life we do not encounter attempts to discredit these 'certainties': no one seriously tries to prove to us that 5×5 does not equal 25, or that the earth has existed for less than 100 years, or that our name is not what we have always known it to be, or that we have been to the moon. These things are not contested.

Wittgenstein explores this concept of certainty by putting it under stress — as one might test the rigidity of a metal in a laboratory. Objective certainty is a human attitude. Wittgenstein is probing it, testing it, by trying to estimate, for himself, how his attitude of being objectively certain of something would fare if he were confronted with unheard-of occurrences in nature, or was contradicted on all sides by the testimony of others, by seemingly authentic documents, and so on.

Wittgenstein's procedure of placing his own 'certainties' under imaginary stress is of deep interest. The outcome seems to be that he wavers between three different possibilities. One possibility is that a particular certainty of his would give way under stress; the certainty would be replaced by doubt; he would question or even give up one of these fundamental certainties; but in doing so would retain his ability to make judgements. A second possibility is that all of his thinking would be undermined; he would be bewildered, disoriented in language and behaviour. A third possibility is that he would, despite all, continue to stand fast; he would refuse to accept any of the apparent evidence against his certainty, no matter how unanswerable it seemed to be.

It is important to notice, however, that Wittgenstein is not trying to *predict* how *in fact* he would react if he were confronted in the next moment or next week, with unheard-of events in nature, or with other apparent evidence against one of his certainties. In relation to his 'belief', 'knowledge', or 'assumption' that his name is L. W., he says:

> What if it *seemed* to turn out that what until now has seemed immune to doubt was a false assumption? Would I react as I do when a belief has proved false; or would it seem to knock from under me the ground of my judging? — But of course what I want here is not a *prophecy*. (Aber ich will hier natürlich nicht eine *Prophezeiung*.) (*OC* 492)

In reflecting on the words 'Nothing in the world will convince me of the opposite!', an exclamation he might make if one of his 'certainties' was challenged, his comment is: 'This does not say (Es ist damit nicht gesagt), that in fact nothing in the world will be able to convince me of something else.' (*OC* 382)

Wittgenstein says that his intention is *not* to try to predict (to prophesy) what in fact he would do, or what in fact would happen to his thinking, if at a future time seeming counter-evidence confronted him. Then what is his intention? I believe that he is trying to determine the *weight* that some one or other of these 'certainties' has for him *now* — not to predict what weight it would have for him on some future occasion. He is trying to define his *present* attitude towards apparent counter-evidence, not what it might be in the future.

This undertaking is complicated by the fact that a particular certainty of his (e.g. that his name is L. W.) does not stand in isolation. It is linked with other certainties — with innumerable memories of what he was always called by his family and friends; with his memory of the name on his passport; with his memory of having published a book under the name L. W.; and so on. The imagined counter-evidence to 'prove' that this is not his name and never has been, would have to attack a vast set of his beliefs and recollections. To doubt all of that would be to become uncertain of his history and identity. Wittgenstein is trying to determine whether any apparent 'proofs' *could* be powerful enough to overthrow, or to threaten, *all* of those countless beliefs and memories.

The result of this thought-experiment in *On Certainty* appears to be ambiguous. Wittgenstein does not seem to succeed in determining a precise weight for any one of his sample certainties, *if* it were to be 'contradicted on all sides'. He appears to hesitate between the three possibilities he discusses: that he might accept the imagined counter-evidence and adjust his thinking to it; that his capacity for any thought or judgement would be destroyed; that he would *decide* to stand fast in his certainty through thick and thin. He asks himself: 'But would it be *unthinkable* that I should stay in the saddle however much the facts bucked?' (*OC* 616) He does not seem to have arrived at an answer that satisfied him.

A problem we have been considering is whether, on Wittgenstein's view, being objectively certain of something guarantees that the thing of which one is certain is *true*. There is a marked contrast here between Wittgenstein and Descartes. The latter thought he had proved that his clear and distinct perceptions *had* to be true, and that he could never have grounds for doubting them. Wittgenstein's position is different. When he weighs one of his fundamental certainties against the imagined extraordinary events that would appear to go against it, no definite conclusion emerges. Whether that certainty would stand fast against the apparent counter-evidence remains unresolved — which means that whether he would still regard it as true remains unresolved.

I take it that Wittgenstein's difficulty in determining a definite weight for a fundamental certainty of his against imagined counter-evidence, is not a matter that is peculiar to Wittgenstein but would be the same for anyone. Any of us who conducted a similar thought-experiment would probably find himself torn between the three possibilities that Wittgenstein considers. Someone might conclude from this that there is *no* objective certainty, that there is nothing which is totally immune to doubt. I believe this would be an incorrect conclusion and will try to explain why.

The things that are 'perfectly' or 'objectively' certain, which are immune to doubt, in regard to which being mistaken is inconceivable, have that status for us only in the *normal* circumstances of human life. The expressions 'I *know* it to be true', 'I can't be mistaken', 'It is absolutely certain', 'It would be senseless to doubt it', etc., are learned and used in life as it is. One could say that their use presupposes that the course of nature will continue to be what it has been (that trees will not turn into men or men into trees, that cows will not speak comprehensible words, that events will not 'gang up' to seemingly prove that one's past history is totally different from what one remembers it as being). Our use of these expressions is at home in the actual world, not in an imaginary world of fantastic events. Our language-games are played in the real world, and their application is restricted to this real world. No wonder then that if we try to project these expressions into an imaginary setting of unheard-of occurrences, *we do not know what to think*!

This illuminates one objection that Wittgenstein has to Moore. When Moore, speaking *as a philosopher*, declares 'I know that that's a tree', Wittgenstein wants to reply, 'You don't *know* anything!': but he would *not* make this reply to someone who made the same utterance 'without philosophical intention' (*OC* 407). When a philosopher states, 'I know that I am now sitting in a chair', this statement seems to Wittgenstein to be 'unjustified and presumptuous' — but not when the same statement is made in some needful context of ordinary life (*OC* 553). Why this difference?

When Moore says, philosophically, that he *knows* that such-and-such is the case, he seems to imply that the such-and-such is true *unconditionally* (*OC* 403). It is then that it is 'presumptuous'. This is not so when there is some occasion for the same utterance in the flow of actual life:

> In its language-game it is not presumptuous. There, it has no higher position than, simply, the human language-game. For there it has its restricted application. (*OC* 554)

The clue to the difference between the philosopher's statement and the same sentence uttered in ordinary life, is that the latter has a *restricted application*! It is not unconditional. It is conditioned by the regularities and vicissitudes of real life, not by the unheard-of occurrences that Wittgenstein imagines in his thought-experiments.

Descartes's certainty that his clear and distinct perceptions are true, was absolutely unconditional. *God would not allow them* to be false! Moore's certainties do not have God's backing: but they have the same flavour — of being completely unrestricted and unconditional.

Suppose that Wittgenstein had been suffering from mental depression and had gone to consult a psychiatrist. In his preliminary examination the doctor thinks it necessary to ascertain, first of all, whether this patient is able to identify familiar objects. So he asks, 'Do you know what that is?' (pointing at a chair); and Wittgenstein replies, 'I know that it's a chair.' (*OC* 355) This would not be a philosophical assertion. Wittgenstein was not being called upon to state what he would think if the 'chair' began to turn into an alligator. In the context of the psychiatric examination, both the question and the answer are restricted to the practical question of whether the patient has the normal ability to identify familiar objects.

In contrast, when Moore declares, as a philosopher, 'I know that that's a chair', his assertion does not pertain to any natural occasion for saying it, and does not have the limited scope that such an occasion would give to it. It is as if Moore were declaring: 'No supposition, even the most extravagant, as to what might happen in the future, could have any bearing on the certainty that this is a chair!' When put like that, Moore's assertion does appear presumptuous — as if God himself could have nothing to say about it! (*OC* 554)

POSSIBLE AND IMPOSSIBLE DOUBT

Wittgenstein says: 'Imagine a language-game "When I call you, come in through the door." In any ordinary case, a doubt whether there really is a door there will be impossible.' (*OC* 391) But immediately thereafter he says: 'What I need to show is that a doubt is not necessary even when it is possible. That the possibility of the language-game doesn't depend on everything being doubted that can be doubted.' (*OC* 392) The sequence of these remarks is puzzling. In one remark he says that a particular doubt is impossible; in the next remark he seems to say that the very same doubt *is* possible. Isn't this a contradiction? Presumably the proposition that there's a door there is to be understood as an example of something that is 'objectively certain' — which is supposed to mean that doubt is logically excluded, that doubt doesn't make sense. If doubt *is* possible, shouldn't this mean that the certainty that there's a door there is not 'objective' but merely 'subjective'?

No. Wittgenstein *does* mean, I think, that a doubt whether there's a door there is *both* possible and impossible. It is impossible in a context of actual life where you have instructed someone to come through the door when you call him. A doubt whether there's a door there would not occur to either of you, and would make no sense to either of you. On the other hand, if you indulged in wild imaginings, such as that what 'looks like' a door changes before one's eyes into a camel, and then asked someone whether *if* that happened would he be right in thinking *now* that there's a door there — then the person might be in doubt as to what to say or think in such a case. Of course there has been a radical change in stage-setting, from the one case to the other. In the ordinary setting for the use of those words, to suggest a doubt whether there's a door there could only be a joke. In the philosophical setting, where 'unheard-of' occurrences are imagined, it is not a joke: but this is not a setting for the employment of language in daily life.

It seems to me that in *On Certainty* Wittgenstein is carrying on two arguments at once. One argument is that the objective certainties of human life are not threatened by the philosophical imagining of unheard-of occurrences: this argument is against Scepticism. The other argument is against the Realism of a philosopher like Moore, who takes these objective certainties as if they are absolutely unconditional. Moore does not give his assertion 'I know that that's a tree' its restricted application to an everyday situation. Instead, he uses this assertion to make a philosophical declaration, by which he seems to say that no happening whatever, however fantastic, could make questionable this certainty of his. It is as if this certainty is so powerful that not even God could so manage things as to make it doubtful. Wittgenstein hits the nail on the head with his remark: 'Is God bound by our knowledge: are a lot of our statements *incapable* of falsehood? For that is what we want to say.' (*OC* 436) We have a philosophical inclination to think like that. In Descartes's theory it is explicit that God is *bound* by our clear and distinct perceptions: for His making them false would be a contradiction of His essential *veracity*, and so is impossible.

DO WE KNOW THAT UNHEARD-OF EVENTS WILL NOT OCCUR?

The temptation to regard knowledge and certainty as concepts of unconditional application, may be expressed in the feeling that the imagining of unheard-of events cannot show that we do not *know* that that's a door and not a camel, or that we do not *know* that our name is what we have always thought it to be — *for this reason*: that *in knowing* that that's a door we *know* that it will *not* turn into a camel; and by virtue of our knowing that our name is what we have always thought it to be, we *know* that future events will *not* gang up on us in such a way as to make it seem that this is not our name. This knowledge of ours reaches into the future and eliminates in advance these imagined possibilities. The imagining of such bizarre occurrences is, therefore, a red herring — *not* because they would not upset our certainties if they occurred, but because we *know* they will not occur.

Let us consider this point. One thing that Moore claimed to know with certainty is that his body has existed continuously since his birth.[22] Imagine that one night after Moore had retired, a member of the family noticed that Moore was not in his bed and could not locate him elsewhere in the house. The rest of the family was aroused, and all of them searched throughout the house without success. The possibility that he had gone outdoors was ruled out by the fact that all the doors and windows were locked from the inside. After two hours of fruitless search Moore was discovered asleep in his bed. The following day all of the family were convinced that Moore had disappeared for two hours. Moore himself had no recollection of having left his bed during the night, or of any unusual occurrence. The others cannot avoid the incredible thought that Moore's body must have ceased to exist for two hours.

Do we *know* that such a thing will not happen, *could not* happen? None of us *believes* that it will or could happen. But do we *know* it? Wittgenstein makes some remarks that are applied to a different example but which apply to this one too:

> One might also put this question: 'If you know that that is your foot
> — do you also know, or do you only believe, that no future
> experience will seem to contradict your knowledge?' (That is, that
> nothing will seem to *you yourself* to do so.) (*OC* 364)

> If someone replied: 'I also know that it will never *seem* to me as if
> anything contradicted that knowledge' — what could we gather
> from that, other than that he himself had no doubt it would never
> happen? (*OC* 365)

If Moore, having declared that he *knows* that his body has existed continuously since his birth, were to declare further that he *knows* that nothing will ever seem to him to contradict this — what would this come to, other than an expression of his *conviction* that such a thing will never occur? Probably most of us share that conviction. But what do we *know* about the matter? Can we *prove* that it couldn't happen?

Here is it relevant to reflect on the extent to which our 'knowledge' rests on things we *believe, accept, take on trust.* Wittgenstein dwells on this in many remarks:

> As children we learn facts; e.g. that every human being has a brain,
> and we take them on trust. I believe that there is an island,
> Australia, of such-and-such a shape, and so on and so on; I believe
> that I had great-grandparents, that the people who gave themselves
> out as my parents really were my parents, etc. (*OC* 159)

> I learned an enormous amount and accepted it on human authority,
> and then I found some things confirmed or disconfirmed by my
> own experience. (*OC* 161)

> In general I take as true what is found in text-books, of geography
> for example. Why? I say: all these facts have been confirmed a
> hundred times over. But how do I know that? What is my evidence
> for it? (*OC* 162)

I believe what people transmit to me in a certain manner. In this way I believe geographical, chemical, historical facts, etc. That is how I *learn* the sciences. Of course learning is based on believing. (*OC* 170)

Knowledge is in the end based on acceptance (*auf der Anerkennung*). (*OC* 378)

What kind of grounds have I for trusting text-books of physics? I have no grounds for not trusting them. And I trust them. I know how such books are produced — or rather, I believe I know. I have some evidence, but it does not go very far and is of a very scattered kind. I have heard, seen and read various things. (*OC* 600)

Must I not somewhere begin to trust? That is to say: somewhere I must begin with not-doubting; and that is not, so to speak, hasty but excusable: it is part of judging. (*OC* 150)

The child learns by believing the adult. Doubt comes *after* belief. (*OC* 160)

These observations apply to every human being. A child could not learn anything if it did not just *accept* many things it is told by parents and teachers. As adults we continue to rely on much of what we read and hear. Descartes's idea that a human being can build up knowledge all by himself was a huge misconception. His supposed procedure of doubting all of his former beliefs was only pretending to doubt them. One thing he never thought of doubting was the *meaning* of the words he used in expounding his philosophical meditations. As Wittgenstein remarks: 'If you are not certain of any fact, you cannot be certain of the meaning of your words either.' (*OC* 114) 'I am not more certain of the meaning of my words than I am of particular judgements.' (*OC* 126) 'If I wanted to doubt that this is my hand, how could I help doubting that the word "hand" has any meaning?' (*OC* 369)

It is extremely interesting that Descartes was challenged on this very point. The authors of *Objections* VI to the *Meditations* wrote:

In order to be sure that you think, you ought to know what to think, or what thinking, is, and what existence is; but since you do not yet know what these things are, how can you know that you think or exist?[23]

Descartes's reply is remarkably innocent:

It is indeed true that no one can be sure that he knows or that he exists, unless he knows what thought is and what existence . . . It is altogether enough for one to know it by means of that internal cognition which always precedes reflective knowledge, and which, when the object is thought and existence, is innate in all men; so that, however overwhelmed by prejudice and attentive to the words rather than their signification, though we may feign that we do not possess that knowledge, we cannot nevertheless really be without it. When, therefore, anyone perceives that he thinks and that it thence follows that he exists, although he chanced never previously to have asked what thought is, nor what existence, he cannot nevertheless fail to have a knowledge of each sufficient to give him assurance on this score.[24]

But Descartes did not invent the words 'thinking', 'existence', 'doubt'. They are words of common language. He never thought of doubting how they are used. If he had, his reflections would have stopped right there. To claim that a person does not have to learn from others the meaning of those words — that a child has an 'innate' knowledge of how the word 'thinking' is used — would be preposterous. Descartes could not even pretend to doubt all things except by not doubting the meaning of the language he used.

Let us return to the question of whether we *know* that unheard-of events will not occur — events of a kind such that if they did occur they would at least *seem* to us to contradict some fundamental certainties of ours. If we reflect on what Wittgenstein reminds us of — that learning is based on believing; that most of what we know or think we know of history, physiology, geography, chemistry, astronomy, physics, is not based on anyone's personal research and verification, but is based largely on *trust* — then it seems clear that not one of us is in a position to *know* that unheard-of occurrences will not take place. Many of us are *convinced* that they will not take place. But if we said that we *know* it, that *would* seem 'presumptuous'.

Someone might agree with the foregoing, and yet insist that he *knows* that even if he were confronted with outrageous happenings his 'certainties' would remain undamaged. But as previously said, if this posture was actually maintained it would have the character of a *decision*. This helps to explain Wittgenstein's remark: 'It is not that on some points men know the truth with perfect certainty. But perfect certainty is only a matter of their attitude.' (*OC* 404) This attitude is in part an expression of *will*. It is a *refusal* to regard anything as counter-evidence. It is well described in the remark:

> I can't be making a mistake; but if after all something should appear to speak against my proposition, I shall stand by it despite this appearance. (*OC* 636)

Perfect certainty about something is not a neutral posture. It is an unwillingness to consider seriously any counter-evidence. It regards that something as *settled forever*.

Let us consider again the question: when your certainty of something is 'objective', does it *follow* that you *know* that the something is so? In the section 'Objective certainty and knowledge' I argued for Wittgenstein's view that this does *not* follow — that when in real life one has an occasion to express such certainty about the truth of something, the meaning of this certainty (namely, that one regards a doubt as nonsense, as logically excluded) rules out both 'I know' and 'I don't know' as things one can rightly say. If we widen the horizon, and consider such an assertion when it is philosophical and unconditional, then there are two reasons against characterizing this certainty as knowledge. First, we do not *know* that bizarre events will not occur, events that would *seem* to contradict our certainty. Second, if we agree to this, but maintain that even if they did occur they would not count against our certainty, this attitude expresses a *decision* rather than *knowledge*.

'SO FAR AS ONE CAN KNOW SUCH A THING'

Wittgenstein says that all of the assertions of the form 'I know that . . .', made by Moore philosophically, could be employed in situations of real life (*OC* 622). When Moore made those assertions he was confronted not by any actual or potential doubt of everyday life, but only by philosophical doubt. Philosophical doubt is not genuine *doubt*, since there is not the normal connection between doubt and conduct. We can be sure that Descartes's philosophical doubt as to whether he was seated by a fire did not prevent him from occasionally stirring the fire or throwing a log on it.

Wittgenstein says that, for each of Moore's sentences, 'I can imagine circumstances that turn it into a move in one of our language-games, and by that it loses everything that is philo-sophically astonishing.' (*OC* 622) I argued in the section 'Objective certainty and knowledge' that when the utterance 'I know . . .' has an ordinary, non-philosophical sense, it is characteristically addressed to some actual or potential doubt, or disbelief, or weak belief. In order to turn one of Moore's philosophical assertions into a non-philosophical one, we need to introduce doubt or disbelief into the situation. Wittgenstein does this with Moore's sentence 'I know that I have never been far from the surface of the earth', when he imagines Moore being captured by a wild tribe (perhaps after shipwreck) whose members 'express the suspicion' that he has come from somewhere between the earth and the moon. (*OC* 264)

Wittgenstein makes it a part of his example that the people of the tribe 'have fantastic ideas of human ability to fly and know nothing of physics'. This has the implication that Moore cannot *explain* to them *why* it is impossible that he should have come from outer space. At first Moore might simply deny that their suspicion is true. But suppose that they did not accept his denial and insist that he *must* have come from outer space, perhaps without being aware of it. Those circumstances would provide an occasion (perhaps an urgent one) for Moore to declare, 'I *know* I have never been in outer space,'

This would be an attenuated use of 'I know . . .': for, because of the difference between his culture and theirs, he cannot tell them *why* their supposition is impossible. Nor do they have sufficient confidence in him to be simply *reassured* by his assertion. His 'I know' would not be functioning in any of the specific ways mentioned in the section 'Objective certainty and knowledge'. Still, something of the ordinary use of those words would be retained; for Moore would be *trying* to convince them that their suspicion or disbelief was wrong. Of course Moore would regard their supposition as nonsense. But his 'I know' would also be an *expression of certainty* in the face of their suspicion, and not *merely* the declaration that their supposition makes no sense. His 'I know' would, in this example, come to much the same as 'I can't be mistaken.' As Wittgenstein remarks, '"I can't be mistaken about it" is an ordinary sentence, which serves to give the certainty-value of a statement.' (*OC* 638)

This imagined case is puzzling. In the section 'Objective certainty and knowledge' I drew attention to several passages in which Wittgenstein was holding that when one's certainty of something is 'objective' (when one regards any doubt about the matter as 'logically excluded'), then it is inappropriate to declare that one *knows* the something to be true. But in *OC* 622 he is saying that every one of Moore's assertions of the form 'I know . . .' could occur in circumstances that would make it 'a move in one of our language-games' — which is to say that 'I know' *would* be appropriate there.

Wittgenstein surely intends to be referring to cases where, for the speaker, doubt is logically excluded — for he says, in *OC* 622, that it is correct to use 'I know' *in the contexts which Moore mentioned*. It was typical of those contexts that, for Moore, doubt was logically excluded. So I take it that this feature of the cases is to be retained. Has Wittgenstein, in his reflections, changed his view of what the correct use of 'I know' is?

It isn't necessary to suppose that Wittgenstein changed his view. After all, in his 'wild tribe' case (*OC* 264) he made a significant change in one of Moore's examples: he changed Moore's audience from philosophers to genuine primitive people who actually suspect that Moore might have come from outer space. So we have a case where a Moore-like assertion would have a *double* role. In part it would express Moore's feeling that his being mistaken about this matter makes no sense; but also this assertion would be an attempt (perhaps a vain one) to remove the suspicion of those people. The assertion would *combine* a conceptual ('grammatical') statement with a genuine expression of certainty in the face of disbelief or doubt. The words 'I *know*' would be appropriate for the second part, but not for the first part. There is no reason why there should not be an assertion which was this kind of mixture. Thus, we are to imagine a case in which a Moore-like assertion would be, in part, a normal use of 'I *know*' and to that extent would cease to be 'philosophically astonishing' (*OC* 622).

Wittgenstein then makes a remark that is itself astonishing:

> What is odd is that in such a case I always feel like saying (although it is wrong): 'I know that — so far as one can know such a thing.' That is incorrect, but something right is hidden behind it. (*OC* 623)

Wittgenstein is apparently envisaging circumstances in which he himself would make a Moore-like assertion (e.g. 'I know that I have never been in outer space'), and where his assertion would be, in part at least, a normal use of 'I know'. Yet he has an inclination to attach the qualification 'so far as one can know such a thing'.

It is surprising that Wittgenstein should have that inclination. If his assertion were, in part at least, an appropriate use of 'I know', why should he want to weaken, or retract it, with that phrase? He even says that this qualification is *incorrect*, but that 'something right is hidden behind it'. Earlier in *On Certainty*, as we saw, he emphasized the differences between an observation of the form 'I know . . .' — 'as it might be used in ordinary life, and the same utterance when a philosopher makes it' (*OC* 406). He went on to remark: 'For when Moore says "I know that that's . . ." I want to reply "You don't *know* anything!" — and yet I would not say that to anyone who was speaking without philosophical intention.' (*OC* 407) So it is a philosophical 'I know' that he criticizes, not an 'I know' of ordinary life. But in *OC* 622 he has imagined that there might be circumstances for a Moore-like utterance, in which it would be (in part at least) an assertion of ordinary language — yet he has an inclination to qualify it with the phrase 'so far as one can know such a thing'.

Let us consider, first, why this qualification would be wrong; and, second, what is the 'something right' that is 'hidden behind it'. It is easy to see what is *wrong* with adding 'so far as one can know such a thing' to one's own assertion that one knows something, when this assertion has a justified place in ordinary life. The phrase 'so far as one can know such a thing' has a normal use in which it *diminishes* the strength of the assertion to which it is attached. If I had occasion to say of two people, A and B, 'I know that A is envious of B', but then added, 'so far as one can know such a thing', this addition would probably be taken as the reflection that it is difficult to know anything with *certainty* about one person's attitude toward another. It would be like saying, 'but of course one can be mistaken about such matters.' Such qualifications Wittgenstein calls 'rules of caution'. He says: 'But these rules of caution only make sense if they come to an end somewhere. A doubt without an end is not even a doubt.' (*OC* 625) He imagines the following being said: 'The English name of this colour is *certainly* "green" — unless, of course, I am making a slip of the tongue or am confused in some way.' (*OC* 626) He adds: 'Wouldn't one have to insert this clause into *all* language-games? (Which shows its senselessness.)' (*OC* 627) The same is true of the clause 'but I may be mistaken'. If one attached it to *every* assertion it would no longer have any function. It is actually used only with *some* assertions, and there it serves to warn the other person not to place heavy reliance on the speaker's statement.

But it isn't merely that the qualification 'but I may be mistaken' would lose its sense if attached to *every* assertion. There are *particular* statements, the Moore-like ones (e.g. 'My name is L. W.', 'I have never been on the moon'), which are of such a nature that, when there are genuine occasions for asserting them, it would be wrong to qualify them with the clause 'but I may be mistaken'. As Wittgenstein remarks: 'If I were to say "I have never been on the moon — but I may be mistaken", that would be idiotic.' (*OC* 662) Also: 'It is right to say of myself "I cannot be mistaken about my name", and wrong if I say "perhaps I am mistaken."' (*OC* 629)

Wittgenstein is supposing, in *OC* 623, that there might be a situation of real life where he had occasion to declare, for example, 'I know that I have never been on the moon.' He has the inclination to add, even in this real-life case, 'so far as one can know such a thing'. But if it would be wrong to add 'perhaps I'm mistaken', it would be just as wrong to add 'so far as one can know such a thing'. Wittgenstein admits this. Yet he says that 'something right is hidden behind' his inclination to attach this qualification. What could that *right* thing be?

WITTGENSTEIN'S 'SCEPTICISM'

Wittgenstein gave no answer to this question. To propose an answer requires a *conjecture*. My conjecture is that something which might be called 'scepticism' emerges from Wittgenstein's reflections in *On Certainty*. It is not what in philosophy is usually meant by Scepticism. Wittgenstein is not holding that all assertions of the form 'I *know* it to be so — it is absolutely certain' are *unjustified*. On the contrary, he insists that often one *has the right* to say, 'I *know* it to be so; I can't be mistaken.'

That which in Wittgenstein's outlook in *On Certainty* I am venturing to call 'scepticism', contains *three* components. The first of these is his reflection that, even in the examples of contingent propositions about which you *cannot be mistaken*, where your certainty is as well founded as any certainty can be, where you cannot *conceive how* you could be wrong, it is nevertheless not impossible that you *are* wrong! As he puts this point in one remark:

> It would be completely *misleading* to say: 'I believe my name is L. W.' And this too is right: I cannot be making a *mistake* about it. But that does not mean that I am *infallible* about it. (*OC* 425; last emphasis added)

And in referring to his assertion 'I have never been on the moon', he says: 'I have a right to say "I can't be making a mistake about this", even if I am in error.' (*OC* 663)

I am repeating the point made in my earlier section 'Objective certainty and truth' — that being certain about something does *not* entail that that something is *so*. It is easy to see this when by 'certainty' we mean 'subjective certainty' — which is simply being convinced, not having any doubt. But when the certainty is *objective*, when truly we cannot be 'making a mistake', when we regard it as *nonsensical* to suppose that our assertion might be false, when we do not *understand* how it *could* be false — then we have a strong temptation to believe that reality *must* agree with our certainty.

I take Wittgenstein to be holding that this is *not* so. The point is difficult to grasp. It almost seems that we are being shown a truth that we cannot express in language. We are being shown that even when our certainty about something is perfectly objective, we can be *wrong* — yet we cannot express this insight in a particular case by saying, 'Perhaps I am wrong.' Now *that* is correct. But it is *incorrect* to think that Wittgenstein's point cannot be expressed in language: for it *is* expressed in the general logical observation that when a person's certainty is objective, it does *not follow* that what he is certain of is true.

A possible source of confusion is the following. Wittgenstein defined the concept of being 'objectively certain' of the truth of something, as meaning that a mistake is *logically excluded*. You may ask: 'If a mistake is logically excluded, then how can that something turn out to be false?' Two things need to be said here. First, Wittgenstein remarks that we must 'make a distinction between the ways in which something "turns out to be false"' (*als falsch erweist*) (*OC* 641). For example, you have put a pan of water on the fire in order to bring the water to a boil. Suppose someone present believes that a spell has been put on the water, which will prevent it from boiling. You might say with irritation, 'Of course it will boil. It's certain that it will.' If the water did not boil but instead turned to ice, you would be dumbfounded! But you couldn't say, 'I was mistaken.' It was not a *mistake* because there was no way in which you could have anticipated that outcome. As Wittgenstein says: 'There is a difference between an error (*Irrtum*) for which, as it were, a place in the game is anticipated (*vorgesehen*), and a complete irregularity that happens as an exception.' (*OC* 647)

The second thing to be noted, is that it is an *individual* who asserts that something is certain. If I am certain about the truth of something, it is *I* who am certain. If I regard it as nonsense to doubt that my name is not what I have always supposed it to be, it is for *me* that being wrong about this is logically excluded. If I have occasion to declare, 'I can't be mistaken about my name', this assertion 'relates essentially to *me*' (*OC* 637). But the existence of the general language-game with personal names does not prevent *me* from being in error about *my* name. As Wittgenstein says:

> The language-game that operates with people's names can certainly exist even if I am mistaken about my name — but it does presuppose that it is nonsensical to say that the majority of people are mistaken about their names. (*OC* 628)

Another component of Wittgenstein's 'scepticism' is his reflection that all of our objective certainties rest on acceptance and trust. 'Our learning is based on believing.' (*OC* 170) 'Knowledge is in the end based on acceptance (*Anerkennung*).' (*OC* 378) 'A language-game is only possible, if one trusts something.' (*OC* 509)

A third component of this 'scepticism' is Wittgenstein's realization that there can be *no guarantee* that one will not be 'contradicted on all sides' by the testimony of other persons (*OC* 420, 503); or that 'unheard-of' events will not at some time disrupt the regularities of nature (*OC* 513).

I am proposing that these three reflections constitute the 'something right' that is 'hidden behind' Wittgenstein's phrase 'so far as one can know such a thing'. According to my interpretation this phrase is *not* serving as a qualification, as a weakening or diminishing, of any of the assertions of certainty one might make when these are appropriate in occasions of real life. Instead, the phrase 'so far as one can know such a thing' operates at an entirely different level — as a highly condensed observation about the presuppositions and limits of human certainty.

Wittgenstein's 'scepticism' is truly *philosophical*, although it is not to be confused with the familiar tradition of Philosophical Scepticism. It is philosophical in the sense of being a set of general observations about the framework and boundaries of the *concepts* of knowledge and certainty, as these figure in the real life of human beings. Wittgenstein's 'scepticism' is expressed by his remark 'It is always by favour of Nature that one knows something.' (*OC* 505)

CONCLUSION

Both Descartes and Wittgenstein regard certainty as a human attitude towards the truth of something. Both understand 'perfect certainty' to be characterized by the impossibility of one's conceiving any ground for doubt, and by the impossibility of being mistaken. Descartes thinks that certainty is restricted: first, to one's own 'ideas'; second, to highly abstract propositions, such as that 'There must be at least as much reality in the efficient and total cause as in its effect'; and third, to whatever can be strictly deduced from a conjunction of the first two. In contrast, Wittgenstein takes certainty to apply to humdrum contingent propositions of daily life, such as 'My name is L. W.', 'I am living in England', 'I have never been to China.' Descartes believes that a single human being can, all by himself, arrive at many certainties. Wittgenstein's view is that anyone's certainty about anything presupposes a mass of knowledge and belief that is inherited from other human beings and taken on trust. Descartes thinks that one's metaphysical certainties have a Divine backing and, therefore, *must* be true. Wittgenstein's view is that when one's certainty of something is 'objective', one cannot understand how it would be possible that one is making a mistake (e.g. *OC* 660) — but that it does *not* follow that one is *right*. He says: 'I can't be making a mistake — but some day, rightly or wrongly, I may think I realize that I was not competent to judge.' (*OC* 645)

Epilogue

In certain respects the *Tractatus* belongs to an old tradition of metaphysical philosophy. This tradition includes such conceptions as that there is an *a priori* form of all possible worlds; that there are simple things which are the ultimate constituents of reality; that these things combine to form states of affairs; that elementary states of affairs can be presented in elementary propositions; that every non-elementary proposition is analysable into an arrangement of elementary ones; that thoughts are structures composed of mental elements; that a thought is an intrinsic representation and a sentence of language a derivative representation of a possible state of affairs; that thoughts and propositions contain their own method of projection; that there is a common nature or general form of all thoughts and propositions; that every genuine proposition can be compared with reality; that when we *mean* or *understand* something, the meaning and understanding is achieved by an inner process of calculation or computation. The *Tractatus* gave these conceptions their most compressed, rigorous, and elegant presentation. In Wittgenstein's new thinking all of these conceptions are swept away.

What are some of the landmarks of the second outlook? One is the rejection of 'essentialism': the assumption that the concepts we employ are governed by necessary and sufficient conditions. Wittgenstein's detailed study of the concept of *reading* (*PI* 156—78) is a model of this criticism. One initially supposes that there must be a difference between reading a sentence in a newspaper and, say, only *pretending* to read it. Employing a series of examples, Wittgenstein shows that there is not *a* difference, but *different differences* in different circumstances. He considers various temptations, e.g. to say that what is essential to reading is 'the conscious act of reading' (*PI* 159); or to say that when one reads printed words aloud the sounds '*come* in a special way' (*PI* 165), unlike the way they come if one is repeating the words from memory or making them up; or to say that the look of the printed words 'guides' the utterance of the spoken words (*PI* 175).

Several connected features of Wittgenstein's new philosophical method are illustrated in this study of reading: for example, the requirement that one must *look and see* whether there is anything in common to all of the applications of a word (*PI* 66); the observation that the applications have only a 'family resemblance' (*PI* 67); the insistence that one must *describe* the use of a word instead of *theorizing* about its meaning (*PI* 109); the close attention to the 'inclinations' of philosophical thinking, but without any assumption that they are 'intuitions' or 'perceptions' of the truth (*PI* 299); the expression of these inclinations mainly in the first person ('I want to say . . .', 'I am inclined to say . . .', 'This is how I think of it . . .') — thereby giving Wittgenstein's writing the directness of confession, and revealing philosophy as a personal struggle with grammatical temptations.

Wittgenstein's thrust against essentialism, and the purpose of his descriptive technique, is aptly characterized in *The Brown Book*:

> It was not the function of our examples to show us the essence of 'deriving', 'reading', and so forth, through a veil of inessential features; the examples were not descriptions of an outside letting us guess at an inside which for some reason or other could not be shown in its nakedness. We are tempted to think that our examples are *indirect* means for producing a certain image or idea in a person's mind — that they *hint* at something which they cannot show. . . . Our method is *purely descriptive*; the descriptions we give are not hints of explanations. (*BB*, p. 125)

Another landmark of the second philosophy is the notion of '*a form of life*'. This expression is found in natural history, where different species of animals are described in terms of posture, locomotion, habitat, feeding, breeding, social organization, the sounds they make, the way they play. Some animals walk on two feet, some on four; some have tails; some live in trees, some in water. Wittgenstein says that what he is providing are 'really remarks on the natural history of human beings' (*PI* 415); that 'Ordering, questioning, recounting, chatting, are as much a part of our natural history as walking, eating, drinking, playing.' (*PI*

25) Using language in many different ways (different 'language-games') belongs to human natural history as much as living in trees belongs to the natural history of monkeys. A language-game is language interwoven with activity, action, *doing* (*PI* 7). 'To imagine a language means to imagine a form of life.' (*PI* 19)

In seeking to clarify the meaning of some bit of language, Wittgenstein persistently asks — with what actions is it joined? What role does it play in our lives? He searches for the connection between an exclamation or assertion and 'its consequences in what one does' (*OC* 363). A philosopher's description of the use of an expression should not be merely an observation about German or English grammar — but 'he must give the circumstances in which this expression functions.' (*OC* 433)

> Ask yourself: on what occasion, for what purpose, do we say this? What kind of actions accompany these words? (Think of a greeting.) In what scenes are they used; and what for? (*PI* 489)

'Our talk gets its sense from the rest of our actions.' (*OC* 229) 'It is our acting which lies at the bottom of the language-game.' (*OC* 204)

This insistence that concepts can be understood only in terms of the human attitudes and actions with which they are linked, was totally absent from the *Tractatus*. Not only was it not there; it *could not* be there. For the fundamental view of the *Tractatus* is that all thinking and all propositions reflect the fixed totality of possibilities that is common to any world, even to one in which there were no human activities. The notion that our language is based on human forms of life is incompatible with Wittgenstein's first philosophy. 'Words have their meaning only in the flow of life'[1] is not a possible remark within the framework of the *Tractatus*.

One significance of the notion of a form of life is that it brings requests for explanations or justification — *for reasons* — to a stop! Counting is something that people do. Is this because it has proved practical (*Z* 700)? Do we have our psychological concepts (e.g. intention) because they have proved advantageous (ibid.)? Do we think because thinking has been found to pay (*PI* 466—70)? No. Counting, thinking, employing the concept of intention — with its special logical grammar and its links with behaviour — are features of the natural history of human beings. They are characteristic of human life — as building dwellings in water is characteristic of the life of the beaver.

Philosophers have typically assumed that the foundations of language and thought are to be found in *a priori* principles, axioms, self-evident truths; or in immediate experience or sense-data. For Wittgenstein the foundations of language and thinking are forms of life.

> In certain circumstances, for example, we regard a calculation as sufficiently checked. What gives us a right to do that? Experience? Couldn't that deceive us? We must somewhere finish with justification, and then there remains the proposition that *this* is how we calculate. (*OC* 212)

There are possible doubts that most of us simply do not have. Someone might believe that *all* calculations are uncertain, and justify this by saying that mistakes are always possible. Can we say he is in error? No. He just reacts differently. 'We rely on calculations, he doesn't; we are sure, he isn't.' (*OC* 217) Without this normal attitude toward calculating there could not be calculating.

We are certain of many things: that *that* is a tree, that *this* is a chair. This certainty is not 'hastiness or superficiality', but 'a form of life' (*OC* 358). It is 'something that lies beyond being justified or unjustified' (*OC* 359). Parents give names to their children and these names have an important role in their lives. What if people forgot their names as they forget telephone numbers? 'It belongs to the language-game with people's names that everyone knows his name with the greatest certainty.' (*OC* 579)

The logic of our language is based on many *facts of nature*, including human nature. An important illustration of this is the fact that we 'go on' in the *same* way, after some technique has been explained to us by examples.

> If we teach a human being such-and-such a technique by means of examples — that he then proceeds like *this* and not like *that* in a particular new case, or that he gets stuck, and thus that this and not that is the 'natural' continuation for him: this of itself is an extremely important fact of nature. (*Z* 355)

The third landmark is an aspect of the significance of forms of life: but it deserves special emphasis. It is the conception that words and sentences can be understood only in terms of the circumstances, the contexts, the life-surroundings, in which they are spoken. This is a teaching that has not, for the most part, been taken in by present-day philosophy. The prevailing assumption is that we understand any sentence that is composed of familiar words grammatically arranged, regardless of context. This is an assumption of the *Tractatus* that still holds sway. Wittgenstein repudiates it in many passages.

> The words 'I am here' have sense only in certain contexts, and not when I say them to someone who is sitting in front of me and sees me clearly — and not because they are superfluous, but because their meaning is not *determined* by the situation, yet stands in need of such determination. (*OC* 348)

There is a philosophical inclination to think that we *understand* a sentence that is uttered outside of a normal context — that what the speaker says is so *obviously true* that his saying it is superfluous, pointless — so we are puzzled not as to *what* he says, but rather *why* he says it. This is an illustration of the observation 'We don't get free of the idea that the sense of a sentence accompanies the sentence: is there alongside of it.' (*Z* 139)

We understand the sentence 'I am here' outside of any context — *only* in the sense that we are familiar with various contexts in which it *would* fit. If, therefore, a person kept interjecting that sentence inappropriately into our conversation, I would not know *what* that sentence meant *there*, or whether it meant anything.

Saying something may be compared with *doing* something. In writing my name I may be *doing* different things in different circumstances: testing a new pen, signing a confession, registering in a hotel. Or I may be doing nothing — just doodling. In uttering the sentence 'I am here', I may be reporting my presence, or expressing my joy at having reached the top of a difficult climb ('I made it!'). Or I may be neither *doing* nor *saying* anything. Wittgenstein says:

> Someone who was considering the thought that he was of no use any more, might keep repeating to himself 'I can still do this and this and this.' If such thoughts often possessed him one would not be surprised if he, apparently out of all context, spoke such a sentence out loud. (But here I have already sketched a background, a surrounding, for this remark, and so given it a context.) But if someone, in quite heterogeneous circumstances, called out with the most convincing mimicry 'Down with him!', one might say of these words (and their tone) that they were a pattern that does indeed have familiar applications, but that in this case it was not even clear what *language* the man was speaking. I could make with my hand the movement which I should make if I were holding a hand-saw and sawing through a plank; but would one have any

right to call this movement *sawing*, out of all context? — (It could be something entirely different!) (*OC* 350)

Wittgenstein remarks that the exclamation '*This* is produced by a brain-process!' may express the philosophical feeling that there is 'an unbridgeable gulf between consciousness and brain-process'. On the other hand, it might be said 'in the course of an experiment the purpose of which was to show that an effect of light which I see is produced by the stimulation of a particular part of the brain' (*PI* 412). These differences of context give different senses to the exclamation.

In talking to someone about my furniture, I might point at a table and say, 'this table is too high.' Here the pointing has sense. But what if I said this to him on the telephone, pointing to the table? What would be the sense of the pointing in that case? (*PI* 670)

'A smiling mouth *smiles* only in a human face.' (*PI* 583) A shrug of the shoulders is a familiar gesture that means something different in different situations. It does not have a *fixed* meaning. Neither does a familiar sentence.

Wittgenstein's repudiation of the assumption that the *sense* of language is independent of the circumstances of life in which the language is used, is perhaps the single most important aspect of his break with what he calls in the preface of the *Investigations* 'my old way of thinking'.

Notes

CHAPTER 1 THE FORM OF THE WORLD

1 *Ludwig Wittgenstein: Letters to C. K. Ogden*, p. 59.
2 Bertrand Russell, *The Problems of Philosophy* (first published 1912). Oxford University Press: New York, 1959, p. 46.
3 Bertrand Russell, 'Knowledge by Acquaintance and Knowledge by Description' (first published 1910—11), in *Mysticism and Logic*. George Allen & Unwin: London, 1949, p. 209.
4 Ibid., p. 210.
5 Russell, *Problems*, p. 46.
6 Ibid.
7 Ibid., p. 47.
8 Ibid., p. 58.
9 Ibid.

CHAPTER 2 LANGUAGE AND THE OBJECTS

1 Hidé Ishiguro, 'Use and Reference of Names', in *Studies in the Philosophy of Wittgenstein*, ed. Peter Winch. Routledge & Kegan Paul: London, 1969, p. 21.
2 Ibid., p. 20.
3 Ibid., p. 22.
4 Ibid., p. 34.
5 Ibid., p. 35.
6 Ibid., p. 46.
7 Ibid., p. 40.
8 Brian McGuinness, 'The So-called Realism of the *Tractatus*', in *Perspectives on the Philosophy of Wittgenstein*, ed. Irving Block. Basil Blackwell: Oxford, 1981, p. 66.
9 Ibid.
10 Ibid., p. 67.

11   Ibid., p. 73.
12   Norman Malcolm, *Ludwig Wittgenstein: A Memoir*, 2nd edn. Oxford University Press: Oxford, 1984, p. 70.

CHAPTER 3 THE ELEMENTS OF REALITY

1   Plato, *Theaetetus*, 188—9, English tr. F. M. Cornford, *Plato's Theory of Knowledge*. Routledge & Kegan Paul: London, 1949, pp. 114—15.
2   *Theaetetus*, 201—2, Cornford, *Plato's Theory*, p. 143.
3   B. Russell, 'The Philosophy of Logical Atomism', in *Bertrand Russell: Logic and Knowledge*, ed. R. C. Marsh. Macmillan: New York, 1956, p. 243.
4   Ibid., p. 252.
5   Alexander Maslow, *A Study in Wittgenstein's Tractatus*. University of California Press: Berkeley, 1961, p. 11.
6   Ibid., p. 12.
7   Ibid., pp. 38—9.
8   Erik Stenius, *Wittgenstein's Tractatus*. Basil Blackwell: Oxford, 1960, p. 84.
9   Ibid.
10   Ibid., p. 85.
11   Ibid.
12   Ibid.
13   Ibid., p. 125.
14   Ibid.
15   Ibid., pp. 122—3.
16   Ibid., p. 85.
17   Ibid., p. 86.
18   Ibid., p. 84.
19   Maslow, *A Study*, pp. 11, 12.
20   Ibid., pp. 38—9.
21   Stenius, *Wittgenstein's Tractatus*, p. 125.

CHAPTER 4 THOUGHTS

1   *Notebooks 1914—1916*, p. 82.
2   Anthony Kenny, 'Wittgenstein's Early Philosophy of Mind', in *Perspectives on the Philosophy of Wittgenstein*, ed. Irving Block. Basil Blackwell: Oxford, 1981, p. 144.
3   John Locke, *An Essay Concerning Human Understanding*, ed. A. C. Fraser, two volumes. Clarendon Press: Oxford, 1894, vol. 2, book III, ch. 2, sec. 1.

4 Augustine, *Confessions*, tr. R. S. Pine-Coffin. Penguin Books, 1961, book I, sec. 8.
5 J. A. Fodor, *The Language of Thought*. Harvester Press: Hassocks, Sussex, 1976, p. 79.
6 David Favrholdt, *An Interpretation and Critique of Wittgenstein's Tractatus*. Munksgaard: Copenhagen, 1967, pp. 82—3.
7 Richard Miller, 'Solipsism in the *Tractatus*', *Journal of the History of Philosophy*, vol. 18, no. 1, January 1980, p. 68.
8 Ibid.
9 Kenny, 'Wittgenstein's Early Philosophy', p. 146.
10 Ibid.
11 B. Russell, 'On Propositions: What They Are and How They Mean', in *Bertrand Russell: Logic and Knowledge*, ed. R. C. Marsh. Macmillan: New York, 1956, p. 290.
12 Ibid., p. 308.
13 Ibid., p. 309.
14 Ibid., p. 314.
15 Ibid., p. 315.
16 Ibid., pp. 315—16.
17 John Searle, *Intentionality*. Cambridge University Press: Cambridge, 1983, p. 1.
18 Ibid., p. 22.
19 Ibid., p. 27.

CHAPTER 7 THE INNER PROCESS OF ANALYSIS

1 William James, *The Principles of Psychology*, two volumes. Henry Holt and Company: New York, 1890, vol. 1, p. 279.
2 Ibid., p. 280.
3 Ibid., p. 281.
4 Ibid., p. 244.

CHAPTER 8 LANGUAGE AS EXPRESSIVE BEHAVIOUR

1 G. E. Moore, 'Wittgenstein's Lectures in 1930—33', *Philosophical Papers*. George Allen & Unwin: London, 1959, p. 307.
2 See Carl Ginet, 'Wittgenstein's Claim that there Could Not be Just One Occasion of Obeying a Rule', in *Essays on Wittgenstein* in *honour of G. H. von Wright*, ed. J. Hintikka. North Holland Press: Amsterdam, 1976, p. 155.
3 See Peter Hacker, *Insight and Illusion*. Clarendon Press: Oxford, 1972, ch. 9.

4 The utterance 'It hurts' has the logical grammar of a first-person psychological sentence.

CHAPTER 9 FOLLOWING A RULE

1 Saul Kripke, *Wittgenstein on Rules and Private Language*. Basil Blackwell: Oxford, 1982, p. 60.
2 Ibid., p. 55.
3 Ibid., p. 62.
4 Ibid., p. 7.
5 Colin McGinn, *Wittgenstein on Meaning*. Basil Blackwell: Oxford, 1984, p. 47.
6 Ibid.
7 Kripke, *Wittgenstein*, p. 96.
8 Ibid., p. 3.
9 Ibid., p. 17.
10 Ibid., pp. 21—2.
11 Ibid.
12 Ibid., p. 22.
13 Ibid., p. 55.
14 Ibid., p. 69.
15 Ibid., pp. 70—1.
16 Ibid., p. 69.
17 Ibid., p. 72.
18 Ibid., p. 77.
19 Kripke's assimilation of 'truth conditions' to 'corresponding facts' was brought to my attention by Dan Rashid.
20 Kripke, *Wittgenstein*, p. 74.
21 Ibid., p. 77.
22 Ibid.
23 Ibid.
24 Ibid., pp. 78—9.
25 Ibid., p. 79.
26 Ibid., p. 86.
27 Ibid.
28 McGinn, *Wittgenstein on Meaning*, pp. 78—9.
29 Ibid., p. 91.
30 Ibid.
31 Ibid., pp. 196—7.
32 Ibid.
33 Ibid., p. 197.
34 Ibid., p. 198.

CHAPTER 10 MIND AND BRAIN

1   John Searle, *Intentionality*. Cambridge University Press: Cambridge, 1983, p. 268.
2   Ibid., p. 230.
3   D. O. Hebb, *Textbook of Psychology*. Saunders: 1958, p. 3. Quoted by David Armstrong, *A Materialist Theory of the Mind*. Routledge & Kegan Paul: London, 1968, p. 74.
4   Armstrong, *A Materialist Theory*, p. 73.
5   Ibid., p. 75.
6   Ibid., p. 91.
7   See Norman Malcolm, *Memory and Mind*. Cornell University Press: Ithaca, 1977, part two.
8   I attempt to unravel it in my 'Consciousness and Causality', in *Consciousness & Causality*, by D. M. Armstrong and Norman Malcolm. Basil Blackwell: Oxford, 1984.
9   Ewald Hering, *On Memory*, Religion of Science Library no. 16. Kegan Paul: London, 1902, p. 39.
10 Wolfgang Köhler, *Dynamics in Psychology*. Liveright: New York, 1940, p. 109.
11 Armstrong and Malcolm, *Consciousness & Causality*, p. 156.
12 Ibid., p. 172.
13 Wittgenstein's argument is expounded and illustrated in chapter 3.
14 One of the themes of the *Tractatus*, as we saw in chapter 4, is that a thought is a 'structure' composed of 'mental constituents'. The criticism of this conception in the present chapter applies therefore to the *Tractatus*. There is no evidence that Wittgenstein endorsed the identity of mind and brain in his early thought. There are, however, some obscure remarks in the *Notebooks* (p. 85) which suggest that he may have been attracted by psycho-physical parallelism.

CHAPTER 11 CERTAINTY

1   *The Philosophical Works of Descartes*, tr. E. S. Haldane and G. R. T. Ross, two volumes. Cambridge University Press: Cambridge, 1972. (Cited here as HR followed by volume and page number.) HR I, 104.
2   HR I, 220.
3   HR I, 101.
4   HR I, 149.
5   HR II, 126.

6   HR I, 147—8.
7   HR I, 150.
8   HR I, 151.
9   HR I, 152.
10 HR I, 221.
11 HR I, 101.
12 HR I, 158.
13 Ibid.
14 HR I, 158—9.
15 Descartes held that God created 'the eternal truths'. God willed that they should be true, but might have willed that they should be false. Descartes concedes that human beings cannot understand how God could have brought it about that it should be false that twice four is eight: but at the same time we should understand that nothing is impossible for God (HR II, 250—1). In a letter of 1644 he says that God was free 'to make it not be true that the three angles of a triangle were equal to two right angles, or in general that contradictories could not be true together' (*Descartes: Philosophical Letters*, edited and translated by Anthony Kenny. Clarendon Press: Oxford 1970, pp. 150—1). In a letter of 1648 Descartes says: 'I do not think that we should ever say of anything that it cannot be brought about by God. For since everything involved in truth and goodness depends on His omnipotence, I would not dare to say that God cannot make a mountain without a valley, or that one and two should not be three. I merely say that He has given me such a mind that I cannot conceive a mountain without a valley, or an aggregate of one and two which is not three, and that such things involve a contradiction in my conception.' (ibid., pp. 236—7) In a letter of 1649 Descartes says: 'And so I boldly assert that God can do everything which I conceive to be possible, but I am not so bold as to deny that He can do whatever conflicts with my understanding — I merely say that it involves a contradiction.' (ibid., p. 241)
16 HR I, 150.
17 Emphasis added.
18 HR I, 102.
19 Wittgenstein, *Last Writings on the Philosophy of Psychology*, vol. I, para. 832.
20 Ibid., para. 834.
21 HR I, 178. The English translation 'I can never be deceived' may be misleading. Descartes's Latin phrase is *non potest ut errem*. This can be translated 'It is impossible that I should go astray', or 'It is impossible that I should go wrong.' Being *deceived* is only *one* form of going wrong. Descartes means that it is impossible that he should go wrong in any way whatsoever!

22 G. E. Moore, 'A Defence of Common Sense', *Philosophical Papers*. Allen & Unwin: London, 1959, p. 33.
23 HR II, 234.
24 HR II, 241.

EPILOGUE

1 Wittgenstein, *Last Writings on the Philosophy of Psychology*, vol. I, p. 118.

Index